Teaching
Children With
High-Functioning Autism
Strategies for the Inclusive Classroom

Teaching Children With High-Functioning Autism

Strategies for the Inclusive Classroom

Claire E. Hughes-Lynch, Ph.D.

PRUFROCK PRESS INC.
WACO, TEXAS

Library of Congress Cataloging-in-Publication Data

Hughes-Lynch, Claire E., 1967-
Teaching children with high-functioning autism : strategies for the inclusive classroom / by Claire E.
Hughes-Lynch.
    p. cm.
Includes bibliographical references.
ISBN 978-1-59363-747-7 (pbk.)
1. Autistic children--Education--United States. 2. Asperger's syndrome--Education--United States.
3. Inclusive education--United States. 4. Behavioral assessment. I. Title.
LC4718. H85 2012
371.9'046--dc23
                          2011037115

Edited by Lacy Compton

Production design by Raquel Trevino

ISBN-13: 978-1-59363-747-7

Prufrock Press Inc.
P.O. Box 8813
Waco, TX 76714-8813
Phone: (800) 998-2208
Fax: (800) 240-0333
http://www.prufrock.com

Dedication

This book is for those who learn differently, my students I taught, my family I love, and the classrooms of the teachers with whom I work.

Table of Contents

Acknowledgements

I would like to thank my editor, Lacy, for her patience, her understanding of my numerous typos, and her ability to balance cheerleading and constructive criticism; and Joel, my publisher, for his faith in me and his willingness to buy dinner!

I would especially like to thank the teachers, students, and interns who have welcomed me into their classrooms over the year and from whom I have learned so much.

I'd like to thank the administration and faculty at the College of Coastal Georgia for supporting my efforts, and Bellarmine University and Harris Manchester College at Oxford for allowing me to begin my study of autism.

Many, many thanks go out to Wendy, who provided suggestions and support and to whom I give full credit!

I'd like to acknowledge that writing this book was an international experience and reflects hours of time in Greek cafés and at Uncle Roger's Cambridge table. I'd like to thank the various waiters, Olga, and Nicki, who all provided sustenance during crunch times.

My mother gets so much gratitude for helping me clarify my thinking and for providing me with a role model. I want to be you when I grow up.

Most importantly, I want to thank James, my husband, who did the laundry and the dishes and kept the uproar down all of the weekends I spent writing. I am an author because you are such a wonderful, supportive husband and father.

And to Annalia and Nick—I love you so much and I'm coming home. You're why I write.

Section I

Understanding High-Functioning Autism

Chapter 1

Overview

The goal of this book is to help a teacher who is not a specialist in autism—a general education teacher, a special education teacher who works with children in multiple categories of special education, or a preschool or daycare provider—work with children who have been identified as having autism, but who are capable of learning content material close to or even above grade level. This book is for those teachers who have a child with an autism label in their classroom and who need ideas and support.

There is clearly a need for a book like this. One study found that 23% of general classroom teachers believed that autism was a temporary disability and that proper treatment, preferably by a pediatrician, would cause it to go away (O'Keefe & McDowell, 2004). Autism is a lifelong disorder, we don't know what causes it, and we don't know how to treat it, much less cure it. But we are learning more and more every day. And kids with incredible potential and abilities are sitting in our classrooms needing our guidance and assistance to learn how to work with this thing we call autism.

This book focuses on five questions critical to teaching a child with HFA:

1. What is high-functioning autism?
   - High-functioning autism is the upper end of autism spectrum disorder, which is tracked on a continuum—from very severe and nonverbal, to more verbal and better able to function in a general education classroom.

○ Characteristics of autism include social deficits, repetitive behaviors, and language impairments that are present from a young age. However, identification may occur later once social demands are greater than the child's capacities (American Psychiatric Association, 2011).

○ There are numerous overlaps with issues associated with giftedness and other disorders as well, including Attention Deficit/Hyperactivity Disorder and obsessive-compulsive disorder (Webb et al., 2005).

○ Autism has been referred to as an "epidemic," and the rates of diagnosis are skyrocketing. Chapter 2 discusses possible characteristics and causes of high-functioning autism and the need to provide services as quickly as possible, and to continue those services through the child's transition to adulthood.

2. Why is a team approach so important to the education of the child with HFA?

○ Teachers and parents have to understand that the child is a whole individual and has to be taught in a comprehensive manner. For this reason, there is a need for general education, gifted education, and special education to collaborate and work together in the identification, programming, and instruction of children (Hughes, 2010a; Hughes & Murawski, 2001; Karnes, Shaunessy, & Bisland, 2004).

○ Parents often have to be the agents of change for this collaboration, because "educators are often so preoccupied with a child's failure, they simply do not look for sparks of extraordinary potential" (Tannenbaum & Baldwin, 1983, p. 192).

○ When a child has HFA, there is a very strong need for the child to perceive him- or herself as capable and integrated, rather than a compilation of separate parts. In order to do this, professionals from various fields have to be communicating with each other, a process that must be facilitated by the parents. The development of this team approach is further explored in Chapter 3.

3. When do you make educational decisions about teaching a child with HFA?

○ During an IEP or 504 Plan meeting, there are a number of crucial decisions made. Chapter 4 focuses on establishing a strong IEP or 504 plan that allows all members to be involved.

4. How can you teach a child with HFA?

○ There are a variety of ways to approach the integrated education of a child with high-functioning autism. It is critically important to look at the characteristics of the child, not the label, in determining appropriate interventions, and to look at a variety of different instructional approaches.

○ The "Give Me a Hand" model provides an overview of the five planes of development and five approaches to teaching. In addition, it is important to look at specific content and level of schooling in order to meet the needs of children. These are further explained in Section II, which covers Chapters 5–11.

5. Where can I find materials and resources to teach a child with HFA?
   ○ A list of resources, materials, and technology is provided in Chapter 12.

Although focused on teachers, this book is also for parents—to give to their child's teachers and to share knowledge so that they may learn what might work in their lives. Parents are the first teachers of children, and as such, any teaching information is for them as well. I hope that they give this book to their child's teachers and ask them to understand that there is always something else to try, something else to do, and more to find out. As we learn more about autism, as autism becomes more common, it is critical that we learn to develop the potential of children—to focus on talent development within a framework of autism.

Chapter 2

What Is High-Functioning Autism?

Autism is so many things to so many people. Autism is a spectrum disorder, which means that there are degrees of severity among a whole lot of different characteristics. The proposed formal definition for autism spectrum disorder (ASD), according to the recently released draft of the American Psychiatric Association's (APA) fifth edition of the *Diagnostic and Statistical Manual for Mental Disorders* (DSM-V; APA, 2011), due to be released in 2013, is composed of three aspects:

A. Persistent deficits in social communication and social interaction across contexts, not accounted for by general developmental delays, and manifest by all 3 of the following:

1. Deficits in social-emotional reciprocity; ranging from abnormal social approach and failure of normal back and forth conversation through reduced sharing of interests, emotions, and affect and response to total lack of initiation of social interaction,

2. Deficits in nonverbal communicative behaviors used for social interaction; ranging from poorly integrated verbal and nonverbal communication, through abnormalities in eye contact and body-language, or deficits in understanding and use of nonverbal communication, to total lack of facial expression or gestures.

3. Deficits in developing and maintaining relationships, appropriate to developmental level (beyond those with caregivers); ranging from difficulties adjusting behavior to suit different social contexts through

difficulties in sharing imaginative play and in making friends to an apparent absence of interest in people.

B. Restricted, repetitive patterns of behavior, interests, or activities as manifested by at least two of the following:
    1. Stereotyped or repetitive speech, motor movements, or use of objects; (such as simple motor stereotypes, echolalia, repetitive use of objects, or idiosyncratic phrases).
    2. Excessive adherence to routines, ritualized patterns of verbal or nonverbal behavior, or excessive resistance to change; (such as motoric rituals, insistence on same route or food, repetitive questioning or extreme distress at small changes).
    3. Highly restricted, fixated interests that are abnormal in intensity or focus; (such as strong attachment to or preoccupation with unusual objects, excessively circumscribed or perseverative interests).
    4. Hyper-or hypo-reactivity to sensory input or unusual interest in sensory aspects of environment; (such as apparent indifference to pain/heat/cold, adverse response to specific sounds or textures, excessive smelling or touching of objects, fascination with lights or spinning objects).

C. Symptoms must be present in early childhood (but may not become fully manifest until social demands exceed limited capacities)

D. Symptoms together limit and impair everyday functioning.

And although not often part of the official diagnostic criteria, the following characteristics are often noted among children with high-functioning autism (Hughes, 2010b):

- sensory under- or overstimulation,
- visual learning styles,
- physical issues such as gait and digestion, and
- discrepant academic abilities.

There are some children who will exhibit mild characteristics and others who will display very severe symptoms. There are many children who do not qualify for services who exhibit some of these characteristics, and other children who do qualify who demonstrate very different characteristics from each other.

There's an old poem that goes something like this:

There was a little girl
Who had a little curl

Table 1

Positive/Negative Views of Similar Behavior

Disabling Descriptors of Behavior	Strength Descriptors of Behavior
Perseverate	Perseveres
Obsession	Interest
Easily distracted	Attention to detail
Overly active	High level of energy
"Professorial" language	High-level, adult-like language
Inability to get along with age peers	Ability to communicate with adults
Easily sensory stimulated	Highly aware of environment
Fearful	High level of imagination
Lacks fear	Adventurous
Impulsive	Makes decisions quickly
Obsessive-compulsive	Neat
Withdrawn	Introverted
Stubborn	Strong-willed
Talkative	Highly verbal
Overly emotional	Passionate
Lacks emotion	Logical
Lacks eye contact	Respects authority
Runs away from conflict	Goes for a walk to process
Stims	Self-soothes

Note. Adapted from "Gifts of Autism," by C. E. Hughes, December 2010, *Parenting for High Potential*, p. 18. Copyright 2010 by the National Association for Gifted Children.

> *Right in the middle of her forehead.*
> *When she was good, she was very, very good*
> *And when she was bad, she was horrid.*

What if the behaviors are the same, but one person sees them as very, very good—while another sees them as horrid?

The context in which a child finds him- or herself is often critical to the success of any intervention. Table 1 describes some classroom behaviors that from one perspective can be considered disabling, but from another can be considered strengths. The difference is in how they are perceived, the context in which they occur, and the degree of problems that are created as a result of the behavior.

The key element is the degree to which these characteristics cause problems in a child's life. If the child cannot function, or cannot learn to function within the environment, there is a problem and intervention is necessary. This difference in views and contexts can sometimes explain why a child functions well at home and not at school—or vice versa. There are a large number of very famous people who have been retroactively diagnosed with HFA, with Bill Gates, Thomas Jefferson, Marie Curie, and Mozart among them (Ledgin, 2005). Clearly, they had much to offer the world and their talents were seen as strengths, not deficits.

Types of Autism

In the upcoming 2013 edition of the DSM-V, the severity of ASD ranges from high functioning to low functioning. This new definition recognizes the similarities between the old labels and reclassifies children based on level of functioning. However, there will be older diagnoses of ASD that may take into consideration the five standard types of ASD. According to the older version of the *Diagnostic and Statistical Manual for Mental Disorders* (the text revision of the fourth edition [DSM-IV], with which some parents and professionals might still be familiar), there are five types of disorders, each with a set of criteria that fall under the category of autism spectrum disorders, including:

- Rett syndrome
- Classic autism
- Childhood Disintegrative Disorder (CDD)
- Pervasive Developmental Disorder–Not Otherwise Specified (PDD-NOS)
- Asperger's syndrome

Rett syndrome is a known genetic mutation on the X chromosome that can cause significant autism-like behaviors and almost always occurs in girls. It is very rare, occurring only in 1 out of 10,000 to 15,000 people, according to the National Institute of Mental Health (2008). It also can be confused with cerebral palsy, because a child's walking gait and movements can be spastic or jerky. Children with Rett syndrome often will have small heads and have little language abilities. They also often have seizures and digestive issues. Children with Rett syndrome often will behave in ways similar to children with autism, but there is a known cause for their actions. It is not considered inherited, because it seems to be a genetic mutation that occurs randomly. Rett syndrome, because of its known etiology, has been removed from the DSM-V category of autism spectrum disorder.

Classic autism and Childhood Disintegrative Disorder are considered to be the more significantly impairing versions of autism. Children with classic autism tend to function in the lower levels of intelligence, due in part to their language skills, which may be significantly lower than the other subtypes. In the past, many people with classic autism were institutionalized and many also had significant health or physical issues as well. However, there is a great deal of confusion in terminology between the word *autism* and the broader term *autism spectrum dis-*

orders, which often includes newer terms for variations of intellectual functioning, language, problem-solving abilities, and times of diagnosis.

According to Dr. Frombonne (2002) of the National Institute of Mental Health, only 1 in 100,000 people demonstrate CDD. This term describes children who develop typically, and then around 3 to 4 years of age begin to regress—to have their development disintegrate—right before your eyes. Children with this form of autism typically end up with more severe forms: very limited language, very limited social skills, and behaviors that are "classically" autistic. This is the version that most people think of when they think of autism.

PDD-NOS and Asperger's syndrome are often considered high-functioning levels of autism, and are included in the emphasis of this book. According to the Emory Autism Center (2009), PDD-NOS is defined as "a general category used to describe a pattern of behavioral differences (which may include deviations, excesses, or difficulties) in the areas of social relating, communication, and attention/interest" (para. 3). I just love this term. "Not Otherwise Specified" is official language for "We have no idea" and "It's not low enough to be called autism." I call it the "There's a problem in development somewhere, and who the heck knows why?" disorder.

Asperger's syndrome (AS) is used to describe children who are on the autism spectrum, but do not have language delay, although they do have communication differences. In other words, it's not the lack of words that is a problem—it's how they use the words that they have. As a result, they also have the social issues and often have the repetitive behaviors and sensory sensitivities of other children on the spectrum. AS is a relatively new diagnostic term that was not included in the autism spectrum until 1995. Thus, most people identified as having AS are still under the age of 25. Older teachers may not have heard of it. It is sometimes known as the "genius" autism, because many children with autism who also score in the gifted range of intelligence often are identified as having this form of autism due to the decreased impact on language development. However, not all children with AS are gifted, just as not all gifted children have AS. Often, children with AS aren't identified until late elementary or even middle school, although more severe cases do tend to get identified earlier. A large number of adults have recently been identified with HFA in their mid-40s (Robison, 2007). These children often grew up being called "geeks" and other not-so-nice labels. It is important to remember that it *is* a problem, and AS does not just represent overlabeling by protective mothers, as some might believe. It is equally important to realize that these children have significant strengths that need focus and specialized development in order to grow.

Additional Labels

There are a number of other labels with which ASD often overlaps. These include, but are not limited to:

- anxiety disorders, including Tourette's syndrome and Generalized Anxiety Disorder–Not Otherwise Specified (GAD-NOS);
- attentional disorders, including Attention Deficit/Hyperactivity Disorder (ADHD) and sleep disorders;
- learning differences, including learning disabilities, intellectual and developmental delays, and even giftedness; and
- medical issues such as febrile seizures and epilepsy.

As you can see, two children who come into your classroom with labels of autism may, in fact, present a range of characteristics, a range of severity, and a range of other, associated issues. There's a phrase among parents of children with autism, "When you've seen one child with autism, you've seen one child with autism." Children with autism are often highly individualistic and require individualized, differentiated intervention plans.

Throughout this book, I will use the term *autism* to describe all of the subtypes of ASD, not just classic autism. When I discuss high-functioning autism, or HFA, I will include all of these labels in the discussion. What I mean by high functioning is *children with autistic behaviors who have the capability of interacting, speaking, and learning general education curriculum in a general education classroom environment with the right supports.* In some cases, they can be identified as gifted as well, but I will primarily focus on the need to identify and teach to their abilities, rather than focusing on their disabilities.

Overlap With Giftedness

There is a tremendous overlap in characteristics between children with HFA and children who are gifted. It is very important that the psychologist who is conducting the testing is aware of the needs of gifted children, in addition to looking for problem areas. See Table 2 for possible differences between giftedness and high-functioning autism.

Autism and the Epidemic Rate

Autism numbers are significantly on the rise. When I was going through a special education teacher preparation program in the early 1990s, autism was focused on during one day of class. It was in a chapter under "Low Incidence" in the general overview of special education labels, and that was the only specific preparation I

Table 2

Differences Between Giftedness and High-Functioning Autism

Characteristic	Gifted (Often, But Not in All Cases)	Autism (Often, But Not in All Cases)
Language	Advanced beyond age peers	Delayed
Social behavior	Often prefers to play alone/introverted; can often do well socially, but may need down time	Plays alone, repetitive play, parallel play
Concepts	Understands concepts beyond age peers; figurative language	Literal concepts
Memory	Strong, particularly in passion areas	Can be strong or weak; wide-ranging abilities
Attention span	Long, if engaged in something of interest; can appear to have ADHD if not	Long, if engaged in something of interest; can appear to have ADHD if not
Sensory stimuli	Very aware of environment; easily responsive	Overly aware of environment to the point that there's a significant problem
Interests	Can appear obsessive	Can appear obsessive
Physical issues	None common; often have above-average health	High level of allergies, digestive issues
Stimming activities	Organizing by specific characteristic, pleasure in the patterns	No immediate discernible characteristic; often just repetitive
Causation	Genetics and environmental interaction	Genetics and environmental interaction

Note. Adapted from "Gifts of Autism," by C. E. Hughes, December 2010, *Parenting for High Potential*, p. 17. Copyright 2010 by the National Association for Gifted Children.

received. In the early 1990s, autism *was* a low-incidence area of exceptionality. It was assumed that if I were to work with children with autism, I would become a specialist—someone with additional training along the way. The chances were 1 in about 10,000 or .01% of a chance that I would work with a child with autism (Kirk, Gallagher, Coleman, & Anastasiow, 2012).

By 2009, that number was 1 in 110, with 1 in 78 boys being identified (Centers for Disease Control and Prevention, 2009). Autism has sharply increased to being a high-incidence category of exceptionality at about 1%. It is still less common than learning disabilities (LD) at 3%–5% or speech and language disorders at 1.6% of the population. It has, however, overtaken emotional and behavioral disorders (EBD) at .7% and intellectual and developmental delays at .8% of the population (Kirk et al., 2012).

The increasing rates of autism are not limited to the United States. According to Dr. Karp (2009) of the University of California, Los Angeles, autism is being diagnosed around the world in increasing rates. In other words, autism is now being found in countries like England, Spain, Holland, and Pakistan, according to Shahina Maqbool (2009), in similar rates to the United States (when using the entire spectrum, rather than the more limited classic autism). Autism is a subject that must be covered in teacher preparation programs now more specifically, simply because of the increasing numbers.

The question, of course, is why? Why this dramatic increase in a decade? With such a sudden burst of referrals, there are a number of guesses why, but little direct evidence. Epidemic? Perhaps, but certainly a real problem. The following is a brief list of suggested reasons that have been put forth about the causes of autism. Some are outdated, some are just wrong, and others still need lots of research.

Refrigerator Mothers

I had to include this as a perception, *not* a cause. In 1943, Leo Kanner, one of the first authorities on autism, noticed that there was a marked lack of affection between mothers and children diagnosed with autism. Furthered by Bruno Bettleheim in 1962, the theory placed the blame almost solely on the environment of parenting. You can hear traces of it in older teachers who say, "Well, just look at that child's parents—they're obviously too permissive/strict/inconsistent. . . . " Clearly, Kanner and Bettleheim (a) did not notice that these same mothers often had very loving relationships with their other children and (b) were blaming the lack of closeness on the mother, not the inherent lack of response on the child.

Dr. Bernard Rimland, in his 1964 book *Infantile Autism*, was the first authoritative voice to debunk Bettleheim's view that the parental bond was the environmental factor and to propose that autism has a neurological and physiological cause. But the damage was done, and we have spent decades since trying to persuade others that our children are loved and not "spoiled."

Genetics

There have been studies that have found links to autism in 113 separate genes, and according to the Simons Foundation Autism Research Initiative (Rudacille, 2011), a great deal of emphasis is being paid to the X chromosome's impact on children with autism. Certainly, autism appears to run in families. However, it's not a clear-cut connection. It appears to be a series of "switches" at the genetic level that have to be "turned on." In other words, it appears that children might be created at conception with the *potential* for autism, which then is triggered by something in the environment or a particular combination of genetic issues that together create autism—both during gestation and afterward. Merely having one genetic marker is not enough—they have to occur together in a particular sequence and interact with each other. Certainly, weeks 8–24 are the time of developing neurological growth during pregnancy, and trauma during this time could have an effect on the brain without causing physical disabilities.

Mirror Neurons

There is a link between the lack of mirror neurons in people and autism, according to Dr. Oberman (2005) and other researchers at the University of California, San Diego. Mirror neurons turn on both when you do something and when you observe someone else doing the same thing. If you see a sad movie and cry, your neurological system is taking the information you've observed and turning on the same neurons that you turn on yourself when you're truly sad. In other words, you can cry at *Beaches* and you don't have to have your best friend actually die in order to feel distraught. Similarly, you can feel joy watching the winner from *American Idol* or anger reading about torture. It doesn't have to happen to you directly to feel it.

People with autism have a dysfunctional mirror neuron system, which means that they don't feel the emotions that other people around them are feeling or have the same awareness of other people's emotions or feelings. In fact, although they may be aware of their own emotions, they might believe that others share their viewpoint. These mirror neurons are responsible for empathy with others, and lack of empathy or even awareness of others' emotions can lead to significant social challenges. This dysfunction of the neural development can account for much of the self-absorption that children with autism exhibit.

Mercury Link/Immunizations

Children with autism act almost exactly like people who have been exposed to mercury. When neurons and nerves are exposed to mercury, they shrink and die fairly dramatically. Fierce arguments have grown up concerning the impact of mercury in immunizations, and numerous conspiracy theories abound about the government's role in promoting immunizations over the health of its children.

Most of the argument is based on a now-retracted study connecting autism with immunizations, specifically the MMR shot, done by Andrew Wakefield—a doctor since found to have changed his results, taken money from companies making alternative immunizations, and thrown out bad data (Hensley, 2010). However, his original 1998 study made a lot of parents nervous, and as a result, many, many parents have chosen not to immunize their children.

Plus, and this is big, folks, there are a lot more things that could more likely cause autism that we are *not* getting upset about. My belief is that immunizations are not necessarily the issue—our global living is—a belief that is shared and being studied now by the federally funded National Children's Study (2011). The amount of hormones and various drugs in our water and meat is staggering. The ubiquitous plastic containers that we store our food in and drink from have harmful substances. There are skyrocketing rates of mercury around the world in our soil, oceans, and air. Just the amount of mercury in our ecosystem has gone off the charts over time. A 1995 study by William Fitzgerald of the University of

Connecticut found that during the last 100 years, the amount of mercury in the air has increased 300%, with most of the increase occurring since 1970. Emissions have dramatically increased in the United States since governmental oversights were removed. Other countries, such as India and China, have almost no governmental oversight. Certainly we see it in the tuna pregnant women are not supposed to eat, the shrimp we're all supposed to eat in moderation, and the smog over our cities. Heck, mercury was in our tooth fillings until recently. The reality is that mercury is in everything—if it's in the soil, the water, and the air, there's nothing we eat, nothing we drink, and nothing we wear that has never encountered mercury. Immunizations are certainly problematic, but there are much bigger problems with mercury and other environmental toxins than the trace amounts found in the MMR shot. Our very ecosystem is threatening us.

Food Allergies

With the issues of headaches, skin problems, digestion, diarrhea, and general bowel disturbances that many children on the spectrum have, there is some evidence to indicate that some children are born with intestinal allergic reactions to irritants, particularly dairy, wheat, and for some children, corn. Certainly the use of corn syrup, gluten, and milk are much higher in our foods today than they were just 50 years ago. In her 2002 book, Karyn Seroussi wondered if such allergic reactions and the consequential autism behaviors mimic typical people's reactions to hallucinogenic drugs such as LSD or "magic mushrooms." Many other parents have noted that their children have inordinately high levels of yeast in their urine and stool. Many researchers, including Drs. Bernard Rimland, William Shaw, and others, have been investigating this linkage between diet and autism for some years now, but the mainline perspective is that it is unproven (see Rimland, Crook, & Crook, 2001, and Shaw et al., 1998).

A friend of mine once referred to children with autism as the "canaries in our world." Living in Kentucky, as we did for a while, mining references are common. In the days before monitors, miners would send down a canary into the mine before the first run to test the air that had been shut up all night. If the canary came back alive, the air was good; if the canary came back dead, the air was bad and they would have to take measures to make the mine safe again. The sheer numbers of children being diagnosed with autism are telling us something; what that something is, however, is hotly debated.

Early Intervention

It's never too late to start focusing on educational issues, but the earlier the better. Often, children with HFA are not diagnosed until they encounter difficulties in school; the average age of an Asperger's diagnosis, for example, is 11 years old (Attwood, 2008). However, at that late age, children have missed a significant amount of time possible for social, language, and behavioral interventions.

Early intervention works. For example, two 4-year-old children with autism were profiled in a newspaper story in Roanoke, VA. Because the children had received individualized applied behavioral modification strategies early, they were going to be placed in a general education kindergarten with no special education supports needed (Cutright, 2010).

Some intervention programs start even before diagnosis. The MIND Institute at the University of California at Davis Medical Center has started an early intervention program for babies as young as 6 months old who are already demonstrating early indicators of autism (Demboski, 2010). Although autism is not often formally diagnosed before age 2 because of developmental differences, children who are not making eye contact, not smiling at people, not babbling, and who are showing unusual interest in objects can receive services early through this program at the MIND Institute; however, it is not yet a national program. The goal of the MIND Institute's early intervention program is to reshape the development process of the brain—to promote neurological synapses that might not occur because of the interference of autism.

Early intervention typically focuses on language development, social games, and pretend play. The Early Start Denver Model has been identified by many programs around the country as effective because of the increased IQ scores and social skills and decrease in negative behaviors of its participants (Dawson et al., 2009). This model uses games such as patty-cake, tickling, peek-a-boo, and other highly socially interactive games that promote eye contact and expressiveness and get the attention of infants and toddlers who are exhibiting a lack of social awareness at early ages.

Transition Needs

Although early intervention is clearly established as a necessary intervention, there are significant needs for children as they develop through the school-aged years and then into young adulthood. Many young adults with HFA can't find jobs when they graduate because of social issues. They may have high GPAs or great computer skills, but no interview skills. "There's a buyer for every house. Why don't we find the buyers for these kids who want to work?" asked Tom Fish (Associated

Press, 2010, para. 7) of the Ohio State University Nisonger Center, a support and research institute for people with developmental disabilities.

According to the Institute for Community Inclusion (Butterworth et al., 2011), national studies have found that only 6%–14% of adults with autism are competitively employed. These same studies have found that, among recent high school graduates with disabilities, those with autism have the highest job-retention rates after more than a year. But 2–6 months into the job, they fare the worst (Butterworth et al., 2011). If they can last, they stay. The solution would appear to be in earlier job planning—in elementary and middle school, not after high school or college.

Key Points From Chapter 2

- Autism is the combination of three major factors: social issues, language issues, and repetitive behaviors that impact a child's functioning.
- There is a movement away from diagnosing different kinds of autism, such as Asperger's syndrome and Pervasive Developmental Disorder, toward describing the impact of autism on the child's functioning. In children with high-functioning autism, this impact is considered to be less severe, but is still a significant issue in a general education classroom.
- There are different perspectives of behaviors related to autism; in some contexts, the same behavior can be considered quite negative, and in others, it can be considered a strength.
- Autism overlaps with a number of labels, including giftedness. These other labels are difficult to separate out from the behaviors of the child.
- Autism numbers are dramatically increasing. There are a number of hypothesized reasons why, including rates of mercury in the environment, genetics, and related allergies. However, ultimately, there is no currently known cause of or cure for autism.
- There is a very significant need for treatment of autism to start as soon as symptoms become apparent and continue all the way through transition to adulthood.

Chapter 3

Building and Working With a Team

In a recent workshop on technology development (Jurvetson, 2010), the speaker noted that there was no one person who knew everything there was to know about Microsoft's Windows program—that the computer runs because of the collective mind power, not a single point of knowledge.

That analogy is particularly important to teachers because there can never be the expectation that one person has all of the information or all of the ideas needed to provide services to a child. Teachers must work in a team environment to identify student needs—and to serve them as well. These team members should include:

- parents, who are the experts on their child and understand the history of their child's development;
- the general education teacher, who understands what typical children are expected to do;
- the special education teacher, who is an expert on differentiation and strategic instruction and who understands how to modify a task and an expectation;
- therapists of all types who have one specific task to accomplish with the child, whether that be physical, occupational, speech, or counseling;
- the child, who doesn't necessarily have to be present at meetings, but should be consulted as often as possible (sometimes, I have to remind myself that "if you have a question about the child, ask the child"); and
- an administrator, who sees the "big picture" of the district, the school, and the needs of all and who can provide support and help make things happen.

However, there are others who should inform the team as well. These people can provide insight, understanding, and lots of ideas. These can include:

- the doctor making the medical diagnosis of autism, who (hopefully) has a great deal of experience with children with autism (may be a pediatrician, a psychologist, a neuropsychologist, or even a psychiatrist);
- community service members who are aware of the resources available within the community, whether that be afterschool care, extracurricular opportunities, or other bridges to the community;
- job coaches and other members of the community who are responsible for hiring graduates; and
- college admissions and counseling service professionals who can help a family and a team plan for long-term educational goals.

Conflicting Viewpoints of Educational Approaches

There are perhaps two different sets of viewpoints that participants may be coming from that can either derail the collaboration process or at least impact it. The first set is the educational/therapeutic dichotomous viewpoints of autism itself, and the second set is the inclusion/continuum of services dichotomy for treatment.

Therapeutic Versus Educational Dichotomy

When working with a team, there are two very diverse perspectives of disability and differences that may be held by different team members and are critical to understand: the medical or therapeutic view, and the social-educational view (Heward, 2008). Although these are theoretical, they are critically important in how someone will identify and provide help to a child with high-functioning autism.

The medical model of exceptionality, which includes the therapeutic view, looks for a cause and a resultant "cure." Therapy, according to dictionary.com, means "the treatment of disease or disorders, as by some remedial, rehabilitating, or curative process." The underlying assumption is that there is a "problem" and that the problem lies within the child. There is a need for experts to identify and remediate this individualistic problem (Gabel, 2005).

Someone with this view is going to emphasize remediation and therapeutic activities—trying to "fix" the child. Services will be significant and focused on developing specific skills. The parents or the therapist will be focused on what is "wrong" with the child and how the child can fit in with his or her peers more easily.

In contrast, the social or educational model notes that persons with disabilities are only disabled within a context, and by changing the context, one can change the impact of the disability. Disability is perceived as a society's response to an identified difference within any minority group, and the effort must be to provide supports within the environment so that discrimination does not continue (Hehir, 2002). The emphasis through a social model is on inclusion and change within the environment rather than within the person.

Someone with this view will emphasize the holistic perspective of a child's experience and focus on inclusion and the acceptance of the child. This is the idea that someone in a wheelchair is not disabled if the classroom has easy access, there is ample opportunities for movement, and chairs, desks, and entrances are accommodating. However, if those things are not available, then the person is "disabled" because of the lack of fit between the person and the place. There is no giving up on skill development, but rather working with the classroom as a whole and encouraging understanding of differences. The focus is often on what is right with the child and how the strengths of the child can be developed.

Theoretically, there is a middle ground of balance, and efforts are made to both focus on the needs of the child, as well as to work within the context of the classroom or environment to change it. However, if you have an IEP meeting where parents lean one direction and professionals lean another, then it is critically important to understand where the other one is coming from.

You can see this shift in models through the language of disability. Children are no longer "autistic"—they are "children with autism." It's called "person-first language," and it is critically important to many, many people. Person-first language is the current language of the various laws, and emphasizes the person first, not the area of difference. Unless, of course, it doesn't. In his essay "Why I Dislike Person-First Language," Jim Sinclair (1999) stated that

> (1) Saying "person with autism" suggests that the autism can be separated from the person. . . . I am autistic because I *cannot* be separated from how my brain works. (2) Saying "person with autism" suggests that even if autism is part of the person, it isn't a very important part. Characteristics that are recognized as central to a person's identity are appropriately stated as adjectives, and may even be used as nouns to describe people: We talk about "male" and "female" people . . . not about "people with maleness" and "people with femaleness." (3) Saying "person with autism" suggests that autism is something bad—so bad that it isn't even consistent with being a person. . . . We talk about left-handed people, not "people with left-handedness," . . . It is only when someone has decided that the characteristic being referred to is *negative* that

suddenly people want to separate it from the person. I know that
autism is not a terrible thing, and that it does not make me any less
a person. (para. 1–4)

Such statements certainly can make one think. I have found that I generally use
person-first language as a sign of respect, and if there appears to be a question, I ask
the parents or the child. My opinion as an educator is irrelevant simply because I
do not have the right to make the choice of perspective for the family.

Inclusion Versus Continuum of Services Dichotomy

Anyone on the collaboration team may have a different viewpoint about
where the child is to be served for special services. Inclusionists favor the general
education classroom as the location for services, while the continuum of services
approach can favor pulling the student out of the classroom for service.

The inclusionist approach tends to favor the bringing of the services to the
child. This approach involves the use of multiple service providers within the same
environment who are jointly serving a group of heterogeneous students (Murawski,
2010). The emphasis is on sharing the instructional tasks for all students and differentiating within the context of the classroom to meet the needs of students with
exceptional needs (Friend & Cook, 2007). Such an approach tends to promote the
blending of special education and general education instructional approaches and
content. With this approach, even a child's strengths and gifts are served within
the general education setting through an acceleration or enrichment of the general
education curriculum (Winebrenner, 2001).

The continuum of services approach emphasizes the diagnostic-prescriptive
approach to services and states that sometimes this specialization of instruction
must occur in locations other than the general education context (Hallahan, Fuchs,
Gerber, Scruggs, & Zigmond, 2010). This approach focuses more on the development of specific skills, rather than the skills already being presented within a
general education classroom. In an approach that emphasizes the development
of talents, complex and advanced material is often provided in separate grouping
arrangements (VanTassel-Baska & Little, 2003).

Despite the fervor and the intensity with which schools debate the placement
of students, the research is fairly clear. In studies of grouping effects, the key to
effective instruction appears to be not the grouping practice, but the effectiveness of the teachers and the appropriateness of the curriculum and instructional
approaches involved (Elbaum, Moody, Vaughn, Schumm, & Hughes, 2009; Kulik
& Kulik, 1984; Rogers, 2002). Thus, a trained teacher with appropriate curriculum
can have a greater effect on students' academic growth than the grouping pattern
that is provided. The keys to a student's growth appear to be teacher flexibility and

instructional appropriateness—or matching the student to the activities you ask of him or her.

Working With Parents

It is perhaps obvious, but really needs to be stated very clearly and firmly, that the parents are the experts on their child. They have lived with their child's unique mixture of characteristics and have an idea of what works and what doesn't. That being said, they understand the growth of their child, not necessarily how that child is in the context of your classroom.

This sense of history is both a help and a hindrance. They might have tried a behavioral strategy 3 years ago and believe that it doesn't work on their child, when, in reality, their child is at a new developmental phase. It's important that both parents and teachers be able to listen to each other and understand the dynamic push-pull of the relationship.

The other factor that parental understanding of the child's history can impact is the different views of growth. Parents tend to look backward; they know how far their child has come. They know how hard and how long the battle to get to this point has been. It can be very hurtful for parents to focus only on the road ahead, when they want to appreciate the growth the child has already accomplished. In contrast, teachers are looking ahead and are aware of how much farther there is to go. They are very, very aware of the gaps that exist between the child and not where he has come from, but where he has to go. Sometimes, teachers' very jobs are on the line in closing that gap between a child and his or her peers. No Child Left Behind did not focus on growth—it focused on requiring all children to get to a particular point. IEPs are not written for backward views, but to close the gaps ahead.

When parents go into an IEP meeting, they are in a place of grief. No one chooses to be part of an IEP meeting—this is not something parents brag about at the playground. According to Elizabeth Kübler-Ross's (1973, 2005) model of grieving, people experience similar reactions to death, divorce, and disability (Boushey, 2001)—a series of identifiable steps that each have their own vocabulary. It is important to know where a parent is in this grief cycle in order to know what to expect and what to say. Saying the wrong thing at the wrong stage of the cycle can have some significant impacts on a teacher's peace of mind, as well as potential legal actions. It is important to know when to offer support, when to offer action, and when to ignore negativity. See Table 3 for a list of helpful and harmful actions.

Table 3

Helpful and Harmful Teacher Actions for Parents at Different Stages of Grief

Kübler-Ross Stage (Straker, 2007)	Typical Parental Actions and Statements	Helpful Teacher Actions	Harmful Teacher Actions
Immobilization/ Shock	Panicky, researching, frozen, asking questions but not listening to answers	Answering questions; providing data numerous times; providing options and understanding why none of them are taken; allowing emotional responses	Rushing to action; stressing immediate response; providing only one option; ignoring emotionality
Denial	Rejecting answers, lots of reading up on those things that reinforce hope; grasping at straws	Listening; focusing on those things that can be done; describing what you see; avoiding use of labels	Debunking myths; becoming part of the establishment that is not listening to possibilities; insisting on use of labels; telling parents what to do and what the data means
Anger	Rejecting answers; full of action and antagonism; looking for solutions to be implemented now	Providing responses and data to what is being done now; problem solving, being available	Resisting ideas; telling parents what to do; taking the anger personally
Bargaining	Trying to get things started, trying to make things happen; focused on action	Providing avenues of action; making suggestions about how parents could be involved; asking for ideas; providing connections to other parents who are in the same stage or who are in depression	Asking the parents to stop; telling them what they're doing is not helping; giving negative feedback
Depression	Stop showing up; inactive, quiet, uninvolved; rejections of possibility of growth	Invite parents to activities; communicate about growth; focus on improvements	Focus on the gap between the child and other children; nag the parents; make comments about how helpful it would be if the parents were more involved
Testing	Willing to try one or two things; small, limited level of involvement	Invite parents to more activities; give the parents specific short-term tasks to be done; educate the parents about new ideas and new strategies	Overwhelm the parents; focus on negative issues
Acceptance	Rational and eager; collaborative	Ask the parents for ideas; provide data and work together; build relationships	Pointing out past issues of the parents; not forgiving of past behaviors

Not in the Club

It is very, very important to recognize that although teachers and parents can both love a child, they do not have the same views on the child. I know what I'm talking about here. My daughter was diagnosed with autism at the age of 2 when she started receiving speech and occupational therapy when she wasn't talking. She was "cured" of autism at age 5 when she no longer qualified for services because she was speaking at age-appropriate levels. However, her intelligence is quite high, and so there is still a gap between what she can think and what she can verbalize. Her repetitive behaviors are managed, and she watches people carefully, trying to crack the code of social behaviors. You might think that I had a great deal to do with helping her, since I am and was a special education teacher. But you would be wrong.

When it comes to my own child, I am a member of the Parent Club. The one where we can only stand by helplessly, watching professionals do their work, hoping that something—anything—is going to improve. The club that wants the professionals to see the glory and the wonder in our children and to work with us on releasing that specialness. The club where we find support, understanding, and a community of people who "get it." The one that so many of us hate being in. It reminds me a bit of the Groucho Marx quote: "I don't care to belong to a club that would accept people like me." We get it, we understand each other, and we support each other, but oh, we miss the days—and sleep-filled nights—of ignorant bliss.

There is no joy in becoming a member of this club—this is no first-round-draft selection, this is no Bid Night for a sorority. But there is comfort in sadness together and there is comfort in the types of joys and celebrations that only another parent of a child with autism, or Tourette's, or bipolar disorder, or twice-exceptionality, or whatever the case may be can understand. And the club is critical to our survival. I only wish I didn't need it. I didn't choose this club—it chose me.

But I am also a member of the Teacher Club. The one who also celebrates growth, who also understands differences and frustrations. The one who recognizes the dynamic relationship between home and school, and that what you see at home may not be what you see at school. The one who loves kids and especially the kids that other teachers don't understand, don't want, or aren't taught how to teach; the kids that other kids don't understand, don't want, or aren't taught how to learn with. The one who seeks the key to teaching like I solve a puzzle. This club, I chose.

There are a lot of similarities in these two clubs, but there are an awful lot of differences. For you see:

- Although parents and teachers celebrate and recognize the very special-ness of the child, teachers do not have the joy mingled with the grief that comes from missing the child who never was—the child that he or she was "supposed to be" but autism got in the way. That grief may come and go, but it is always, always there.

- Although both teachers and parents are focused on growth, teachers measure progress by how far a child has to go, while parents measure progress by how far their child has come. Parents have a memory of the battles—for identification, for services, for stability, for growth—those that have already been fought and those that have been lost. This memory—biological in its "fight or flight" response—is as old as their child, and those memories are dredged up in every conflict. There is no new fight; there is just a continuation of the same fight—it might ebb and it might flow, but it's still the same fight. But to teachers, new conflicts are new. New conflicts are time-bound, issue-bound, and related to situations that are happening right here, right now. Parents are aware of the cost and the struggle that have already been spent and want acknowledgement for the progress of the battle. Teachers often focus on the cost and the struggle yet to come and want support for the battle ahead.

- Although parents see their child as a constellation of needs—medical, educational, therapeutic—teachers see the child in a constellation of others: part of a group and the actions and reactions and interactions of needs that come from a multitude of children. Teachers are constantly balancing the needs of the child with the needs of the many. As parents, we have one child with many needs we're trying to balance.

- Although parents will be working with their child's autism for the rest of their lives, teachers only have the child for a short time. Their relationship with their child, and autism, is often bigger than a marriage, bigger than financial solvency, and bigger than anything we might have ever imagined. As teachers, we leave at the end of the day. We leave at the end of the year. We pick up our own lives at that point, which might include disability, illness, and other issues that are bigger than we are, but the professional part is limited by time and location. We do our best for 6 or 8 or 12 hours a day, often more time than we spend awake with our family, but we leave it behind. Parents pick it back up every day of every year. They don't call it "commitment" for nothing. Being in this club is a lifetime sentence.

I often present a 6-hour professional development workshop for teachers titled "How to Communicate With Parents of Children With Autism." There is an incredible need to be able to respect each other, talk to each other, and understand each other. There are all sorts of typical communication strategies, such as active listening and providing time for communication, that teachers must learn, and they also need to know the points where communication tends to break down—delivery of bad news, legal understandings, and so on. Teachers are so often caught between many things: the school system and the parents, the legal and financial constraints of a system, the needs and desires of the families, and sometimes, the desire to keep your job and to do a good job.

Both teachers and parents know that they have to learn to communicate with each other. They know that everyone's job is easier, that the child benefits, and that progress is made when communication happens. But it's important to know that although we're in the same book, and hopefully, the same chapter, we are not, very definitely not, on the same page.

Communication Strategies

There are effective ways to handle parental responses, and then there are highly ineffective ways. Teachers need to validate and sympathize, *not* empathize. To empathize is to share those same feelings. To sympathize means that you understand and you "get it." To sympathize is to support, or to say things like:

- It must be very hard to hear that . . .
- I can see that you're upset . . .
- It's very difficult to . . . especially when . . .

Teachers, well-meaning, kind, caring people that they are, should *not* say things like:

- I know what you mean.
- I understand where you're coming from.
- I feel that, too.

It comes off as patronizing. It comes off as the precursor to that most dreaded of communication breakdowns—what I like to call the *YeaButs*. Parents or teachers who are wanting the best, trying to understand, and trying to bridge that gap may say "I understand that . . . yea . . . uh-huh . . . yea, but . . ." That "but . . ." is emphasizing the different point of view, the gap, the different page. Just as M. C. Escher drew different ways of seeing the same thing, parents and teachers, by definition of their relationship to the child, are in different places from each other.

Because the reality is that when you're a teacher, you have a different goal, a different purpose. Even if you're a parent of a child with exceptionality, even when you're a member of the club in a different place, when you're in the role of a teacher talking to parents, you have a different context. You have the context of school. You have the stage setting of your classroom in which you, and others like you, control the play and the actors, and the parent is but an audience member or maybe a stagehand. You each have the same desire for growth, but you have different views, different directions, and different needs. And these differences can cause serious distrust, serious miscommunication, and serious conflict if handled incorrectly.

If you're a parent reading this or if you're a teacher reading this . . .

- What is needed is understanding.

- What is needed is respect.
- What is needed is an acknowledgement of differences, while appreciating what makes you different.

After all, you're not in their club. And *who* you are and what role you're playing is very important to the success of the education of that child.

Working With Professionals

There is a wide range of professionals who could be involved in the education of a child with high-functioning autism and a whole host of collaboration strategies available for professionals who are working together for the education of a child who has multiple and potentially conflicting needs.

The Language of Autism

It's important when talking to different professionals to be able to understand the lingo. There's a whole host of official jargon that you will have to plow your way through. When I teach college students in their teacher preparation programs to start speaking "educationalese," I teach them to think of it like learning another language. Autism has yet again a whole new set of words to learn, even if you already speak education lingo. Words you thought you knew the meanings of don't quite mean the same thing in the context of autism. This is not even close to an exhaustive list, but it's a starting point for you. For more information, please see the Resources list in this book.

- *Typical and atypical*: These are words to describe what *most* children do at a specific age in a specific time and place. It is important not to think of them as normal and not normal, although most people do. Normal implies judgment—something you want your child to be. It is considered typical of a 4-year-old child who just moved to a new town to act out and cry while she is in the new grocery store. However, is acting out and crying considered normal when she is accustomed to the grocery store? Normal doesn't really take background situations into consideration. In typical/atypical, you look for things that aren't really explained by the age or the situation. There are *lots* of young children who act out, scream, and focus on objects, but for how long, at what age, and what else is going on?
- *Spectrum*: Autism is a spectrum disorder, which means that there are degrees of severity among a whole lot of different characteristics. There are some children who will exhibit mild characteristics and others who will have very severe symptoms. There are many children who do not qualify for services who exhibit some of these characteristics, and other children

who do qualify who demonstrate very different characteristics from each other. The phrase I often use is "children on the spectrum," which can include all of the various forms of autism, Asperger's syndrome, PDD-NOS, and Rett syndrome.

- *Characteristic*: Children might show a certain behavior, and many other children with autism have this same type of behavior. But it may not be enough to qualify for a label, or there may be other significant characteristics that are missing. It's a bit like looking at one puzzle piece and saying, "Yes, that looks like it goes to that puzzle, but without the other pieces, it's hard to say." Children may exhibit autism-like characteristics and not qualify for autism, but they still act differently.

- *Criteria*: This is the official term for the level of intensity and combination of characteristics that have to be there to qualify for the label and in order to be treated or receive services. Criteria do not imply severity; just that according to an outside authority, the child meets the standards for that label on multiple characteristics. For example, children with social impairments and repetitive behaviors but without language delays might fit the criteria for Asperger's syndrome, but not for PDD-NOS. There are *educational* criteria and *medical* criteria, and it's important to know which type you're working with.

- *Dysfunction*: This means that something does not work well or the way it's supposed to for others of the same age. "Social dysfunction" means that children don't socialize the way that other children do. It's a global term that tries to take the judgmental aspect out without going all the way to the term "disorder." According to my husband and mother, I have an organizational dysfunction, but it's not a significant problem for me. It's annoying for my husband, who has to see my bedside table piled with things that I'm doing at the time—a sewing project, three books, several cards in process of being written, random earrings I took off and didn't take back to the jewelry box—but not a real problem in my life. I can find things I need and my life is not deeply affected. Still, a dysfunction *can* become a disorder or disability if it gets too significant in a person's life.

- *Disorder*: This term implies that the ability that is impaired is creating a significant problem in a person's life. However, disorders are not assumed to be permanent and can sometimes be "cured" when given appropriate treatment or developmental growth. However, it is important to know that disorder treatment is not an equation: There is never one known right way. There may be many, many strategies and treatments available that may or may not be effective for a particular child.

- *Disability*: To use the term disability means that there is a dysfunction that creates significant problems for a child, and it is assumed to be a permanent situation. However, although it may be permanent, there is still teaching and learning that can help the child learn to cope. Many people have learning or behavior disabilities, and they can be taught to cope with them. I teach my prospective teachers that you can't teach someone to overcome his disability, but you can teach him how to learn *around* it or to cope with it. An example of a disability would be someone with artificial limbs. He can learn to run again with a prosthetic leg, but he can't ignore the fact that his original leg is missing. Likewise, someone with a learning disability can learn to cope and function, but she can't ignore the fact that she learns differently.

- *Handicap*: This is the old term for disability, but there is an underlying assumption that the condition cannot get better. Thus, you have handicap parking because the problem that created the need for a person to need to park close to a store is not going to get better. A friend of mine had a handicapped sticker because she had a serious heart condition. That heart condition could not be "taught" to get better.

- *High functioning v. low functioning*: High-functioning autism (HFA) is a difficult term. There are no clear-cut differences between high-functioning and low-functioning children with autism—no cut-off IQ scores, no reading score, no social ability index. It is a nontechnical term. The informal understanding is that children who are high functioning have stronger language and problem-solving skills and have slightly below average to above average and even gifted intelligence (Hughes-Lynch, 2010). Children who are low functioning tend to have characteristics that are more severe, have lower language skills, have lower intelligence scores, and often have other issues as well. Traditionally, Asperger's syndrome and PDD-NOS are considered higher functioning, while CDD and classic autism are lower, but these labels can vary widely from child to child. When I describe one child as high functioning, I am trying to imply that she is a little below or even above grade level in most academic subjects, struggles with language to some degree, has some sensory and social issues, and you might not even know that she had autism if you met her. On the flip side, a student who is low functioning may have very limited language, just got potty trained at age 11, and may be in a self-contained classroom. There are lots of children in between, above, and below them—all of who have autism and yet all of who are unique.

Collaboration Strategies

There are a number of resources available to professionals who are collaborating and working together. In an ideal situation, all of the educators are working and collaborating together to create a unified educational experience for a child that consists of blended components of their various areas of specialty, rather than segmenting the child's day up into separate sections with so many minutes of his day allotted to each professional. This minute-by-minute service approach ends up segmenting the child so that he would be in gifted instruction for an hour a day, need social skills instruction for another hour, and then focus on his language skills for yet another hour. In between, he is to learn science, math, and social studies. It is much easier for everyone if specific skills can be worked on in conjunction with content, rather than as a set of isolated skills.

In order to provide this unified approach, Friend and Cook (2007) discussed five models of interaction that educators can use, with the general education classroom as the focal point of instruction:

1. *One-teach, one-support* is where one teacher is the lead instructor and the other takes notes, assesses behavior, or monitors behavior. It is important that the knowledge of the special educator be implemented, so that the special educator is not used as a glorified paraprofessional.

2. *Station teaching* is a commonly used approach where each instructor works with children in a small group as groups cycle through the stations. The stations can be differentiated by interest, readiness level, and learning styles to better meet the needs of all students.

3. *Parallel teaching* occurs when the class is divided in half and each teacher is responsible for instruction of the same material.

4. *Alternate teaching* occurs when teachers take turns teaching a small group who may need either advanced activities or additional practice while the other teacher is providing instruction to the larger group. Care should be taken that this is not a "resource room without walls" in which the special educator works only with her students. Rather, this is an opportunity for both teachers to provide focused instruction to different students at different times.

5. *Team teaching* is when both teachers are the focus of instruction. One can be talking while the other is taking notes and asking "dumb" questions—the questions that they know that children might have, but are too afraid of looking "dumb" to ask. They can model, dramatize, and play off of each other. Such teaming requires a greater level of trust and a relationship between the teachers, but can be incredibly rewarding for both teachers and students.

These various models can be employed using a "while one professional is . . . , the other professional is . . ." planning model (Murawski, 2009). The use of such a model allows professionals opportunities to work together to integrate their content and skills together. I've also found them to be excellent prompts for the question of "Okay, what shall we do today and how can we ever get it all done?"

Types of Professionals

The list of professionals is a long one; the characteristics of the disability tend to frame the people with whom you'll be working. However, there are many, many variations of the following.

General education teachers. General education teachers are trained to take the state's expectations, as stated in the general academic standards—whether that is identifying colors in preschool or describing the elements in the periodic table of elements in high school chemistry—and translate these standards into instruction. They tend to teach in a whole-class method and to the middle of the class's ability level. They are perceived as content experts, have a strong background in the content that they are teaching, and understand how what they are teaching will lead to further growth in the content areas. When I work with secondary teachers, because secondary teachers tend to be the most content focused, I ask them what they teach. The answer is often "geometry" or "English." "No!" I inform them. "You are teaching geometry and English *to* children. You are *teaching* children."

Most general education teachers do not refer to the literature or to doctors about the characteristics and needs of children with autism; a recent study found that a large majority of them rely on the special education teacher as the sole source for information and feel very uneasy about teaching children with autism (Schwarber, 2006)—a statistic that demonstrates the importance of the knowledge level of the special education teacher.

Special education teachers. Special education teachers traditionally have little content background, but have extensive training in strategies and differentiation. They can take a typical assignment, strip it down to its essential components, teach it in a different manner, change the classroom environment, and adapt the instruction to the individual child. They are trained to identify and describe exceptionalities and scaffold instruction to meet the needs of the child. They typically are less content focused and may have less knowledge of grade-level methods of instruction because of the range of ages and readiness levels with which they work. Special educators who graduated more than 10 years ago may not have had extensive education regarding autism because the label has only taken off in the last decade.

Gifted education teachers. Gifted education teachers are similar to special education teachers in that their training is primarily focused on implementing strategies, but their focus is on the instructional processes of acceleration and enrichment. They have been trained to identify strengths and to develop a child's abilities, so they tend to be a very positive type of instructor and one with high expectations. It is important when working with a gifted educator that she or he be familiar with the concept of "asynchronous development" so that he or she will not be expecting a child with high-functioning autism to act the same as other gifted students.

Working With Specialists and Therapists

There are a variety of specialists you might be working with—ranging from someone who sends a report that you're supposed to read, understand, and incorporate into your teaching, to someone who you call in tears because you don't know what else you can do.

Specialists are generally either provided by the school system through the IEP, provided through the medical insurance of the parent, paid for independently by the parents, or a combination of all of these. The particular mixture of specialist services is often determined by the parents' pocketbooks, their ability to get what they ask for, and what is available in their area. It can be a very confusing array—particularly if different therapists have opposing strategies. You will need to communicate with the parents to determine the degree to which they are advocating a particular approach. You may have one set of parents who are emphatic about a particular diet, while another set of parents are equally emphatic about the use of a particular biofeedback strategy. It is important to keep an open mind, and to keep the focus on the child and his or her "fit" within the classroom. If you're confused or irritated because of confusing messages, imagine the parents' distress, angst, and determination to find something to help their child.

Generally, specialists fall into three primary categories directly related to the characteristics of autism. These include:

- *behavioral specialists/therapists* for behaviors related to autism, such as repetitive behaviors, stress-related behaviors, tantrums, and social engagement with others;
- *speech therapists* for communication issues, word-finding and articulation, prosody, and pragmatic language issues; and
- *occupational therapists* for sensory issues, daily living skills, handwriting, grip, muscle tone, and gait.

Often, depending on the specific issues of the child, there may be other therapists involved as well:

- *biomedical therapists*, who focus on biofeedback or other biological approaches, such as magnetic therapy;

- *cognitive therapists*, who focus on thinking skills and how the child can frame his or her experience;
- *developmental therapists*, who focus on assessing and facilitating a child's growth in the planes of development—physical, social, language, cognitive, and emotional. They often work with younger children before they get into school, although some may work with school-aged children;
- *nutritional therapists*, who work with children's eating habits and digestive issues. They may prescribe certain diets to be followed. Numerous families are asked to follow a gluten-free, casein-free (GFCF) diet, or some other variations such as phenol-free, probiotics, uses of essential fatty acids, or sugar-free diets;
- *physical therapists*, who tend to work on various gait issues and any unusual patterns of movement;
- *play therapists*, who encourage children to work out their issues and anxieties using structured and unstructured play with objects and with others. During these play experiences, therapists watch and may interact with the child to encourage problem solving;
- *psychiatric therapists*, who may work with the child and family on various medications to control the symptoms of autism;
- *sleep therapists*, who may work with the child and family to develop healthy sleep habits—something that eludes a lot of children with autism;
- *social skills therapists*, who work with the child on improving social interactions. Commonly, they use social stories, social scripts, or social thinking programs to help children recognize and determine appropriate social skills;
- *visual therapists*, who work with the child on improving the "eye" part of the hand-eye coordination aspect. Specific skills include fine and large motor issues, including reading, writing, and general clumsiness; and
- *vitamin therapists*, who work with the family on a regimen of vitamins that some families find to help their child. Often, doses of Vitamins A, C, and B6 and magnesium are common treatments.

If there are comorbid conditions, such as Tourette's syndrome or epilepsy, you might work with yet even more specialists.

Clearly, there are lots of overlapping areas that different therapists may address. For example, social interactions—always an area of challenge—may be addressed through a social skills therapist, behavioral therapist, speech therapist, play therapist, or even a developmental therapist. It is important to remember that there are many different ways to address a problem; just keep an open mind and listen, while knowing that you are an expert in the particular social dynamics of your classroom.

It can't hurt to try something new, but you want to keep things as consistent as you can in your classroom—for your sanity and that of your students!

Behavior Specialists

Behavior specialists are just what their title implies: They are experts at working with behaviors that impede learning—in other words, the reasons that a child with autism can drive you crazy. You will often be working with a counselor who may have access to social skills programs, a behavior interventionist, or an Applied Behavior Analysis (ABA) specialist. Specific social skills programs will be discussed in Section II, but it is critically important to coordinate social skills programs so that the instruction from the counselor or therapist matches the instruction in the classroom. Ask for a curriculum or weekly updates and again, ask what you can do or should not do.

Some behavioral specialists may see content learning as part of their behavior focus, but most do not. Most are working on the management of social skills, attentional skills, and repetitive behaviors. A Board-Certified Behavior Analyst (BCBA) will be certified through the Behavior Analyst Certification Board (BACB), while others may be certified as Behavior Support Specialists (BSS) through your state department of education. Any certification implies graduate-level work beyond a bachelor's degree with emphases on behavior management and therapy.

The language of behavioral therapists. It helps to speak the specialist's language. Behavioral therapists will toss around certain terms, and it will help you if you understand where they're coming from. It's as easy as the ABCs of behavioral therapy (Santrock, 2012):

- *Antecedent*: Antecedents are those events that precede a behavior, sometimes called a *trigger*. In the case of an undesired behavior, the antecedent is something you want to change in the behavior response; for a positive behavior, you want to increase the response. For example, one child I knew was triggered by perfume—just the smell alone of a perfume was enough to produce a tantrum.
- *Behavior*: According to dictionary.com, behavior is "the way in which a person acts in response to a particular situation or stimulus." More than that, in behaviorist terms, behavior is observable and measureable. Because it is observable and measureable, changes can be documented. Replacement behavior is a behavior that the therapist selects as one to encourage as a replacement for the negative behavior. For example, for the child triggered by perfume, the therapist worked with the child to have the child leave the area of the offending smell, rather than having the tantrum.
- *Consequence*: A consequence follows a specific behavior and has the possibility of increasing or decreasing that behavior. If a mother always gives

in to her son's whining for candy in the grocery store line, the child is more likely to whine while standing in line. The giving of candy was supposed to decrease the whining, but in fact, it will increase the likelihood that it will occur again. There are three types of consequences: reinforcers, negative reinforcers, and punishment.

- Reinforcers are any sort of provided consequences that are likely to increase the desired behavior. In the example of the whining and the candy, the candy is likely to reinforce the whining.

- Negative reinforcers include the removal of something undesired in the case of a positive behavior. If the child stops whining once he gets his candy, the mother is more likely to use candy as a means of getting him to stop.

- Punishment is the least effective consequence, because it only stops behavior, rather than increasing or decreasing specific behavior (American Academy of Pediatrics, 2004). When children are presented with punishment, there is not an emphasis on what *to do*, but rather an emphasis on what *not to do*. Therefore, punishment has been found to be short term in its effectiveness, because it does not replace the response to the antecedent.

- *Discrete Trial Training*: This is the process through which a student is gradually rewarded for getting closer and closer to the eventual goal. For example, in the first trial, a child might be rewarded for saying "P" when asking for something. By the fifth trial, the therapist requires the child to say "Pul" when asking for something, and by the 20th trial, the student is expected to say a complete "Please." Each skill that is learned is specific and predetermined as to what the end result is going to be.

In addition to the general behavioral terms, there are essentially five ways you can describe a child's behavior. Use the terms correctly, and you've got clear information with which to work. These terms form the foundation of the data that has to be gathered to make data-driven decisions:

1. *Characteristics*: What does something *look* like? It's a way of describing *what* a child is doing:
   - What words are being used?
   - What expression is on her face?
   - How does the child hold her pencil?
   - What does she say to other children?
   - What is her tone and facial expression?

2. *Frequency*: How *often* does a certain behavior occur and over what time frame? Hint: "Always" and "never" are trigger words for the need to collect data here. You need numbers, not impressions.
   O How often does a "repetitive behavior" occur?
   O How many times did the child get out of his seat and in what time frame?
   O How long did the child sustain attention?
   O How many back-and-forth interactions were you able to hold?

3. *Latency*: How long after you ask for a certain behavior does a child do it?
   O How long does it take to get a child to respond to his name? Typical kids will respond immediately to their name. Our friend Gus sometimes would appear to have to think about what his name meant before he would turn toward you.
   O How long does it take for a child to get back to work once you've asked her to?

4. *Duration*: How *long* does a behavior last?
   O How long does a tantrum last?
   O How long does she wander around the room?
   O How long does he rock?

5. *Intensity*: How loud or soft or hard or big or small (the size of something) is the behavior?
   O It's one thing to shut the door. It's a whole 'nother thing to *slam* the door. Middle school kids are prone to issues of intensity and when you fuss at them, the response typically is "WHAT? I was JUST (dropping my books, closing the door, getting out a pencil, setting the table . . . you name it)." Intensity has to do with degrees. It's typical behavior that's just, well, more intense.

Behavioral strategies. There are a wide variety of behavioral strategies that a specialist may focus on, depending on his or her training. Most of the time, behavioral specialists will focus on identifying triggers of behaviors, identifying and describing specific behaviors, and determining reinforcers. Many will work with Applied Behavior Analysis strategies.

Applied Behavioral Analysis (ABA) is the gold standard of working with children with autism. A recent study by the Center for Autism and Related Disorders (CARD; Faller, 2010) in Phoenix found that 43% of its children ages 2–5 who were treated with ABA techniques were "cured" or no longer required services. However, ABA in its therapeutic version is one-on-one, requires someone with advanced training in ABA techniques, and can require up to 40 hours of intervention per week. In other words, it's very expensive and it's very intense. But it works.

In a school setting, behavioral therapists might work on specific skills related to social interactions or how to deal with frustration. Rewards might include M&Ms for very concrete children and "class dollars" for more advanced children. I personally have always hated the use of candy as a reward, because (a) candy itself might be a trigger for autism, according to some theorists, and (b) you ruin their lunch or dinner and eating is often an issue for these children. Find something else: a happy stimming activity such as playing with a spinning top or computer time that the child wants to work toward. The behavioral specialist is a fabulous resource for you to work with in setting up reward and consequence systems in your classroom.

Speech and Language Therapists

Speech therapists tend to work in isolation; that is, they have the child in for therapy within the therapeutic setting. Some very proactive ones will include you in the process, so you need to find out what your role is expected to be. However, at a minimum, ask the therapist what specific skills she is working on that week, what you can do, and what you should *not* do. I've seen a number of teachers undo the good work of the speech therapist by overdoing their role in speech production. For example, a therapist was working on a child's development of initial sounds. The child was essentially nonverbal, and the speech therapist was encouraging the child to make an initial sound that closely approximated the actual word. The teacher, young and gung-ho, started asking the child to verbalize everything he wanted, eventually placing so much pressure on the child that he shut down and retreated again. It is important to do—and not to undo—what the speech therapist is focusing on. I know of several teachers who coordinate with the speech therapist to align their phonics instruction with the emphasis that the speech therapist is focusing on in speech, so children get initial sounds both orally and visually and ending sounds both by speaking it and reading it. Speaking can be very difficult for children with autism—if you can teach them to read the sounds at the same time, you can sometimes help both processes.

Speech and language therapists focus on two aspects of speech:
- improving production of speech, and
- improving communication.

This list includes working with the articulation of words, the finding of words, the use of language in different settings, swallowing and use of the tongue and mouth, naming of things, parts of speech, appropriate endings, nonverbal communication, and even the rhythm of words. Basically, if an issue involves the mouth and communicating, it involves a speech therapist.

A certified speech and language therapist—also called a Speech and Language Pathologist (SLP)—will have a graduate degree and be certified by the state where she works. Most therapists will also be certified with a Certificate of Clinical Competence in Speech-Language Pathology (CCC-SLP), a credential offered by the American Speech-Language-Hearing Association (ASHA).

The Language of SLPs. You would think that a specialization that emphasizes the improvement of communication would have easily understood terminology. But such is not the case. This is a list of some of the more common terms, but certainly not an exhaustive one. It would be advisable to communicate with the student's SLP if you have questions about what he or she is working on.

- *Apraxia*: According to the American Speech-Language-Hearing Association (ASHA, 2011), childhood apraxia of speech (CAS) is a motor speech disorder. Children with CAS have problems saying sounds, syllables, and words, but not because of muscle weakness or paralysis. The brain has problems planning to move the body parts (e.g., lips, jaw, tongue) needed for speech. The child knows what he or she wants to say, but his or her brain has difficulty coordinating the muscle movements necessary to say those words. Sometimes, children with autism will have difficulty forming words because of apraxia. Apraxia is often used synonymously with the term "dyspraxia." Some specialists will focus on the difference, with apraxia meaning "without speech," and dyspraxia as "difficulty with speech" (SpeechPathology.com, 2005), while others define dyspraxia as a disorder with sensory integration while planning speech and apraxia as a disorder in executing speech (Cermak, 1985). You will need to ask your SLP if he differentiates between the two and if so, how he defines each one.
- *Articulation*: The clarity of speech and the intelligibility of the various words and sounds are issues of articulation. When an SLP is focusing on articulation, he or she will be focusing on the formation of the sounds, using the tongue, the mouth, and the teeth. Although the development of language is important, the clear communication of that language is the focus in articulation.
- *Assistive and augmentative communication* (AAC): When the mouth and the formation of language is exceedingly difficult, SLPs might consider the use of AAC, devices that provide the communication for the student (Mirenda, 2001). These devices range from talking computers to Picture Exchange Communication Systems (PECS) in which students select a graphic of the concept or idea that they want to convey.
- *Expressive language*: To communicate what you want, what you are thinking about, and what you are feeling are all aspects of expressive language. It is critical that students be able to select the right word for the right pur-

pose and state them using the right tone and pitch with the corresponding body language in order for their message to be clear.

- *Fluency*: The speed and flow of words and sentences impact fluency. Stuttering, although not often an issue in autism, is related to anxiety issues as well. However, many people with autism do have issues with smoothness and dynamics of speech.

- *Language*: According to ASHA (2011), language "is made up of socially shared rules that include the following: (a) What words mean, (b) How to make new words, (c) How to put words together, (d) What word combinations are best in what situations" (para. 3). Thus, language is both spoken, written, verbal, and nonverbal and is housed in context and culture. Children with HFA, as part of the definition of autism, have difficulty with some aspect of language.

- *Oral motor exercises*: This refers to "sensory stimulation to or actions of the lips, jaw, tongue, soft palate, larynx, and respiratory muscles" (McCauley, Strand, Lof, Schooling, & Frymark, 2009, p. 343). Speech therapists will encourage such experiences in order to help a child feel how he is to form sounds and words. Often, children with autism will place things in their mouths as a form of sensory stimulation; therefore, this therapy can use an action they are already doing to help them with their speech.

- *Phonological processing*: This is the understanding of separate and distinct sounds that a child has to process and produce. For example, the difference between "car" and "cars" can be very important when crossing the street.

- *Pragmatics*: Saying the right word in the right way in the right place for the right purpose; language determined by the context (Peppé, McCann, Gibbon, O'Hare, & Rutherford, 2006). I can talk like a professor in faculty meetings, but it's not appropriate to talk that way to my family.

- *Praxis*: Being able to complete a skilled movement. In speech, this refers to the movements made with the mouth and tongue, such as swallowing, or saying the letter "o." It refers to the brain planning to move the muscles of the mouth in the proper shape to make the proper sound. However, it is also a word that occupational therapists use, and with an OT, it has a slightly different contextual meaning.

- *Prosody*: The rhythm and music of speech, also known as *intonation*. Each language has its own distinctive prosody. Children with autism often have issues with prosody (Peppé et al., 2006) and are said to sound like "little professors"—a term that I, personally, find rather offensive!

- *Receptive language*: In order to communicate, it is important to understand what is told to you. Receptive language is the ability to understand and comprehend language, both spoken and nonverbal.

- *Speech*: According to ASHA (2011), speech "is the verbal means of communicating" (para. 4). There are three types of speech disorders, including (a) fluency, (b) voice, and (c) articulation. A child with autism may have all of these, or none of these. As part of the definition of autism, there must be a problem with language, and certainly language production can qualify as a communication issue.
- *Diadochokinesis*: if you really want to impress your SLP with your desire to understand his or her area of expertise, try this word. Here is a syllable breakdown so you can even pronounce it correctly: die-uh-doe-ko-kin-ee-sis. Diadochokinesis is the rapid repetition of several different sounds in a row. This is a traditional oral motor exercise, used to improve the quick lip and tongue movement required to produce clear speech (Speech Therapy on Video, 2006).

Speech-language strategies. The SLP has an enormous range of strategies that she can draw upon when working with children. She might work on everything from teaching the child how to read directions, to multistep directions, to word-finding strategies, to articulation issues. The list of what the SLP might work on is far beyond the scope of this book, and I recommend that you talk with your SLP for ideas.

Occupational Therapists

Occupational therapists focus on the daily living skills that a child needs at a particular age within his environment. They often work with children and families on daily living skills such as brushing your teeth, gross motor skills such as riding a bike, and fine motor skills such as using a pencil grip. In the case of children with autism, that point of contact between the demands of the child's environment and the child's response to those demands becomes the central area of emphasis. Often, skills such as self-regulation, learning how to focus, and appropriate ways to express feelings are emphasized.

According to the Bureau of Labor Statistics (2011), an occupational therapist will have a master's degree and be certified by the state. Although not required, many occupational therapists are registered with the National Board for Certifying Occupational Therapists, and will have the initials OTR after their name, indicating Occupational Therapist Registered.

The Language of OTs. OTs seem to have fewer terms, but they are very precise with their definitions.
- *Fine motor skills*: The skilled use of hands and fingers.
- *Gross motor skills*: The coordinated body movements made with the large muscle groups, such as running, biking, or swinging the arms.

- *Visual motor skills*: Related to hand-eye coordination, in that they are the skills necessary for knowing where things are in space. Writing, tracing, pointing, and grasping are involved in these skills.
- *Visual perceptual skills*: Different in that they do not necessarily involve the body, but are the skills needed to determine an object from its background or to interpret the visual field. These abilities significantly impact reading, copying, and even tasks like tying shoes.
- *Bilateral coordination skills*: The ability to use both sides of the body. I was told once by an occupational therapist not to allow my younger children to sit in a "w" shape with their bottoms on the floor, their knees in front of them, and their legs out to the side, because the shape did not cross the mid-line and did not develop neurological connections. I don't know the research behind it, but I was amused at the idea of a biological necessity for the seated "criss-cross applesauce" that is often taught in kindergarten.
- *Sensory processing skills*: Related to how a child receives information from his or her environment. An occupational therapist can teach a child who is either understimulated or overstimulated about how to interact with her environment.

Occupational therapy strategies. It is especially critical that you communicate regularly with a child's OT because "living skills" mean how he functions within your classroom. You will want to provide information to the OT, as well as reinforce the skills the OT is working on. Occupational therapists typically deal with both the fine motor and sensory issues that plague children with autism. Therapies range from the provision of materials, like the use of pencil grips and balance chairs, to more significant therapies, like brushing the skin with a hard plastic comb and balanced musical interludes.

The OT may use a variety of techniques, some of which, frankly, I found really odd when I first started working with an OT. They often use strategies like rocking, wrapping a child in a hammock and spinning her, or even having her play in a ball pit to calm down an agitated nervous system. The first time I was asked to "brush" a child with a hard plastic brush, I really wondered about the educational value of such strategies. However, I found that the children tended to calm down and could focus better as a result. Some schools in collaboration with their OTs have instituted "sensory rooms" for their children with autism in their buildings—rooms that look very much like the effects of hallucinogenic drugs with lights, sounds, and colors all over the place. However, again, these experiences are for sensory systems that are not functioning appropriately and are valid alternatives to seclusion and restraint (Champagne & Stomberg, 2004).

Occupational therapists will also often use an object, a weighted vest, or a seat cushion to provide sensory input to a child. These almost all have weight and heft to them, as well as a variety of textures and bumps. These can be used in classrooms or even carried around with a child to provide appropriate stimulation. Some schools, in collaboration with their OTs, have found other strategies such as yoga, dance, and the use of music to improve children's time on task within a classroom.

As an educator, I had a hard time letting my students go to these rooms to "play"—or to use their "toys"—and yet, I found that if I did not, their level of agitation would increase to the point that they were unable to calm themselves down and they were not learning anything anyway. A classic example was a 10-year-old child I knew who, while very verbal and extraordinarily good at math and reading, would put things in her mouth—pencils, book edges, hair—you name it, she chewed it. You could tell when she was agitated because she would start gnawing and breathing rapidly. The OT suggested that when it became apparent that chewing and oral issues were a problem, she could be given gum to chew. An easy solution, yes, but it required that I get over my inbred teacher reaction of "NO GUM!" However, with gum smacking away, she was able to stay in her seat and respond appropriately most of the time. I realized that I could not stop her autistic tendencies, but I could reduce their impact on the classroom community with the inclusion of such strategies. And what I found was that such activities seemed to help many of my other students as well!

Medical Specialists

A number of parents work with various medical specialists. The list can range from a general pediatrician, to a pediatric neuropsychologist, to a nutritionist. It is especially important to have an open discussion with these medical experts, because often all you will get originally from them is a written report. This written report might have medical information that is related to diet or medical, bodily interventions, but it often can venture into educational psychology. When the report provides information that is relevant to classroom functioning, it is also often full of "helpful" strategies that tell you how to run your classroom. I tend to see two reactions when teachers read these types of reports: an open, interested reaction or one that discounts the information as not relevant to their classrooms. Take the report with a grain of salt—the information can be very helpful, but at the same time, the specialist does not work with you, your classroom, your school, or the other children within the classroom. That doesn't mean that you can't incorporate some of the ideas, but be sure to read the report with an eye for the most important suggestions and see how they are related to the child's individual needs. I have read reports from one doctor that recommended one-on-one reading support—a reality that just was not feasible in my self-contained classroom of 15 high-needs students and no paraprofessional. But I did incorporate some volunteer grandparents from a local nursing home, trained them on how to read to children with disabilities, and thus, we had one-on-one reading support.

Often, parents will try to use these medical reports as evidence for asking for more supports for their child. Remember, more support is always a good thing, but you are the curriculum expert. I had one group of parents who were bound and determined to incorporate a particular computer program into our school—a program that we did not have either the money or the training for. The psychological report asked for this program by name, and I was asked to explain why my reading program would suffice in place of this particular computer program. It was a very uncomfortable position to be in, but I also knew that I had been trained in a different reading program and that my reading background would allow me to meet this student's needs without the added expense of the new program. I did not "take on" the parents, but I was asked to provide backup for my curriculum choices by my principal. Luckily, I read up on the program and could walk the parents through it and show them how I was going to be able to incorporate most of the elements within my classroom. In these situations, remember that (1) the parents are just frantically looking for something to help their child, and (2) if you are knowledgeable about what you're doing, you can defend your choices. Both of you are focused on helping the child—just with different tools.

Working With Doctors and Medications

Although you won't be prescribing medications, chances are very good that you will be consulted about the need for, and the effects of, various medications on a child with autism. As many as 80% of children with Asperger's syndrome or autism are prescribed a psychiatric medication of some kind (Brice, 2007). Only Risperdal and Abilify have been approved by the FDA for use with autism; the others are used to treat the symptoms of autism. Although there is no medical cure for autism, there is a large list of commonly prescribed medications. Common types of medications include ones regularly prescribed for ADHD, depression, bipolar disorder, seizures, and antipsychotics. However, this list is constantly changing. Medical interventions and tests are being conducted at a very rapid rate these days. According to autismhealingthresholds.com (2011) and National Institute of Mental Health (NIMH, 2009), the medications in Table 4 are the most commonly prescribed among children with autism.

Key Points From Chapter 3

- Working with a team is critical to the success of teaching a child with high-functioning autism.
- Teachers have the need to understand the various viewpoints that can conflict about how best to serve a child with HFA and the needs of parents and strategies to communicate with them.

Table 4

Common Medications for Autism and Common Side Effects

Medication	Used to Treat	Common Side Effects
Risperdal (risperidone)	Aggression, irritability, bipolar, mania, schizophrenia	Weight gain, increased appetite, sleepiness
Abilify (aripiprazole)	Depression, irritability	Agitation, sleep problems
Adderall (amphetamine)	Hyperactivity, impulse control	Zombie-like behavior, drug dependence
Anafanil (clomipramine hydrochloride)	Obsessive-compulsive disorder (OCD), repetitive behaviors	Increase in suicidal thoughts
Ativan	Anxiety	Aggression, agitation
Carbatrol, Equetro, Tegretol	Seizures, mania	Blood disorders, rashes
Clonidine	Impulsiveness, aggression, hypertension	Tiredness, fatigue
Clozaril, FazaClo (clozapine)	Hyperactivity, fidgeting, aggression	Seizures, blood disorders
Haldol	Tics, antipsychotic, aggression	Sleepiness, muscle stiffness
Klonipin (clonezepam)	Seizures, panic, anxiety	Habit forming
Lamictil (lamotrigine)	Mood stability, irritability, hyperactivity	Rash that can be deadly
Luvox (fluvoximine maleate)	Depression, OCD	Suicidal thinking in younger people
Pepcid	Stomach acid, reflux	Constipation, diarrhea
Prozac (fluoxetine hydrochloride)	Depression, OCD, anxiety, aggression, panic attacks	Suicidal thinking in younger people
Tenex, Intuniv (guanfacine)	High blood pressure, inattention, Tourette's, ADHD, sleep disorders	Constipation, possible change in heartbeat
Topomax (topiramate)	Irritability, self-injurious behaviors, convulsions	Acidic blood
Thorazine (chlorpromazine)	Severe behavioral problems—explosiveness, aggression	Zombie-like behavior

- The different terms used by educators must be understood, along with the vocabulary and strategies for working with professionals who are not teachers, including:
    - behavioral therapists,
    - speech therapists,
    - occupational therapists, and
    - medical specialists

- The potential side effects of common medications and how they can affect the classroom must be considered by teachers. Table 4 includes a list of medications students with autism may take.

Chapter 4

Writing a Strong IEP

One of the biggest differences between medical diagnoses and educational labels is the emphasis on need for services. Special education in public schools is defined by the federal Individuals with Disabilities Education Act (IDEA), and autism is defined in Section 300.8.c.1.i as a "developmental disability significantly affecting verbal and nonverbal communication and social interaction, generally evident before age three, *that adversely affects a child's educational performance*" (USDOE, 2004, para. 8, italics added). Schools have to assess a child's cognitive and academic levels in addition to communication and social behaviors in order to determine if special education services are needed. This may mean that parents can bring their child to school with a medical diagnosis, and yet not qualify for services under IDEA, a situation that can lead to confusion and distress if not explained well. If there is an impact on learning, a child may qualify for either an Individualized Family Services Plan (IFSP) if the child is younger than 3, or an Individualized Education Program (IEP) if the child is between ages 3–22. If there is a disability and the child requires accommodations in order to learn, but there is not enough of an impact for special education services, the child may qualify for a 504 Plan. The line between a 504 Plan and an IEP is a fine one, and it's often determined by the administrators of the district. You should find out what your school district considers to be "adverse" effect, which is often a particular set of scores on specific tests and measures, before you advise parents or make suggestions about what they can do if they've just gotten a diagnosis from a doctor. This degree of adverse impact can be particularly important, because many children with HFA may have a medical diagnosis of autism, but not an educational label. As a teacher, it may mean that you deal with the characteristics of autism, but without the support from special education.

Although not all students with HFA will qualify for an Individualized Family Services Plan (IFSP), an Individualized Education Program (IEP), or a 504 Plan, it is critically important that for those who do, the plan helps the teachers and parents focus on developing the strengths of the child while remediating areas of difficulty. IFSPs are for children younger than 6 who qualify for Early Intervention services; IEPs are required only for students with a qualifying label in public schools from grades K–12 or up to age 21, who qualify for educational interventions because of a perceived need.

Special Education in Public Schools

The following is a synopsis of special education. For more information, please go to the NICHCY (http://nichcy.org), Wright's Law (http://www.wrightslaw.com), or U.S. Department of Education's Office of Special Education Programs (http://www.osepideasthatwork.org) websites. As a teacher, you need to know the rights and responsibilities that parents and teachers have under the law.

Funding Issues

Public education is free—all of it. If specialized programs, equipment, technology, and services, including individual persons, are deemed necessary to help a child, all of it is free to the parents. However, it is important to realize that as a school system, we have to operate under significant financial constraints, and all of our dealings with parents will take that into consideration, even though legally, we're not supposed to. Susan Senator (2005) referred to it as the business model of education, not a bad metaphor.

Special education in the public schools is required by federal law; also known as the Individuals with Disabilities Education Improvement Act and commonly called IDEA. Significant changes are made to this law every 7 years. The last round of changes were conducted in 2004, so the most recent law is called IDEA 2004. About 1/3, or 33%, of the federal education budget is taken up with special education. Because approximately 10%–20% of students in schools are in special education, there is an unequal distribution; it is clear that it is more expensive to educate children with disabilities.

However, all of this federal money only pays for approximately 7% of the actual cost of special education borne by a school district (New America Foundation, 2011). The remaining 92% of the monies has to come from the state and the district—most often from the district. IDEA has been very close to an unfunded mandate from the federal government: Districts are required to follow very specific procedures and to provide specific services, and yet are given very little money to do so by the federal government. In cases where districts have claimed that they are unable to provide such services because of their economic woes, the Supreme Court has told them that they must—and they must simply take the costs from other operating expenses. Thus, it is in the interest of school systems to keep their special education costs under control, but provide enough services that students benefit.

There is a legal definition of the word "benefit" as well: The education for any one child has to provide a setting in which it is expected that that child will make progress. It is *not* required that the educational experience be maximized for optimal growth of that child, nor purely for social reasons. This means that school districts are always trying to balance what is a "good enough" education for a child and the desires of the parents. When I teach a Special Education law class, I tell my students that special education has been shaped by court cases, and that while individuals may want to do the best for children, the system has to maximize its public tax dollars for all children. Thus, there is an inherent tension built in between the needs of the school district to provide adequate education for all of its children with the budget that it has and the needs of the parents to have excellent educational opportunities for their child.

This doesn't necessarily mean that the process has to be overtly adversarial, though. Districts and parents are not automatically on opposite sides; in fact, they do have the same goal—to educate the child in the best manner possible and to help him grow. It's just that the word "possible" means different things depending on which side of the table you're sitting.

IEP Versus 504

All public schools are required to serve all of their students, so special education is designed to work with students who (a) have a disability, *and* (b) have some form of school problem that *only* a change in instruction would address. If there is an adverse effect on educational achievement, but a change in the accessibility to the instruction would address it, students may have a disability, but not qualify for special education.

If this is the case, but they still need some accommodations or modifications in order to perform well in school, parents have the right to ask for a 504 Plan. Section 504 is part of the Rehabilitation Act of 1973 that requires employers to provide equal access to their employees in order to do their jobs; they cannot discriminate, based on the employee's disability and the employer's requirement to provide access. For example, if your office is on the second floor, you are not allowed to deny a person in a motorized chair a job if he or she would be capable of doing the job once he or she had access to the office. The employer has to provide ramps or elevators or some form of access. If you think of children with disabilities as employees, they have the right to access the traditional school curriculum and not have their disability get in the way of that access. Schools may have to make accommodations. A 504 Plan is where the school, the parents, and sometimes the child, plan what kinds of accommodations are needed to access the regular curriculum. Students on a 504 Plan do not need specialized instruction, but they may need more frequent breaks, opportunity to move around more, or even special equipment. Often, children with HFA are served under a 504 Plan because they may be at or near grade level for their academic work, but may need accommodations in order to remain there.

A 504 Plan protects both the district and the child. An individual, fabulous teacher might make some classroom accommodations for a child—allowing him to get up out of his seat or giving him extended time for projects and tests. But if the child moves to a teacher the next year who is more inflexible, then a 504 Plan will *require* that teacher to make specific changes to her classroom. She does not have to change the curriculum, but she will be required to change how she instructs, based on the specific needs of the child. The district will be protected by a 504 Plan, because it documents that it is not discriminating against a child with a disability and that it is providing access to the curriculum.

There are fewer parental rights under a 504 Plan than there are in an Individualized Education Program (IEP). However, parents do have the right to call a 504 Plan meeting at any time to review its effectiveness, request additional assessments, and so forth.

If a child qualifies for a disability, *and* it is determined that he or she needs particular services in order to progress, an IEP will be written. An IEP spells out what the educational plan is for *that* child, based upon her strengths and areas of challenge. They are not supposed to be "cookie cutter" plans in which every child in a classroom is working on the same goal. They are supposed to be specific to the child and followed by every teacher and professional within that school. All teachers—both special education and general education—are held to the requirements within the IEP. A teacher cannot choose not to follow the IEP; it is a document full of legal protections for the child and the parents that specific steps will be followed, or there can be legal repercussions.

Such repercussions are rare, but a long, protracted legal battle is one that can be avoided simply by following the IEP. However—and unfortunately—the IEP process often is based upon an adversarial relationship, rather than a collaborative one. Each "side" tries to get what it needs, and the IEP process is designed to find the balance. Sadly, schools do not have the funding to have fabulous services for all children, but parents want the best for their child—this tension between money and need is one that is constantly under discussion. Once the IEP has been established, it is in the best interest of the child for the individual teachers and families to work collaboratively, which is sometimes difficult to do after a challenging IEP meeting.

Special Education Processes

Getting to an IEP is often a long and frustrating process. The process is firmly established by federal law and has to be adhered to. However, there are small but significant differences between states and districts in the way they translate the law. You will need to check out the specific processes for your individual state. Essentially, there are seven steps:

- *Initial Problem*: The child is observed by the classroom teacher to have difficulties or problems in school. Problems can be academic, behavioral, or social. Or, the parents can bring the plight of the child to the attention of the team, sometimes called a Student Support Team (SST), a Response to Intervention (RtI) team, or a Prereferral Team.

- *Prereferral Team*: The teacher (or the parents) brings the name of the child to the team and a description of the problem. The team generally is a group of general educators, with some limited participation by special education professionals. The parents are rarely directly involved at this point, but do have the right to be there, and are notified of the team's decisions. The team then makes recommendations that can be implemented relatively quickly as well as any screening assessments that might be done by teachers. In a school system that is following Response to Intervention (RtI), these recommendations have to be carefully documented and based on researched strategies. A waiting period of about 6–9 weeks generally is recommended to give the strategies time to work and time for documentation to be gathered to determine the effectiveness of these new strategies. The idea is that perhaps a child doesn't really have a disability; there's just a mismatch between the educational environment and her learning style. In other words, if the school changes the educational environment, the child might catch up.

- *Referral Team*: Once the data of the prereferral strategies have been gathered, the referral team will make a decision on whether to move forward. If the strategies were effective in bringing about changes in the child, then it usually is decided that there probably wasn't a disability, but a gap in the learning process. However, if little to no progress happened, the team can make an official recommendation for formal assessment. Parental permission is required, and generally, the school psychologist becomes involved. In more progressive school districts, special educators and school psychologists are involved early in the process. In some states, they are prohibited from doing so. It is important to note that when a parent insists on assessment, or when a child comes to a district with a diagnosed disability that has already received services, such as autism, most school districts move directly to the assessment step.

- *Assessment*: The purpose of the assessment process is to determine the nature of an educational problem, whether academic, behavioral, or social. Assessments can be tests, observations, interviews, or checklists. Often schools use a multidisciplinary assessment that explores all of the needs of the child within a school environment. You may have a fully developed autism diagnosis, but the school will still need to do a thorough assessment for educational purposes. Once the assessment is completed, there has to be an eligibility meeting.

- *Eligibility*: Required by federal law to be held within 60 days of the parent's written consent to formal assessment recommendation (the definition of days as calendar days, school days, or business days is up to the state, and if a parent never formally signs consent on paper, no timeline is started), the IEP eligibility meeting determines if the child meets the educational definition of disability. Each state has a slightly different version of its eligibility requirements. You will need to check with your own state to see if it follows federal suggestions, the DSM guidelines for autism, or its own guidelines. I joke with my students, with no real sense of humor about it, that the best way to "cure" some disabilities is to move to a different state. It is also important to know that there is a difference between educational and medical definitions of disabilities. This distinction is most commonly seen in the issue of dyslexia, which is a more medical/psychological term for great reading difficulties. Dyslexia can fall under the educational term of "specific learning disability," but it doesn't always. A child might meet the definition of dyslexia provided by a private psychologist, but not meet the definition for learning disability. Although somewhat historically rare for children with autism, there are a growing number of cases where a school system has denied services because the child doesn't meet the educational definition of autism. If this is the case, the parent needs to get a written copy of what the educational definition of autism is, because the federal suggestions mirror medical guidelines. However, some states have placed more restrictions on their autism label and have excluded some of the more higher functioning children. If parents are unhappy with this decision, they often have a fight on their hands.

- *Need for Services*: This decision usually is conducted at the same meeting, but it is a federally defined separate decision process. The team then decides if the child not only meets the definitional test but also needs specially designed instruction in order to benefit from schooling. If the child has a disability, but does not need specialized services, she may be eligible for a 504 Plan. But if she *does* need specially designed instruction (SDI), she is to receive an Individualized Education Program (IEP).

- *IEP Meeting*: Generally immediately after the Need for Services decision, but not always, an IEP is written if the child was found eligible for special education. In the next major section, I detail the parts of an IEP, but it should be emphasized that the IEP is written by the team; it should never be the sole creation of a single person—teacher, therapist, or parent. Although most teachers and schools may come in with a draft of goals written ahead of time, all of them are up for discussion and negotiation. The IEP spells out what it is that the schools are going to do for a child, and it is an agreement regarding the services and programs that will be provided. Schools *must* provide the services, programs, and accommodations that are listed on the IEP.

Rights Under IDEA

There are several basic assumptions that IDEA is founded on. These all translate into specific parental rights. These include:

- *Zero Reject*: No child, no matter how profoundly disabled, can be denied educational services. This does not guarantee all children rights to the *same* educational experiences, but all children have the basic right to an education that is appropriate for them.
- *Free Appropriate Public Education* (FAPE): This is the underlying assumption of the law, and it is defined by the Supreme Court. According to the Learning Disabilities Association of America (2004):
  - Free requires that the education of each child with a disability must be provided at public expense and at no cost to the child's parents. The only exception is that incidental fees normally charged to nondisabled students or their parents as part of the regular education program also may be charged to students with disabilities and their parents.
  - Appropriate means that each child with a disability is entitled to an education that is "appropriate" for his or her needs. Appropriate education is determined on an individual basis and may not be the same for each child with a disability. Appropriate does *not* mean "best"—a distinction that parents often miss. It means "conditions under which it can be reasonably assumed the child will make progress." A very different concept from "best," indeed . . .
  - Public refers to the public school system. Children with disabilities, regardless of the nature or severity of their disabilities, have the same right to attend public schools as their nondisabled peers. The public school system must educate students with disabilities, respond to their individual needs, and help them plan for their future. Private schools

are not held to the same requirements to provide services as the public schools.

o   IDEA is an education act that guarantees that eligible children with disabilities will receive a public education that includes special education and related services as directed by the child's IEP, based on the child's individual needs. (Section 2)

- *Assessment*: Assessment shall be given in the child's strongest language, if English is not his first language. This is to make sure that children who come from a second language background are not found to be performing poorly because they were tested in English, rather than their native language. However, if they are stronger in English, they can be evaluated in English.

- *Due Process*: Districts must follow due process, which means that they must follow the rules that they set for themselves. If they do not, the parents can hold them liable. If schools state that they operate within a time frame, they must follow that time frame. If they state that they have to communicate in writing, they have to communicate in writing. Parents and school districts might disagree, but if the school districts did not follow due process, they have no hope of winning.

- *Parent Inclusion*: In the law, Congress states that one goal of IDEA is " . . . strengthening the role and responsibility of parents and ensuring that families of such children have meaningful opportunities to participate in the education of their children at home and at school" (IDEA, 2004, SS1400, Section 5-B). In other words, the school district *must* make an attempt to include parents at every step along the way.

- *Least Restrictive Environment* (LRE): Children with disabilities have the right to be educated to the greatest extent possible with their nondisabled peers in the Least Restrictive Environment. This means that separate classes, programs, or schools, or other removal of children with disabilities from the regular education environment, occur only when the nature or severity of the disability is such that education in regular classes with the use of supplementary aids and services cannot be achieved satisfactorily. If schools are to provide separate experiences, they must justify such placement.

- After reviewing the educational data available, the IEP committee must design special educational instruction to meet the unique needs of the child with a disability, coupled with any additional related services that are required to assist a child with a disability to benefit from that instruction.

Other Parental and Family Rights

Before you go into any official meeting, it helps to know what parents have the right to ask for. Because of the litigious nature of the IEP meeting, it is very important that the teachers present know what is legally required and what is not. For more complete lists of parent rights, please go to your state's special education regulations or to http://www.wrightslaw.com. WrightsLaw has an excellent description of the various laws and their application to parents. Parents have the right to:

- Be present at all school meetings about their child. The school can hold the initial set of meetings without them, but they must be invited to the eligibility, determination of need, and IEP meetings in writing. As a teacher, you *must* invite parents, multiple times, to any "official" meeting about the child in which decisions are made. If it doesn't fit into their schedule, schools have to try to work around this issue—and prove that they did so.

- Bring anyone else they want to any of the meetings. I have been a parent advocate at numerous meetings because I speak "educationalese" and can facilitate the process for them. Know that if they do bring in an advocate, you must be on your best behavior and make sure that all paperwork is done absolutely correctly, because the presence of an advocate can be the first step in a lawsuit and the focus of the meeting can shift away from meeting the needs of the child to the district covering its legal bases.

- Give or refuse assessment of their child. If they want their child assessed by the school district, then that permission must be granted in writing.

- Have an independent educational evaluation (IEE) that has to be considered in addition to the data provided by the school-based assessment team. Parents have the right to have this information, but they might have to pay for this independent evaluation themselves. For example, the school might find that a student does not meet eligibility based on the evaluation results. However, an independent psychologist might very well find different results. Schools have to take both sets of data into consideration.

- Ask for mediation, an impartial due process hearing, if they are not pleased at the process or the outcomes of the meetings. Mediation is designed to avoid a court case if possible. Parents and the school both have the right to request mediation and then move to a court case if the decision in mediation is not acceptable. If parents request a court case and lose, however, they may be required to pay the court costs.

- Inspect and review their child's educational records.

- Be given written prior notice on matters regarding the identification, evaluation, or educational placement of their child.

- Be given a full explanation of all of the procedural safeguards. They also can ask questions about what the jargon means.

- Appeal the initial hearing decision to the State Education Agency (SEA) if the SEA did not conduct the hearing (the school district has the right to do this as well).
- Have the child remain in his or her present educational placement, unless the parent and the school agree otherwise, while administrative or judicial proceedings are pending.
- Participate in, and appeal if necessary, discipline decisions regarding their child.
- Call an IEP meeting, even if it is not the scheduled time, to address concerns or changes that have occurred.
- Receive special education services until the child is 21 or until he or she graduates high school with a regular diploma, whichever comes first.

Writing a Good IEP

The IEP is made up of several interrelated and significant parts. These include:

- *Present Levels of Performance or Present Levels of Educational Performance* (PLOP or PLEP): These statements summarize any testing data that is present on the child and any documented progress or changes in the child. PLOP can include information on a child's behavior, academic levels, or social/emotional states. They also include statements of student strength and areas in which the child is making growth. These statements of performance must then directly lead to the child's goals. There cannot be a goal written unless there is documentation that such a need exists in the PLOP.
- *Annual goals*: Must be measureable and objective. They should be as specific as possible. This means that vague, fuzzy terms like "appreciate" or "understand" should not be used. Even fuzzier goals like "improve social interactions" should be made much more specific. IDEA 2004 took away the short-term objectives that may have guided schools in their determination of progress. I teach my students to follow a "formula" for goal writing—ABCD:
  - *Antecedent*: Under what circumstances?—"Given a 3rd grade level book SWBAT (Student Will Be Able To)"
  - *Behavior*: The verb involved—"describe"
  - *Condition*: What it is that the child is working with—"the plot of the story"
  - *Determinant*: The degree to which the child should master the skill or behavior *and* how it is to be measured—"at a proficient level, as determined by the classroom teacher." Examples:

○ Given a fourth-grade writing prompt, Elizabeth will be able to construct a five-sentence paragraph, using correct grammar, spelling, and punctuation with a graphic organizer to display her paragraphs.

○ During one-on-one conversations, Ray will be able to maintain appropriate eye contact with intermittent and appropriate glances for a 10-minute conversation.

○ During passing periods, Aaron will be able to monitor his own behavior with appropriate calming strategies that do not include calling out or tantrums, for 4 out of 5 passing periods.

- *Program provided or special education services provided*: You will have to describe how long the services provided will be and where they are to take place, keeping in mind the need for the LRE. Similarly, the amount of time that the child will interact in the general education program must also be specified. Some districts have a more inclusive approach than others. Inclusion, simply defined, is the concept promoting that rather than have the student move to the special services, the services come to the child. The child tends to stay in the general education classroom, and special education teachers and other specialists come into the classroom to provide direct services to the child. Generally, teachers collaborate, co-teach, and plan activities together that allow the child to participate as fully as possible in the general education curriculum. However, there may be many variations of this model in a school. Other districts may rely more on the "continuum of services" model in which students might go to a resource room for a smaller student-teacher ratio during specified periods of time. Or, students might be in a self-contained class or even a special school. You will have to decide which approach is more important to you.

- *Related services provided and length of time provided*: All of the services, such as occupational therapy, speech therapy, and adaptive physical education, and the length of time that service is to be provided have to be specified. Sometimes, this is provided in minutes over the course of a week or a month. You will want to make sure that the child sees the therapist for as long as is needed at a consistent time every day or every week; consistent time frames allow you to plan more coherently than a "well, I'll pick him up when I have time" form of service. The longer the time frame stated during the IEP, the more likely it is that the therapist may not be providing exact amounts of service per week. You should ask for it in terms of the smallest increments you can get the therapist to agree on. How long each day does the child see the specialist, and does service within the room count? Once a day for 15 minutes in your classroom to emphasize the concepts you're working on might be more effective than a pulled-out session twice a week for 30 minutes or 120 minutes each month that might come all in one session. You will have to decide this as a team. But you can certainly always ask for as much service as you feel would be beneficial.

- *Modifications and accommodations*: These are the changes that are necessary within a classroom that will allow the child access to the general education curriculum; modifications are changes in the standards, while accommodations do not require changes in the general education curriculum. They generally inform you of the changes that you will need to make, such as preferential seating, allowing frequent breaks, extended time on tests, or a scribe to write for a child. This section also can include various forms of technology that may need to be present to help the child communicate, such as a Picture Exchange Communication System (PECS) or a computer with vocal abilities. Many of the strategies and ideas in the upcoming chapters can be written directly into the IEP as suggested modifications, as long as there are some data that such accommodations are effective. That means that you have to collect data on the strategies that you're trying.

- *Means and frequency of communicating to parents*: Provision of a student's progress reports documenting his progress toward his goals has to be specified in the IEP. Often, this is on the same schedule as other students' report cards. However, parents might request more frequent communication if there is a new therapy or strategy they are trying at home. Also, the assessments and methods of evaluation toward the accomplishment of the goals must be specified. Schools are required to collect, monitor, and analyze IEP progress data throughout the IEP timeline. Parents have the right to ask to review samples of evidence to ensure that the regular reports are not simply a hunch or unspecified observation but rather a systematic process designed to ensure that SDI is working or not. This means that it is very important that teachers keep track of their schedules for (a) data collection, (b) data analysis, and (c) communication to parents on each of their students. While you hope you never have a lawsuit, if you do not keep the timelines for communication and data collection, you can be found liable.

- *Testing accommodations, if any*: When students are given high-stakes tests that determine their progression to the next grade or the school's overall performance on its goals, some students are allowed to receive alternative tests. However, such alternatives are limited by the state to around 2% of the population and are generally limited to students with more profound disabilities. If you have concerns with the administration of inappropriate tests, you should talk to your school administrator about this. However, sometimes administration of these tests can be modified, such as given in a smaller environment, read aloud, or other accommodations.

- *Time frame of the IEP*: Generally, IEPs are good for a year, but IDEA 2004 allowed states to choose to do 3-year IEPs if parents agree in writing. Most states still require an annual IEP review and meeting to write new goals for the next year, but some are considering moving to a more flexible, long-term format.
- *Statement of transition*: By the time the child is at least 16 years old, although some states require it at the age of 14, the IEP team must start thinking about the goals of the family and child after high school. Adult services start getting involved at this time so that the movement from school placement to adult living is as smooth as possible.

Professional Boundaries

What is notable because it is missing are the specifications of educational approaches or therapies. Rarely does the IEP tell teachers and therapists how to do their jobs; it just specifies what they are to have accomplished at the end of it. It assumes that teachers are professional enough to be able to select the most effective instructional approach and does not require additional teacher training. If parents have a particular therapy program that they have been using that has been successful, they can request that it be put into the IEP. *However, there is no legal right for a parent to name a particular program in the IEP.* The IEP does recognize that you are a professional and that you have the right to make instructional decisions for a student. But I would recommend that if a child has a history with an effective program, you consider it, if possible. It can be very confusing to a child to switch from one therapy program one year to a different one the next year, so you should consider the educational, behavioral, and social impact of such changes. Particularly because children with HFA often have a difficult time with transitions and change, it might be worthwhile to seriously look at what has been done in the past before you fit the child into the way you do things in your classroom. It's what I call the "square peg in the round hole" phenomenon. Sometimes, it's easier to dig out the hole than to whittle down the peg.

Getting the Most Out of Your IEP Team

Realize that an IEP meeting is a negotiation. It is in everyone's best interest to collaborate and provide a plan for your student's educational experience. There are a number of things that you can do to help facilitate this process.

Attitudes. Believe that the parents, other teachers, and administrators involved ultimately have the child's best interests at heart. They may have different rules and different expectations, but we are all in the profession of helping children.

Recognize different areas of expertise. Parents are the experts on their child and they may have a better idea than anyone about what might and might not work for the child. However, the professionals involved have been trained in disabilities and may have expertise in a process of education that you do not. The IEP meeting is an excellent way to match the child's needs with the variety of strategies that the district can offer. All of the people involved can learn from each other.

Be prepared to be very firm on some things and to allow the parents some leeway as well. Be prepared to give in, and be prepared to insist.

Be prepared for "happy talk" that says very little. "Kaneisha is delightful" makes everyone feel good, but it is not useful in order to write a goal. "Kaneisha should be provided puzzles in order to strengthen her spatial abilities" is more specific and practical.

Relatedly, be prepared to insist on the IEP addressing the child's strengths as well. An IEP meeting is designed to meet the needs of the whole child. That can include areas of strength. They just have to be documented and stated in the PLOP. Most people tend to focus on the "cannots," while the IEP also should focus on the "cans."

Be prepared for the parents to feel some discomfort. Private matters have significant implications on educational interventions. A child's potty training history, who lives with the child, and the relationship between the parents are all relevant information to your student's educational progress.

Before the meeting. Be prepared. Come early, and have all of the student's documentation. Plan through what you would like to see happen at the IEP meeting. Familiarize yourself with the format of the IEP form so that you can more easily discuss it. Have some draft goals you might like to see happen.

Familiarize yourself with the child's testing and evaluation data before the meeting. You have the right to see it ahead of time.

Ask if you can talk with the parents ahead of time. Have them visit your school or classroom if possible.

During the meeting. Teachers may want to do the following during the IEP meeting:

- Take thorough notes. Ask those speaking to slow down if you need them to.
- Document any disagreements in writing.
- Make sure that the goals are challenging, yet realistic.
- Make it clear that no decisions have been made prior to the meeting—that all parties have to discuss and agree in order for any programming changes to be made. Research on the effectiveness of IEPs found that the parents who were the most unhappy with the process were involved in IEPs where

it appeared that decisions had already been made and they were being presented with the final outcome (Henderson & Hughes, 2011).

- If anyone gets upset, ask for a moment to calm everyone down. Most members of the team will understand.
- Make sure the paperwork is done correctly. If there is a lawsuit, it will start with an examination of the IEP meeting.
- Translate to the parents, even if they don't directly ask. Often, the school professionals outnumber family members. You may be very familiar with each other and the process, so there is a tendency to steamroll right over the parent. Make sure that they understand everything—it's well worth the effort. If you don't take the time now to make sure they understand and get their input, you might be spending it in lawsuits later. Don't allow yourself to be bullied, but also don't be a bully. Just maintain as calm an outlook as possible.
- Listen very carefully to what is being said. Teachers and administrators often are not able to say things that parents can, but you can delicately suggest to the parent what is possible. For example, when I was a teacher, I could not suggest that children be evaluated with a nonverbal IQ test, because that would make the school district liable for the cost of the evaluation and it was something that was outside the normal evaluation process. But I *could* say "Do you have any nonverbal IQ information for your child?" Most parents don't know about the existence or power of a nonverbal IQ test. Similarly, I used to carefully explain their rights to parents when I felt that the district was taking advantage of them. I couldn't tell parents what to do, because my job would be in jeopardy, but I could let them know they could do something. Often, teachers are as frustrated with the "system" as the parents, but parents are allowed to ask for things, whereas you could lose your job. Walk this line carefully, but always stay within the spirit of the law and keep the interests of the child in mind.
- If the child is not present, you can ask the parents to share their fears, and their child's fears, about the process to the team. If there will be changes, the parents can share probable reactions of their child. If the child is present, be sure to facilitate the child's communication with the team. Help members of the team speak to the child, and help the child speak with them. Be sure to redirect some questions that you know that the child can answer. You are an advocate for the child as well as a professional in your role.
- If you have any questions about the IEP, you can take a few days to sign it. You do not have to sign it right then and there. However, even if you do, you are not necessarily agreeing with the conclusions of the IEP team. You have the right to convene them again if you have concerns or ques-

tions. Whatever your choice of program, remember that every choice can be changed. Most parents end up doing an amalgam of educational placements, from private school to homeschooling to public school in different combinations. As a child grows, her needs change and the effectiveness of the educational placement can change. Remember that you are but a small part of the child's overall educational experiences. Stay on top of things, and be an active member of the team where all members are working to help the child. Begin with trust in the process and the people involved, be aware of your possibilities, be aware of your limitations, and be cautious. Remember that most of the time, we're all trying to help a child; we just can't agree on how to do it.

Key Points From Chapter 4

- It is important to know the parts of the IEP and what is legally required of the IEP process. A child may need a 504 Plan instead of an IEP, and the rights under the 504 Plan are very different.
- It is critical that you understand the rights of the parents before you go into an IEP meeting. It is also critical that you understand the flexibility and the limitations that an IEP places upon a teacher.
- Key to the success of an IEP meeting is the feeling by the parents that the decisions have not been made ahead of time (Henderson & Hughes, 2011). You need to have ideas that you are ready to present, but you cannot have it look as if you have already made those decisions ahead of time.
- Although you have to balance the needs of the district with the needs of the family, you can get yourself sued if you don't follow the legal requirements of the IEP. When in doubt, make the choice that is in the best interest of the child.

Section II

What Can I Do?

Chapter 5

Developing a Framework of Interventions

There's a phrase out there—"If you've met one child with autism, then you've met one child with autism." There are so many variations and differences among the population, that it's impossible to describe the best way to teach a child with high-functioning autism. It is very important when looking at the educational experiences of a child with HFA that there is a significant focus on a child's areas of strengths, rather than on the child's areas of challenge. The other critical aspect is the mindset of the teachers and parents. HFA and giftedness often look very much like each other (Hughes, 2010a). What is a problem in one context can actually be a strength in another. As a teacher, you need to establish a context so that children can learn to work with their differences, rather than fighting their own natures.

In addition to establishing a mindset, there are numerous approaches to teaching, much less teaching a child with HFA. When I work with teachers, I find that they often follow a "hit and miss" approach: "Let's try this . . . then this . . . then this. . ." We call it our "teacher toolbox," and the idea is to have a variety of tools to reach for in different situations. However, such an approach does not allow teachers to determine anything other than a list of teaching ideas—ideas that might need to be changed later in the year as the child develops or even in the next half hour if there is a conflict in the classroom. Good teachers are responsive to their students and let their students "tell" them what approach is appropriate at a given time through careful observation and a plan to follow. In addition, good teachers have an understanding of how one can approach general teaching, and then match instructional approaches to student characteristics and needs.

Five Approaches to Teaching

There is a wide range of possible ways that teachers can instruct and conduct a classroom. Each teacher's classroom is as individual as he or she is, and is the result of the interactions of the teacher, the particular students, and the administrative support. When I teach preservice teachers and they make a comment such as "It's a typical fifth-grade classroom," I interrupt them and say, "There's no such thing." My class last year was similar to, and yet very different than, my class the year before. And I can assure you, my classroom has some components that are similar to my neighbor's, Mr. Smith's, but there are many, many things that are different.

Despite the individuality of each classroom, there are some similarities in how teachers approach the processes of teaching and learning. According to most texts (Joyce & Weil, 2009; Ormrod, 2010; Santrock, 2012), there are three primary approaches to teaching that most teachers select from, either in combination with each other or leaning heavily one way or the other:

1. *behaviorism*, which focuses on teacher actions;
2. *information processing*, which focuses on student actions; and/or
3. *constructivism*, which focuses on group and environmental actions.

Most teachers select a combination of these. I use a lot of strategy instruction, groups, and reward systems. I also get students' attention, and I try to teach them ways to remember things. My teaching style is a combination of different approaches. But what I have found is that knowing different approaches to teaching can help me figure out what else I can do when my "usual" isn't working for a particular child.

Behaviorism

Under Behaviorism, there are two primary areas of focus:
- *direct instruction*, in which information is directly and explicitly provided to the student; and
- *behavioral interventions*, in which the antecedent, behavior, and consequences in the forms of rewards or consequences are determined. It is critical to determine those things that are preceding and reinforcing certain behaviors and what function a particular behavior has for a child.

For ease of remembering these approaches, I have called these:
1. Teach, and
2. Time.

This approach primarily focuses on teacher actions and observing and monitoring student behavior in response to teacher actions. The teacher is considered the agent of change, and the job is to facilitate the desired responses of the child.

Teach. The teach strategy has been more clearly defined through the TEACCH program, developed at the University of North Carolina (Schopler, Mesibov, & Hearsey, 1995). Although this book does not go into specifics denoted by the TEACCH program, structured teaching is defined as the explicit manipulation of:

- the physical environment and determination of where specific tasks are to be done,
- visual schedules that provide information to students,
- development of specific work systems that specify independent work, and
- task organization that provides specific information about how a task is to be done.

Time. All behavior, according to behaviorists, is to either (a) get something or (b) get away from something (Carr, Horner, & Turnbull, 1999). A teacher then has to figure out what a child is wanting (e.g., power, attention, food) or what the child is trying to get away from (e.g., anxiety, failure, punishment). Knowing the function of a behavior then allows the teacher an opportunity to intervene and either provide something else that the child wants or something else for the child to get away from. According to behaviorists, everything you can watch about a child is defined as behavior, from learning the multiplication tables, to getting along with group members, to diagramming sentences. As such, behavior is observable and measureable. Concepts like "thinking skills" or even "emotions" are not things that can be observed or measured, so they aren't concepts that can be impacted by a teacher.

As mentioned in previous chapters, Applied Behavior Analysis is the gold standard of autism interventions (Granpeesheh, Tarbox, & Dixon, 2009), and has been found to be highly effective when working with children with autism. ABA is the system through which children are taught to stop doing inappropriate behaviors and to adopt appropriate behaviors using rewards. It is a very clearly established process by which a target behavior is determined, the steps to reach that behavior are identified, and the child is rewarded when he begins to come close to that desired behavior. It's a process of breaking down a goal into very specific steps to master first. It's very similar to the system your grandmother used when she said, "When you eat all of your dinner, you may have dessert." Formalized by Dr. Ivar Lovaas in the 1960s, ABA has been found over and over again to work for kids with autism. It's the most successful treatment and is even recommended by the U.S. Surgeon General. It's often the *only* thing to help students with low-functioning autism. The philosophy has many names—discrete trial teaching, behavior modification, stimulus-response—but any program that uses the word "behavior" or "skills" in it is probably rooted in this philosophy.

ABA is structured around the understanding that kids will change their behaviors in response to appropriate reinforcers. Schools often will use ABA in their approach to teaching. They will offer rewards and consequences to encourage children to behave, learn, and engage socially. In a general education classroom, I used a Pizza Friday reward if everyone could behave well enough that they would not receive a single "code" for 5 days. For Greg, I developed a behavior contract that if he could stay in his seat for more than 10 minutes at a time, I would give him a point. He could then cash in his points for rewards. I have seen a kid stop making moaning sounds for 5 minutes in order to get a single Skittle. I have seen kids learn to point in order to get the lollipop afterward. ABA does not care *why* kids change their behavior; just that they do.

There are some amazing computer programs that have emerged out of this philosophy (collecting points and getting scores are used in these programs as forms of reinforcers). These cutting-edge programs are teaching kids with autism what to say in different social situations, to identify the emotions on people's faces, and to replace repetitive motions such as handflapping with more socially acceptable ones such as foot tapping. Some of these are listed in the Resources section, but new applications are being designed every day.

There are many people who object to ABA for several reasons, not the least of which is that it is very similar to animal training. Whether you're teaching a child to say "Hello" at appropriate times and rewarding him with hugs and praise or teaching a dog to come to you with treats, ABA uses the same foundational principles of rewarding appropriate behaviors and then fading the reward once the behavior has been learned. I used to laugh that I got a puppy at the same time I started my teacher education program, and obedience classes and my discipline classes were very similar. I was a better teacher because I was a dog owner. In her 2004 book, *Animals in Translation: Using the Mysteries of Autism to Decode Animal Behavior*, Temple Grandin noted that she often feels more at home with animals than she does people—she understands how they react to things. Now, I happen to adore my dog and have no issues recognizing the underlying similar motivations in both of us. But others do.

The other concern that some people note is that ABA works on the symptoms, but not the underlying causes or issues. You can teach specific skills, but because generalization is so difficult for children on the spectrum, they often don't move those new skills forward on their own. Aspy, Grossman, and Myles (2007) highlighted the ABC-Iceberg model. Although it is still important to understand the antecedents, define the behavior, and determine the consequences, in their model, there are numerous underlying factors related to the condition of autism itself that provide additional compounding factors.

Information Processing

In contrast to the ABA model that implies a logical connection focusing on measureable results, the teaching model of information processing places the emphasis on the procedural aspects of learning—from getting and maintaining attention, to storage and retrieval of long- and short-term memory. There is much attention placed on brain scans, the biology of the learning process, and how we can influence the responses of the brain.

The information processing model concerns itself with how students activate and maximize their brain development. Brain arousal levels, types of memory, and metacognition are of concern to teachers using an information processing approach to teaching.

Getting and maintaining attention is a significant issue for children with high-functioning autism (Dawson et al., 2004), particularly:

- social attention, or paying attention to people. Most children prefer to watch people instead of things and are very responsive to facial expressions. However, children with HFA often watch people *as* things and have difficulty with eye contact and interpreting the meanings of facial expressions;
- joint attention, or having attention drawn by means of nonverbal communication, such as pointing a finger. Children with joint attention issues will focus on the finger, not the thing at which the finger is pointing; and
- attention to others' distress, or being aware of distress sounds as separate from environmental sounds and responding to the sounds with appropriate emotional sensitivity.

Although these are primarily social in nature, there appears to be an underlying issue with language as well. A study by Mayes and Calhoun (2007) found that when matched for intelligence, children with autism performed less well on attention and processing speed tasks than their peers and in manners very similar to children with ADHD.

In addition to getting a child's attention, teachers have to work with children on remembering information. Children with HFA often have difficulties with memory as well, particularly working memory (Mayes & Calhoun, 2007). I equate working memory with packing for a trip—you might have a wonderfully organized closet (long-term memory), but your ability to be comfortable on a trip is directly related to how much stuff you can put into the suitcase. Working memory is how much a child is able to remember at any one time. A classic test of working memory is asking a child to repeat a list of numbers or letters backward. Despite their limitations of working memory, however, children with HFA often have very strong spatial and visual memory, meaning that memories are found through visual encoding, not through language encoding (Koshino et al., 2004). Creating strategies for children to encode and find their memories of tasks, skills, and concepts is very important for a teacher. Because children with HFA often remember things when presented visually or with images, a teacher's job, then, is to make visual as much of the instruction and information as possible.

Cuing can be a tricky thing—it can become very frustrating to a teacher to remind a child over and over again. I find that I often use counting as a coping strategy when I want to say, "How many times do I have to tell you to . . . ?" When I hear myself thinking that, I stop and start counting. I learned this strategy from a very wise teacher. When my son was 3 and in an inclusive preschool, I went to pick him up. The teacher had "that" look, and I asked what had happened that day. "Oh, he just needed reminding to keep the outdoor toys outside," she said with a small smile. "Oh?" I asked, knowing that there must be more to this story. "Seventy-four times," she finished. "Seventy-four times?" I said. "Yikes!" "Yes," she said. "But at least it didn't take 75 times." And he never again "forgot" to leave the outdoor toys outside. She had kept her temper in check by counting every reminder, and my son learned that she was more stubborn than he was.

Lastly, beyond asking students to pay attention, and to remember what you tell them, teachers of children with HFA have to help them learn how to do the task (e.g., write a paper, read and remember the main point, make friends) on their own. We know that we can't always be there, and so part of our job is teaching students how to learn without us. I have always laughed that my job as a teacher is to work myself out of a job.

This process of independence is accomplished through the process of meta-cognition. Metacognition means "thinking about itself," and is the process through which students ask themselves the right questions when presented with a new situation. It has been clearly established that teaching children with learning disabilities to use metacognitive strategies in new learning situations can dramatically improve their academic abilities and the ever-important test scores (Deshler & Lenz, 1989; Harris & Graham, 1999), and that the use of such strategies holds great promise for children with HFA (Reaven et al., 2009; Wood et al., 2009). Presenting children with a script or a series of steps to think about allows them to free up working memory in order to solve the problem. Rather than focusing on *how* to perform a task, students can focus on *doing* the task.

For ease of remembering these approaches, in addition to the first two teacher-focused set of strategies, I have called these student-focused strategies:

1. Train, and
2. Think.

This approach focuses primarily on training and changing student thinking patterns in order to effect change. By paying attention, maintaining attention, and thinking structured thoughts, students are able to change their outcomes. The emphasis is on the student actions of attention and memory, while the role of the teacher is to facilitate the student activation of these skills.

Constructivism

Constructivism focuses on how a child makes sense of the world and his or her own learning (Santrock, 2012). Unlike behaviorism, which focuses exclusively on observed behavior, constructivism assumes that future behavior is dependent on what the learner feels and understands, rather than a mechanical response to a stimulus. These feelings and understandings come about through social interaction with others, and language is of critical importance for this process. Under constructivism, there are two primary areas of focus:

- *social constructivism*, in which children form understanding through social interactions with others; and
- *environmental cues and climate*, in which the setting and social environment of the child impact his or her learning.

Social constructivism means that the teacher's focus is not just on the child with HFA, but rather on the inclusion of the child with HFA—both his responses to his peers, and his peers' responses to him. It is this group dynamic and behavior between children that a sensitive teacher will be aware of and will monitor. Explicit group facilitation and a welcoming, inclusive approach in both tone and atmosphere are aspects that a teacher who is focusing on social constructivism will develop. The teacher will pay particular attention to the classroom—the arrangement of the classroom, the management system, the use of group development processes, and scaffolded instruction that allows students at different levels to engage with the content. What is said, what is done, what is placed where, and where children and adults sit and stand are all target areas.

For ease of remembering this set of strategies that focus on the context of the student learning, rather than teacher behaviors or student thinking, I have called this approach:

1. Together.

This approach places the learning of the child within a dynamic context, rather than the isolated actions of either the teacher or the child.

Summary of the Five Approaches to Teaching

For ease of comprehension, and to make the list of possible strategies easier to remember, I have renamed the educational approaches:

1. *Teach*, which includes the approach of direct instruction;
2. *Time*, which includes the approach of behavioral interventions;
3. *Train*, which includes the approach of information processes;

4. *Think*, which includes the metacognitive approach; and
5. *Together*, which includes the approach of social constructivism.

Five Aspects of Development

There are also essentially five aspects of development: physical, language, emotional/moral, cognitive, and social (Santrock, 2012; Sternberg & Williams, 2010). These aspects are not independent of each other, because physical growth can impact cognitive development, and language development can also impact emotional development and social development. Each aspect is related to the other aspects. However, we can watch different actions and classify them into the developmental aspects. Thus, how a child moves falls under physical development, how a child relates to other people fall under social behavior, and what a child says and how he says it fall under the language development aspect. The different aspects provide useful targets for intervention and improved outcomes.

As children age, their development can be relatively synchronous, with all five aspects developing at similar rates, such as a typical child whose physical development, cognitive level, language level, social level, and emotional level are similar to that of his or her physically aged peers. When children are different in any one or more of these aspects, we start applying labels to them in order to describe those differences. Thus, a child with physical differences, such as deafness or blindness, would be described as having a physical disability, whereas a child with cognitive differences might be described as having an intellectual and developmental disability (IDD) or even giftedness, depending on whether the cognitive difference was delayed or advanced. To be identified with HFA, a child has to have disorders in language, emotional, and social interactions, and yet have some areas of strength. However, the specific classroom behaviors that are the translations of these general characteristics can be highly individualized and specific to the child. Autism is incredibly pervasive and can affect every developmental aspect of a child. For this reason, this book focuses on how high-functioning autism can affect a child's ability to:

1. *Move*, which includes the physical development of a child;
2. *Communicate*, which includes the language development of a child;
3. *Feel*, which includes the emotional development of a child;
4. *Think and learn*, which includes the cognitive development of a child; and
5. *Interact*, which includes the social development of a child.

I often attend professional development workshops, and most of the time, I walk away with some wonderful, specific strategies that I can use right away. The

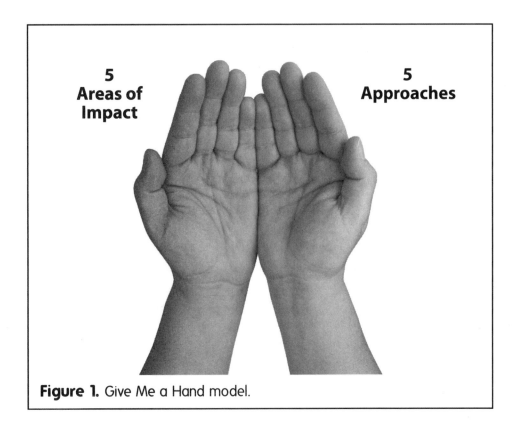

5
Areas of
Impact

5
Approaches

Figure 1. Give Me a Hand model.

problem occurs when I can't immediately implement a strategy, or it's a great idea, but not for the kids who I have this year. I then file the idea, the handout, or the PowerPoint and promptly forget it. I have forgotten so many great ideas and strategies, simply because I have many, many files and no way to connect them with other ideas and strategies that I know.

Teaching a child with HFA is a process of matching the developmental characteristics and specific issues that the child is exhibiting with an intervention determined by the educational approach, as seen in the "Give Me A Hand" model in Figure 1. Remembering these five areas that autism is likely to impact and the five approaches to teaching can help you remember some of the "tools" that you have to work with. The more tools in the toolbox, the more arrows in the quiver, the more ideas a teacher has for working with diverse children, the more effective the teacher (Joyce & Weil, 2009). It is useful to determine what aspect of the child needs intervention and how one can go about intervening. Such a framework approach allows the teacher to pick and choose interventions, as well as to know what else to try when nothing is working.

Chapters 6–10 provide much more in-depth descriptions of various ideas and strategies that you can use, but no book can give you everything. What the Give Me a Hand model allows you to do is classify new strategies you may learn and give you a way to remember them. I joke with teachers that whether you're using your two hands in prayer or wringing them together in frustration, the Give Me a Hand model can help you remember something else you can do. Table 5 provides a list of suggested ideas and strategies to frame your classroom interventions.

Key Points From Chapter 5

- There are five approaches to instruction that a teacher can choose, including:
  - *teach*, which includes the approach of direct instruction;
  - *time*, which includes the approach of behavioral interventions;
  - *train*, which includes the approach of information processes;
  - *think*, which includes the metacognitive approach; and
  - *together*, which includes the approach of social constructivism.

- High-functioning autism can affect five areas of development, including how a child:
  - moves,
  - communicates,
  - feels,
  - thinks and learns, and
  - interacts.

- Together, these form the foundation for the Give Me A Hand model, which allows a teacher to select a particular set of strategies based on a particular issue of a child.

Table 5

Strategies for Using the Give Me A Hand Model

Autism Impacts		Instructional Approaches				
Developmental Aspects		Teacher Focus		Student Focus		Social Focus
How a Child:	Common Issues:	Instruction *Teach*	Behavioral *Time*	Attention/Memory *Train*	Metacognition *Think*	Environment *Together*
Moves	Gait Clumsiness Need to move	Physical therapy Occupational therapy	Behavior contracts	Environmental Assistive technology	Cues	Classroom arrangement
Communicates	Expressive Receptive Pragmatics Self-Talk	Speech therapy Scripts Vocabulary development	Fluency graphs ABA	Visual cues Prompts	Cue words Scripts Visualization techniques	Cooperative learning Language-rich environment
Feels	Regulation Sensory Central coherence Comorbidity Repetitive behaviors	Emotional management strategies Replacement behaviors Therapy strategies (e.g., occupational, counseling)	Escalation cycle Behavior contracts Social modeling	Visual cuing Stims Calms Fidgets Use of music, yoga	Self-scripts Sensory stories Stress thermometer Reframing	Climate/culture Peer partnerships Environmental Mindsets Safe areas Anti-bullying
Interacts	Mindblindness Small group Large group Greetings Conflicts Self-help	Replacement behaviors Social stories Scripting Moral development	Modeling Responses Behavior contracts Power cards	Physical environment Visual cuing Prompting Choices/control Animal therapy	Self-scripts Self prompts Self-advocacy Goal-setting Social stories	Circle of friends Classroom arrangement Rule development Procedures Climate/culture
Thinks/ Learns	Attention Memory Organization Processing Speed Focused Interests Piagetian stage Creativity	Question-response Task analysis Tiered instruction Scaffolding Bloom's taxonomy Remediation Prescriptive Assessment Acceleration Enrichment Creativity skills	Modeling Charting Progress monitoring Fluency graphs	Learning styles Cuing Prompting Mnemonics Number +- Time +- Spacing	SRSD KU-SIM Choice Goal-setting Problem finding/ solving Visual organizers Graphic organizers	Climate/culture Cooperative learning Peer tutoring Brainstorming Aesthetics

Chapter 6

Physical Development: Autism Impacts How a Child Moves

Although physical development isn't one of the defining characteristics of autism, there are impacts of autism on the physical development of a child. Primarily, these include gait issues, stances, general clumsiness, and tics (Hansson et al., 2005). In other words, how children walk, stand, and move is impacted by autism and appears related to issues within the basal ganglia and cerebellum (Rinehart et al., 2006). Other physical issues, such as diet and biological approaches to treatment, are decisions typically handled and administered by the family. It is important to ask if the family is following a biological approach, so that you can collaborate with them, but you are not responsible for such programs.

Physical development is often not within the purview of the classroom teacher, but there are a number of issues that clumsiness and "oddness" in stance and walk will create within the classroom setting. This book touches on physical issues, but teachers should feel assured that other professionals such as physical therapists will more directly handle any physical issues for your students with autism. However, in addition to gait and clumsiness issues, some children with autism have a need to move in order to learn—in other words, they cannot learn unless they're moving (Hannaford, 1997). Such need to move is often characterized as ADHD, but in reality, it's the brain's need for physical movement in order to facilitate neurological linkages, rather than a direct attentional issue.

Teaching Strategies

To deal with any physical issues related to autism, it is particularly important as a classroom teacher to work with the child's physical or occupational therapist. Therapists have strategies in their repertoire that are not often taught in a teacher preparation program. They can provide direct instruction and practice to the child in the appropriate ways to stand or move and to improve motor fluidity. They may also be able to provide any assistive technology that might be necessary such as a standing frame or a weighted vest. Similarly, some students may need assistance in how to hold a pencil or how to sit in a chair. For example, "four on the floor" is a timeless direct teaching strategy for keeping kids seated and not leaning back in the chair, balanced on two legs.

One interesting strategy that has been suggested for students with sensory processing issues, such as students with HFA, is the use of different glasses and lenses, such as Irlen lenses, ambient lenses, and even computerized glasses. Irlen lenses, developed to treat what's called scotopic sensitivity, can be (1) colored transparencies placed over reading material and (2) tinted glasses that improve visual perception. Although there is limited research about the efficacy of Irlen lenses, there are many anecdotes of improved reading comprehension, attention, and basic academic skills, particularly with children with learning disabilities (Simpson, 2005). Donna Williams (1995), a woman with HFA, reported on her improved ability to integrate parts of a face into a cohesive whole and make eye contact with the use of such lenses. Similarly, ambient lenses and prism lenses are designed to help children make sense of their world by changing the quality of the light. Improvements in posture, head positioning, and motor movements, such as reduction in toe walking, have been found (Kaplan, Carmody, & Gaydos, 1995). Recently, glasses have been developed that contain a small camera and a tiny computer that can interpret people's facial expressions—often a challenge for children with HFA—and provide feedback to the wearer. A green light indicates a positive facial expression, while a red light indicates a negative facial expression (Adee, 2011).

Timing Strategies

Using a behaviorist perspective, practice and use of these lessons can be rewarded through a behavioral contract or some other form of reward system. Such measuring and monitoring of physical activities can provide the physical or occupational therapist with invaluable information for their treatment programs, as well as allowing you an opportunity to support the results of what the therapist is focusing on. I have often found that asking the child to name a reward she wants to work toward is particularly helpful. Figure 2 is an example of such a behavior

I _____ (my name)

agree to: _____

_____

_____

_____

Insert picture of student doing the task here

For:

_____ amount of times

(or within a certain time frame)

When I do this, I will get :

_____

_____

_____

_____

Insert picture of reward here

and a Happy Note sent home to my
family and the principal.

Signed:

Student: _____

Witness: _____ (teacher)

Date: _____

Status report:

1) Date: _____ Progress: _____

2) Date: _____ Progress: _____

3) Date: _____ Progress: _____

Figure 2. Behavior contract.

contract. Note the visual nature of the behavior contract; students with HFA often understand better when there is a visual image, instead of words. The visual images are key to developing a contract that they understand and are motivated by.

Training Strategies

The goal of information processing approaches in the physical realm is a matter of drawing a child's attention to the physical demand needed for a task such as reminding her to stand in a certain manner (e.g., not slumped over) and how to remember the physical demands of tasks such as holding a pencil. Some forms of assistive technology, such as pencil grips or air cushions for sitting on, allow children with HFA to pay attention and remember the physical skills in which they have been instructed.

Thinking Strategies

Perhaps the classroom teacher will play the most active role in developing a child's physical development by cuing him when to use the strategies provided to him by the occupational or physical therapist. Reminding a child to use certain skills does not mean that the classroom teacher has to know or teach these skills—teachers have enough to do without adding a whole new set of skills!—but it does mean that rather than yelling at a child for forgetting, the child needs to be reminded through cuing. Some children may need reminding one or two times before they learn to use their skills. Others may need 360 times. Stay patient—they may simply need more time to learn the skill.

It is critically important to teach a child exactly what to do when you provide the prompt, because she may be unable to figure it out on her own. For example, many children with autism get in trouble in settings when the teacher places her pointer finger on her lips. They do not interpret the movement as replacing the words for "everyone be quiet now," and so they continue to talk. I once worked with a child who did not have the same sense of personal distance that the typical American person has. He had to be taught to measure out one arm's span between himself and another person. When he started creeping up on us and making us nervous because he was too close, we would prompt him by pointing to our arm. In addition, the whole class was taught the prompt, and it helped his social relationships tremendously.

Using visual imagery is also key to metacognitive cuing. If the child simply needs reminding to slow down or to focus on his movements, a visual cue can help him. Touching your nose, making "walking fingers," or using some other such visual reminder can help a child. Some teachers have placed duct tape on the floor around children's desks to visually remind them that it was their space and that in order to cross into another child's space, they would need to ask permission. Montessori programs, for example, place a great emphasis on a child's learning space, often using small rugs or placemats to designate a learning space that is to be respected by others. Some teachers have blocked off a "pacing zone" with duct tape on the floor for some children so that they can move around. Such an arrangement allows children to remain focused on their work, yet able to move within a confined space while respecting the work of others.

Together Strategies

Tics, toe walking, "noodle" posture, outbursts—all of these can affect the classroom environment. Children notice differences, particularly in how one looks or moves. One of the best strategies to promote within your classroom environment is probably the easiest to say, and the most difficult to do: Accept. Acceptance means that when a child makes a repeated noise, the other children ignore it. Acceptance means that when a child walks on his tip-toes, the other children wait for him to catch up, and don't laugh. Acceptance means that children understand that there is a range of possible noises, actions, and movements that all of us can do and that the job of the classroom is to encourage improvement, and to accept a child for who he or she is.

I learned this lesson my second year of teaching when I had Jason, a kid who made hooting noises like an owl when he was focused on something. For a while, I tried to remind him to be quieter, I tried moving him away from the others, and I tried a white noise machine to drown it out. I learned the power of acceptance when I was preparing to move a divider around him, and one of the other students told me "It's okay, Ms. Hughes. I think he hoots when he's happy. We really don't mind. It's just what Jason does." I left Jason in his seat, and for the rest of the year, we had a small hooting sound in the background that we didn't even really notice after a while. It even became part of a really nice memory of that class. It was, after all, just what Jason did.

In addition to the attitude of the students in your classroom, your classroom arrangement can take the child's physical issues into consideration. Be sure to place the child away from objects that can be overturned if he is clumsy. Do not place the child near another child with aggressive impulses who will snap if the child with HFA bumps into him. More than placement can be involved in the classroom arrangement. Some classrooms have moved to optional stand-up desks with swinging footrests to allow children an opportunity to move while learning—desks that would be very appropriate for students with attentional issues as well as any child who need to move in order to learn.

In addition, the rest of the class can be alerted and taught how to arrange the classroom for maximum learning benefits. Building a class culture where movement is permissible, as long as one child's movement does not impact another child's learning, allows children to monitor their own learning needs. The teacher does have to reinforce the rule that children cannot bother one another, but a successful inclusive classroom cannot require children to remain seated for extended periods of time.

Key Points From Chapter 6

- Although physical development issues are not indicators of autism, autism can impact how a child moves and relates to her world physically, particularly affecting tics, gait, and clumsiness—issues all related to brain differences.
- *Teaching* strategies focus on specific skills and use of technology, if necessary. There are a variety of lenses that have been used with students with HFA and other technologies to address physical issues. You can also directly teach proper body positioning and actions.
- *Timing* strategies allow teachers to construct behavior modification charts to encourage the child to use appropriate actions and movements. An example of a behavior contract is provided in Figure 2.
- *Training* strategies focus on reminding the child to use appropriate strategies for movement. A physical therapist or occupational therapist may have some assistive technology that helps a child move his body appropriately.
- *Thinking* strategies allow a child to structure her thoughts about her movements. "Arm's distance" for personal space and the use of duct tape to define movement zones are examples of visual, concrete movement reminders.
- *Together* strategies involve the whole classroom. An inclusive classroom should encourage movement and acceptance of numerous differences. Stand-up, swinging desks are available to help the classroom environment become one that works with differences rather than combating them.

Chapter 7

Language Development: Autism Impacts How a Child Communicates

Speech and language issues are probably the most significant characteristics of children with autism; they often cannot either find the correct words or use language appropriately for the social situation (Siegel, 2003). Almost all children with HFA will either be receiving services from an SLP or will have received services for communication that can be reinforced by the classroom teacher.

Although the child may have received services from an SLP, there are still going to be some significant communication issues related to autism. A child with HFA may have issues with *expressive* language, where he has difficulties expressing himself—finding words; using appropriate prosody, rhythm, and intonation; and finding the right word for the right situation. Interestingly enough, possibly because of their difficulty with understanding abstract concepts, children with HFA often have difficulty with pronouns. Aaden, a child I knew who was in the seventh grade, often called girls "he," scrambled possessives, and sometimes referred to himself in the third person. In one really confusing encounter that I remember clearly, he told a girl in class that "She can get his book and come over to Aaden," when what he meant was "You can get your book and come over to me." Similarly, these children can get confused with *receptive* language—the volume, pacing, and flow of language can overwhelm them so that they may observe details, but miss the overall meaning. They may miss fine levels of meaning between various words and are unable to either summarize their overall understanding or the purpose of the communication (Norbury & Bishop, 2002). The level of expressive and receptive vocabulary is one of the defining differences between children diagnosed with PDD-NOS and those diagnosed with Asperger's syndrome; children with AS typically score much higher on receptive and expressive vocabulary than children with other forms of autism (Szatmari, Archer, Fisman, & Streiner, 1995).

Although some children with HFA can be quite strong in their expressive and language skills, most have issues with *pragmatics*, or the appropriate use of language for certain social skills (Norbury & Bishop, 2002). Expressive language is three-fold: being able to find a word, articulate a word, and make sure it is appropriate for the situation in which it is being used. It is this social component that often distinguishes the child with HFA.

In addition to the challenges with the finding and use of language for communication with others, children with HFA also may have difficulty with self-talk, or metacognitive structuring of their language experience (Sze & Wood, 2007). Although they may have strong memories for particular words, they are not often able to find the appropriate words for their own questions or concerns. Thus, when looking at behaviors of children with HFA, they are unable to demonstrate an internal dialogue that controls emotional self-regulation.

Many, many adults with HFA remark that they often feel like "aliens" or "foreigners" in that they struggle to understand the language and social cues around them (National Public Radio, 2010). Indeed, if you Google "autism" and "alien," you will find numerous sites that claim that children with autism are actually a result of alien abduction! I *strenuously* object to such characterization because it removes the very humanity of these children—a humanity that is necessary to understand and appreciate them. However, I have found it easier to understand autism myself by thinking of these children as from another culture. Mesibov, Shea, and Schopler (2004) noted that

> in a sense, autism functions as a culture, in that it yields characteristic and predictable patterns of behavior in individuals with this condition. The role of the teacher of a student with autism is like that of a cross-cultural interpreter: someone who understands both cultures and is able to translate the expectations and procedures of the non-autistic environment to the student with autism. (p. 19)

I have found that often, the same strategies I use with my English Language Learners are effective with my students with autism as well.

Teaching Strategies

Because of the specialized instruction for language development used by SLPs, most classroom teachers are not in the position of having to provide direct instruction in the development of speech and language skills. However, it is critically important that you support and reinforce the skills that are being taught. Ask the SLP to keep you up to date about concepts and ideas to reiterate and build up, and be sure to share your upcoming units and content map with the SLP so that he can prepare his lessons for the student as well.

However, there are numerous classroom vocabulary skills that you can directly teach. These include scripts, call-and-response activities, and content-specific vocabulary words.

Scripts are words and phrases that are to be used in specific order in specific contexts. Teaching children appropriate greetings is a method of scripting. For example, a child may have read the word "salutations" in the book *Charlotte's Web* and learned that it is a greeting, but not understand that "salutations" is not often a socially acceptable greeting in ordinary contexts. Teaching greeting and leave-taking scripts can help a student know what to say in those situations. Similarly, teaching the art of question-asking can provide students with the vocabulary that they need to engage in classroom instruction.

Call-and-response activities include direct instruction where the teacher directly teaches specific language and immediately seeks feedback, using a highly interactive and engaging style. For example:

Teacher: This unit is about the Civil War. What is this unit about?
Students: The Civil War.
Teacher: That's right! The Civil War involved two sides, the Union and the Confederacy. What were the two sides?
Students: The Union and the Confederacy.
Teacher: Exactly! The Union was composed of the states that supported a centralized federal government, and most of them were in the northern part of the country. What do you think we called the Union states?
Students: The North!
Teacher: That's it! The states in the North were called the ____?
Students: Union!

Call-and-response strategies are not scripted strategies, but are ways to keep students engaged in short, vocabulary-focused bursts of instruction that are designed to promote memory enhancement. Care should be taken that such call-and-response strategies are covering new material not previously learned. If this strategy is used for review of thoroughly mastered material, there is a strong possibility that the child will become bored by the activity and disengage from all communication activities, particularly if the child is a high achiever.

Content-specific vocabulary words allow the student to learn the vocabulary words associated with the particular content. Each content area has a specific vocabulary, and it is important to be very specific when teaching the meaning of the various words. However, it is not enough to teach just the definition (e.g., that a noun is "a person, place, idea, or thing"). Students must be taught how to apply their knowledge of the vocabulary. They must learn to recognize a noun, understand where in a sentence most nouns go, and pinpoint typical endings for nouns. Because children with HFA tend to be rules-focused, they must learn the rules of the vocabulary, as well as the exceptions to the rules. The use of language is not something that comes naturally to them, and so they must be taught it.

I have found that with the provision of rules, many children with HFA can actually do quite well in language arts. When words become tools that follow certain rules, they are able to manipulate words, not from an intuitive level, but from a technical level. One child with HFA that I know actually won a national poetry contest because of her ability to find the correct words for the correct meter. When words are taught as tools, kids with HFA can analyze them, and make patterns of them—a challenge always interesting to a kid with HFA!

Timing Strategies

With the use of behavioral interventions and observable documentation of change, classroom teachers can document the number of words that a student with HFA is able to use in specific contexts and chart this improvement over time. The key to any use of a timing or behavioral strategy is the identification of a specific goal that can be measured over time. Skills such as the correct use of greetings, vocabulary usage, appropriate articulation, and the appropriate manners to ask for directions can all be scripted, monitored, and then rewarded.

Although many teachers dislike specifying the length of a written assignment, it may be necessary for a student with HFA. They can become very focused on the communication of information and neglect to elaborate or provide examples. Denise, a seventh grader with HFA I once worked with, would provide me with one-sentence responses to questions asking for literary analysis. Although technically her response would be correct, I learned that I had to provide clear, numeric expectations of writing assignments such as "This paper should be at least 1.5 pages long." When I did that, I would get exactly 1.5 pages, but it would be more elaborate than her previous responses. An example of a behavior contract that could be adapted for vocabulary development can be found in Figure 2.

Training Strategies

Training strategies involve the use of getting, directing, and monitoring a student's attention or focus on a particular piece of information that you want them to learn. One of the key means of getting and keeping the attention of children with HFA is through the use of a visual stimulus rather than a verbal prompt. In fact, children with HFA appear to process information as well or even better than typical children when the stimulus is visually presented (Heflin & Alaimo, 2007).

One of the key elements of teaching children to communicate through visual means is through the use of visual cues. Cues can be devised and taught for many issues of communication present in children with HFA, including volume, turn-taking, length of conversation, appropriate topics, and common articulation errors. Some examples of cues I've seen include:

- Most people know that a finger on the lips can mean "hush." It's the use, and the consistency of its use that is important with children with HFA. Most teachers use a "hush" and the finger on their lips is their secondary backup signal. For kids with HFA, the finger on the lips is the first signal to which they respond.
- Our cafeteria used an actual stoplight to change the volume level during lunchtime—green meant "free conversation," while red meant "silent lunch" or time to focus on eating.
- Another teacher I know would use her finger as a cue to children to indicate when it was their time to talk. She would point to the child she was talking to and indicate that it was his turn.
- Yet another teacher used a ball of yarn that she would wind up—as long as she was drawing yarn up into the ball, the child was free to talk, but as soon as she stopped, the child had to stop talking.
- I used a "V" that got lowered or raised, depending on if I wanted a child to lower or raise the volume of her speech.
- I also used the sign language for the letter of difficulty when I wanted to cue a child that his articulation was slipping. I taught the class that the "L" and "R" signs meant that someone needed to focus on those letters when he was talking.
- To ask a child if he needed to use the restroom without breaking the flow of what I was doing, I would flash the "T" sign. Because "t" is not a common articulation error, I co-opted it for "toilet." I sometimes felt like an umpire, flashing letters and signals all over the room, but I found that sign language was a very effective medium for communication with children who have communication issues, but visual strengths. Figure 3 includes the sign language alphabet.

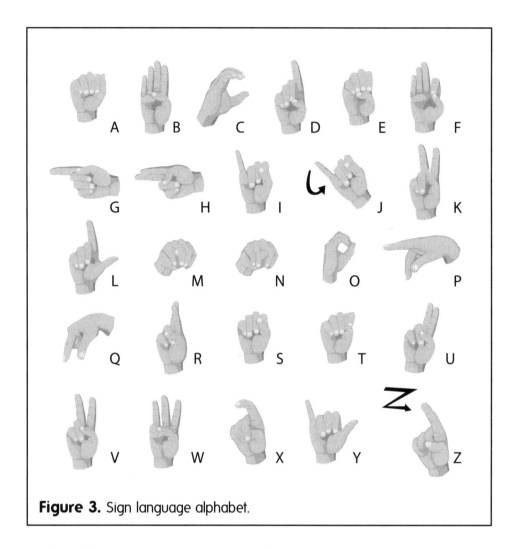

Figure 3. Sign language alphabet.

In addition to cuing strategies, visual representations can also facilitate the development of vocabulary through visual connections and the emphasis of visualization techniques. Two common vocabulary strategies include the Word Splash strategy (Allen, 1999) and the use of the Frayer vocabulary model (Klausmeier & Frayer, 1970). I have also used the vocabulary web concept, developed by the Center for Gifted Education (1996b) at The College of William and Mary in my classes.

Word Splash

A word splash is a graphic representation of the pertinent vocabulary words within a chunk of meaning. Words become elements of an artistic representation of the words themselves, and turn into visual elements that can reinforce the meaning of the word. Figure 4 demonstrates a word splash for the word "autism" and some of

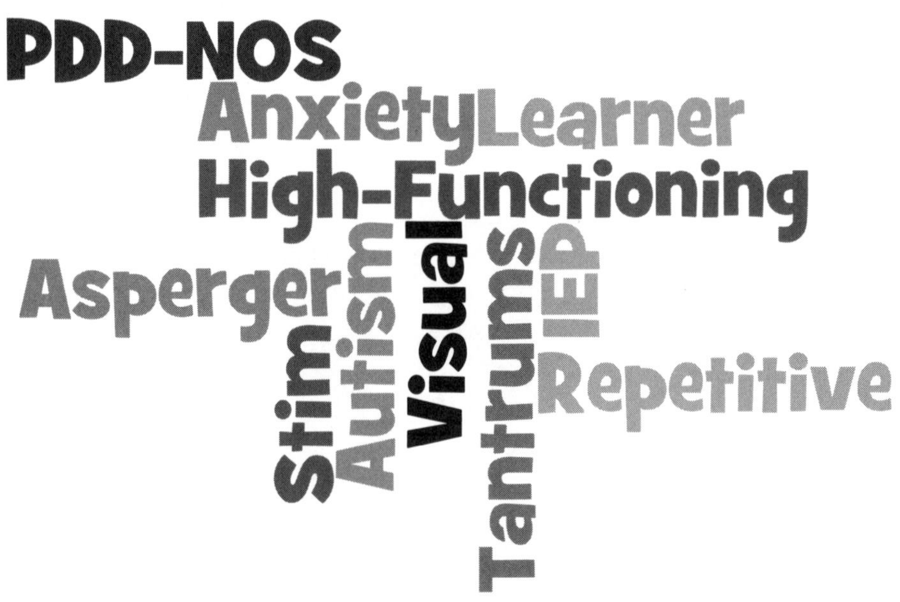

PDD-NOS
Anxiety **Learner**
High-Functioning
Asperger **Stim** **Autism** **Visual** **Tantrums** **IEP** **Repetitive**

Figure 4. Word splash of vocabulary words associated with autism.

the accompanying vocabulary. Word splashes could be made for "ways to say hello," "addition terms," "words to use instead of 'said,'" "topics of conversation interesting to other children," and so on. The list of word collections that can be visually drawn together is endless.

Frayer Vocabulary Model

The Frayer vocabulary model has been found to be intensive in terms of time, but also highly effective for building vocabulary understanding within the content areas (Greenwood, 2002). The model has several versions, depending on the age of the child and the child's ability to think beyond the concrete representation. The Frayer model graphically organizes a word so that the child can see how the elements of a word form a larger understanding of the word. In the center of the graphic is the word of focus. Above the word are the "meanings" of the word—the definition—listed in the upper left quadrant, and the characteristics—or other words that are related to, part of, and connected to the meaning of the word—listed in the upper right quadrant. This upper component "places" a word in context to other words, reinforcing the meaning not only of the word in question, but in relationship to other words.

The bottom portions of the graphic are the ways in which the word is found in experience. The emphasis on the bottom aspect isn't on other words, but on a child's experience. Examples of the word are described in the bottom left quadrant, and

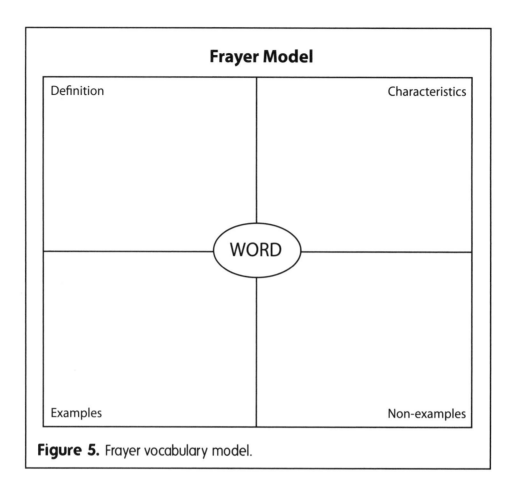

Figure 5. Frayer vocabulary model.

these can either be verbal or pictorial. If a child is struggling with the language of the word, attaching a picture of what the word looks like in the real-world experience can provide an excellent visual connection. Similarly, in the bottom right quadrant, nonexamples are demonstrated either verbally or visually. Some teachers will use "synonyms and antonyms" for these bottom quadrants, but I have found that there are very few vocabulary words with perfect opposites, and children with HFA often interpret antonyms as needing to be completely opposite. I have found that nonexamples are a better way of showing the concept of "lack of" or "not there." See Figure 5 for an example of a Frayer vocabulary model.

Vocabulary Web

The vocabulary web developed by the Center for Gifted Education (CFGE, 1996b) expands upon the Frayer model by drawing relationships between words, based not only on related ideas, but also through word analysis—a skill in which children with HFA often are strong. The CFGE vocabulary web allows children with HFA to draw relationships among words based on their historical roots and to relate new words to each other using those roots. The use of "stems" allows further analysis of vocabulary words, using prefixes and suffixes as well as the language of origin. The complexity of the word study allows a child with HFA to not only memorize a series of vocabulary words, but to understand the relationships of words to each other—a very important skill for children who struggle with communication issues. See Figure 6 for an example of a vocabulary web.

Thinking Strategies

Thinking strategies involve providing the child with the thinking skills necessary for the skills and knowledge that you're trying to teach him. Because verbalization is so difficult, many of these children simply don't know what to think in certain situations and get in trouble or have emotional difficulties—not because they haven't learned the skills, but because they don't know when to use them. Two of the most common strategies I have seen used for encouraging metacognitive communication are the use of cuing through specific words and rhythms of language and the use of reading.

Cuing

An effective metacognitive strategy is to teach children with HFA to recognize cue words. We use cue words to guide our conversations, our arrivals and leavings, and our written language. Phrases and words such as "well, then," and "for these reasons," and "so" are designed to move the communication along. These cue words are often the ones that a child with HFA misses, so that she is caught unaware when a person appears to bolt from a conversation because the child missed the relevant cues. Similarly, there are words that drive math problems, paragraphs, and directions. Many of these cue words are ones that typical people tacitly understand, but may need to be specifically taught to children with HFA.

One strategy I have employed with children with HFA is the use of connecting visual images with rhythms of speech. When a person is trying to change the subject, move away, or change the flow of language, his breathing and the rhythm of his words change. You can teach a child to "see" these rhythms in a manner similar to synesthesia. Synesthesia is the ability that some people, including children with HFA, have where they "taste" colors or see colors related to numbers. Synethesia combines two senses with a concept. In his book, *Born on a Blue Day: Inside the Extraordinary Mind of an Autistic Savant*, Daniel Tammet (2006), who has HFA, discusses how numbers have certain colors associated to each one, and as a result, he constructs rainbows and art in his head as he solves math problems and memorizes strings of numbers. Although you can't teach synesthesia, you can encourage it. Because children with HFA have difficulty processing the language that is used,

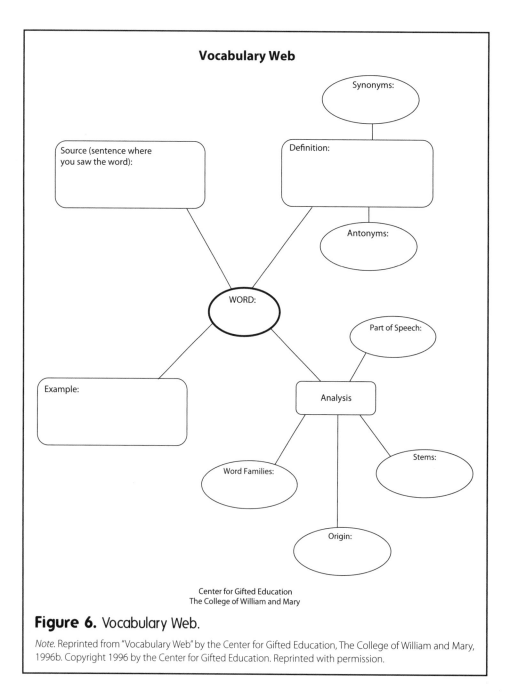

Figure 6. Vocabulary Web.

Note. Reprinted from "Vocabulary Web" by the Center for Gifted Education, The College of William and Mary, 1996b. Copyright 1996 by the Center for Gifted Education. Reprinted with permission.

using other senses to monitor the use of language can allow them to focus on the meaning of the language. For example, when someone starts shuffling her feet, losing eye contact, and "ummm"ing, the rhythm can be visualized to change from a vibrant, engaged yellow, to a lackadaisical gray-blue. When a child "sees" the conversation turning from yellow to faded blue, he can then be triggered to change the subject or to end the conversation.

Such use of colors or cue words can be used to script a child's thinking patterns: "Oh, I recognize this pattern. What is it that I'm supposed to do next?" The same scripts that were taught directly by the teacher as a teaching strategy can be used as a metacognitive prompt to generalize, when provided the appropriate cue words and prompts. It is very important that children with HFA who are taught scripts be taught when and where they might use them in other settings. Teaching the cues or pattern recognition is a very important skill in generalizing. It's one thing for a child to make conversation in the classroom or in the therapy setting with a speech pathologist; it's an entirely different thing to recognize those same script prompts in new settings. Cuing a child to look for those similarities is the first step to generalization.

Reading

Many practitioners have hypothesized that children with ASD would learn to read best using a whole-word technique because of the highly visual nature of children with autism; however, studies have found that children with ASD are as diverse as typical children in their reading abilities (Nation, Clark, Wright, & Williams, 2006), and there is some evidence that children with HFA can often be hyperlexic or able to decode words at very high levels. Some practitioners advocate for a whole-word approach to reading, because of the visual learning style favored by so many students with HFA, while others note that the use of phonics is critically important in the use of writing and technology (Blischak & Schlosser, 2003). The biggest discrepancy appears to be in their reading comprehension, not their oral reading fluency or ability to decode (Cardoso-Martins & da Silva, 2008). Visualization techniques have been found to be effective in improving reading comprehension with children with language processing disorders (Joffe, Cain, & Marić, 2007).

Visualization techniques can be as simple as encouraging your students to take time to visualize in their minds what the words are saying. This allows for additional processing time to connect visual images and experiences with specific language. However, more complex and more instructional visualization techniques employ the use of specific questions:

- What can you see happening here?
- Who do you see involved here?
- Where do you see this happening?

Notice that the "why" and "how" questions are not asked. The first level of engagement with words is the translation to a visual image, and thus, very concrete images must be formed first. Once these images are formed, then the teacher can ask the student:

- Why do you think this is happening?
- Does this look like something else we have studied? How?

Literature web. One strategy that I have used to help students learn how to analyze literature that they may not completely understand is the Center for Gifted Education's (1996a) literature web (see Figure 7). The literature web allows students to begin to analyze literature through the use of a visual web—breaking the cognitive task that involves words into smaller, more discrete parts that use visual relationships. The reading, or piece of literature, is in the center, so that students with HFA understand that they are discussing one piece, rather than pulling from their often-extensive knowledge of other material. Rather than telling what the story is about, the student can describe what words are key to the meaning of the story, what visual images are used, what the simple main idea might be, and how the structure of the piece reinforces the main idea. One adaptation I have made, however, is in the "Feelings" section. Because children with HFA are often not aware of their feelings, or able to communicate those feelings, I ask, "What feelings does the author *want* the reader to feel?" This seems to remove the challenge of the personal response to literature and make it more analytical. Often, children with HFA are aware of what emotions are theoretically expected in certain situations; they just don't recognize such emotions in themselves.

The emphasis of the reading instruction is on the translation from the written word to the visual image—a process that Temple Grandin (1996) called "thinking in pictures." Visualization using written words can work backward as well. Some adults I know with HFA—several of them public speakers and teachers—"listen" to people talk by visualizing the words written out as people are speaking. They can then see the words that are being spoken to them, visualize what they would say back as if they were reading the conversation, and then respond to people around them. I was cued into this interplay between reading and spoken language when a good friend of mine, searching for a word, said, "I can tell you how to spell it, but I don't know how to pronounce it." When questioned, she admitted that when she listened to me speak, she envisioned the words appearing on a page. Such manipulation of visual and spoken language requires a great deal of cognitive energy, but it provides a means of compensating for the difficulty in understanding spoken language.

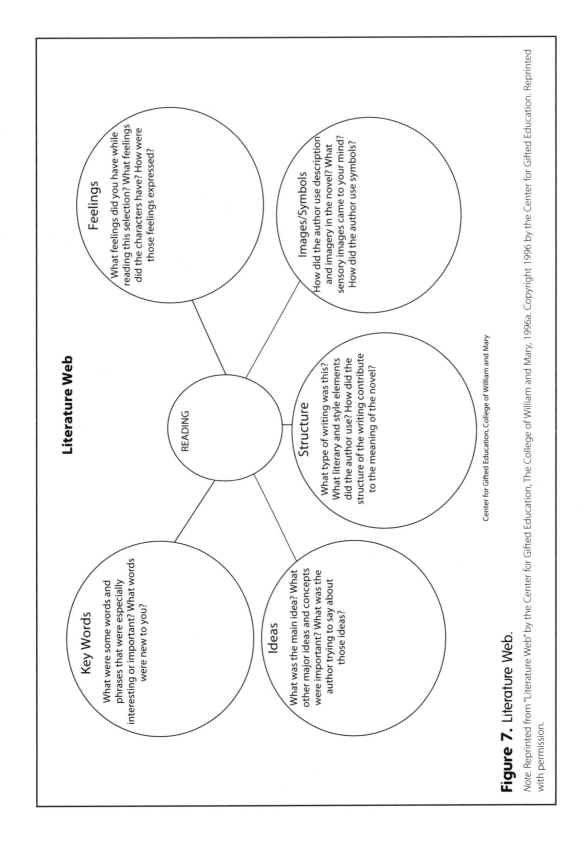

Figure 7. Literature Web.

Note. Reprinted from "Literature Web" by the Center for Gifted Education, The College of William and Mary, 1996a. Copyright 1996 by the Center for Gifted Education. Reprinted with permission.

Together Strategies

The best classroom environment for children with HFA is one in which it is understood that not all children communicate in the same manners and do not use the same strategies. Children with autism can be perceived as similar to English language learners (ELL) or to children who are hearing impaired, because they all may use different means of communicating. The primary difference, of course, is that children who are hearing impaired and children who are ELL have a baseline of language to which they can compare and translate standard English, whereas the child with HFA is struggling to understand the demands of language in general. The use of cooperative grouping and student-to-student interactions can allow children to "translate" for the child with HFA and to the rest of the classroom what the child might be trying to communicate. A classroom in which communication differences are addressed and dealt with openly is one in which children can appreciate and accommodate for each other's differences.

Echolalia

This openness to different forms of communication can lead to a greater understanding of the use of echolalia in children with HFA as a means of communicating. Echolalia is when a word or phrase that has been heard by the child is then repeated to the listener out of context (Siegel, 2003). Children with HFA will not be able to find the appropriate words for their intended purpose, and so will find another set of words that may or may not meet their needs. Often, they are selecting words or phrases in an effort to connect with someone, to engage with them, but with an underlying lack of understanding (Siegel, 2003). When receptive language is significantly impacted, there is a greater use of nonmeaningful echolalic phrases; however, when receptive language is higher, there is a greater use of meaningful echolalic phrases (Roberts, 1989). Children with HFA often have higher levels of receptive language, and so their echolalic phrases may appear to be random, but carry some level of meaning. A supportive teacher and classroom will attempt to make some sense of the odd songs, phrases, and dialogues that can emerge from a child with HFA, even if the only sense that one can make is that the child wants to engage with you. One child I knew could quote entire songs from Elmo's World, and yet many of the songs she chose had some form of relevance to the situation. We soon came to listen to her songs as means of gaining some insight into her mind—she could not find her own words, so she borrowed words from others.

Language-Rich, Visual-Rich Environment

Although it is common for preschools and classrooms of young children to have labels on items, it is a practice that fades within a few years. However, for children with HFA, having labels on common things allows students to make the connection between the word and the visual thing. Again, if the teacher can think of HFA in a manner similar to acquiring a second language, it becomes less problematic for teachers who say, "But she's too old for that."

Similarly, if a teacher and a classroom understand that some children do not learn as well using words, the use of visuals becomes very important to the communication of a classroom. Pictures can be used for directions, schedules, and questions. Information can be presented using videos in addition to lectures and notes and verbally engaging activities. When looking at content or instructing students, the teacher needs to be both internally asking, as well as modeling for the other students, the question, "How else can I say this, and can I show it rather than say it?"

If children and teachers become used to using multiple modalities for communication purposes, then there can be greater communication between all students. Two strategies for building in classroom interactions and movement in order to help students learn vocabulary are the "Give One-Get One" and the "Inside-Outside Circles" techniques.

Give One-Get One. Give One-Get One is a strategy that links prior knowledge and vocabulary to new concepts and new vocabulary, as well as encouraging social interactions and movement—all aspects that can promote learning.

1. Have students individually fold a piece of paper into two columns and label the columns "Give" and "Get."
2. Pair students up.
3. Ask the pairs to list important words or ideas they wish to remember about a topic in the "Give One" column.
4. Ask the whole class to stand up and raise their hands when they are finished.
5. Ask students to find someone to high five. You might need to preteach that a high five is a gentle slap of hands, rather than the ornate, multistep greeting it becomes between some students.
6. In the new partners, partner A shares something from his or her Give One column. If Partner B doesn't have it on his or her list, he or she records the idea in the Get One column. Then Partner B offers an item from his or her Give One column, and Partner A records it in his or her Get One column. A variation of this game gives 1 point to each student for every item they have in common and 2 points to the student who had something to give.
7. Partners split up, raise their hands, and look for another partner to high five.

8. The process repeats itself until the teacher calls time.

9. Each student has a list of ideas and/or important information for reference. If points are being taken, the original partner pairs can add their points together for recognition of the most unique ideas given.

10. In addition, if there's time, some teachers will ask students to create a review poster of their Give One-Get One items.

Inside-Outside Circles. Another strategy to use movement in the classroom and to develop communication is the "Inside-Outside Circles" technique.

1. Students are divided into small groups.

2. Students write review questions or unit facts on an index card. You may have to provide some students with specific questions to ask if they are unable to think of any questions on their own.

3. Each team member checks the validity of facts or answers to questions with the other members of the team. Answers to questions are then written on the back of the card.

4. Teacher numbers off the class, giving students either #1 or #2.

5. The ones form a circle facing outward.

6. The twos form a concentric circle outside the ones. Pairs should then be formed with the ones and twos facing each other.

7. The ones read their question to the twos, then wait for a response, coaching if necessary.

8. The twos read their question to the ones, then wait for a response, coaching if necessary.

9. The teacher gives directions such as "Ones, please rotate to your left." You can specify how far to rotate, depending on the total number of people in the class.

10. Repeat with the twos moving in another direction.

Key Points From Chapter 7

- Speech and language issues are one of the defining features of children with HFA. Understanding, finding, using, and expressing themselves with appropriate inflections and prosody can be very difficult for students with HFA. Typically, students will receive services from an SLP. Numerous people draw a comparison between children with autism to children from a different culture.

- *Teaching* strategies focus on specific skills to be used with language and communication. Strategies such as scripts, call-and-response activities, and content-specific vocabulary words can allow students to learn how to engage.

- *Timing* strategies allow teachers to construct behavior modification charts to encourage the child to use appropriate words and interaction sequences. An example of a behavior contract is provided in Figure 2.
- *Training* strategies can develop a student's ability to connect words together in meaningful manners. Strategies such as the Frayer Model, the Word Splash model, and Give One-Get One provide visual relationships of words.
- *Thinking* strategies provide alternative means for students who are struggling to understand spoken words. Encouraging the use of visualization techniques, including the use of written words, can provide structure for the child. In addition, cuing the child to use other senses beyond auditory meanings, such as analyzing rhythms of language, can enable the child to become better at the appropriate use of language.
- *Together* strategies can mean that all of the children in the classroom support and try to understand the meanings behind a child's use of echolalia and repeated statements. In addition, having a classroom that is rich in language and visual images can provide support to a child who is struggling to communicate.

Chapter 8

Emotional Development: Autism Impacts How a Child Feels

There are a number of factors that impact the emotional behaviors of children with HFA. Underlying these behaviors are some specific issues related to autism:

- emotional regulation (Laurent & Rubin, 2004),
- sensory integration and processing differences (Iarocci & McDonald, 2006),
- weak central coherence and poor joint attention (Morgan, Mayberry, & Durkin, 2003),
- mindblindness or theory of mind (Frith, 2001), and
- other comorbid disorders (Leyfer et al., 2006).

Such a list indicates that emotional issues are significant within the classroom, where children with HFA may exhibit behaviors such as:

- irritability,
- tantrums, and
- repetitive behaviors.

Comorbid Conditions

Although many of these issues may seem minor to an adult, or even a peer, the child with HFA is also often impacted by other compounding mental health issues. In addition to dealing with issues related to autism, more than 65% of children with HFA are likely to exhibit symptoms comorbid with other psychiatric disorders (Ghaziuddin, 2005) including:

- 44% with a specific phobia (Leyfer et al., 2006),
- 37% with obsessive-compulsive disorder (OCD; Leyfer et al., 2006),
- 37% with significant depression (Ghaziuddin, Ghaziuddin, & Greden, 2002), and
- 31% with ADHD (Leyfer et al., 2006).

Emotional Regulation

I once worked with Stefan, a 7-year-old with Asperger's syndrome, who had a cat that he loved named Smoky—all of his writings were about his cat, his conversation focused on his cat, and we were told in great detail on a daily basis about Smoky. This lasted until one Tuesday, when he started talking about trains. The next week, I expressed delight to his mother that he was expanding his areas of interest, and she told me that Stefan had seen Smoky get hit by a car the last Monday. I will admit that I knew less then about autism, and I perceived that Stefan had no emotions about losing his cat, and simply replaced his love of the cat with a love of trains. I was horrified. However, after watching him closely, I noticed that he changed the subject whenever cats came up, and he walked away from classmates who were discussing their cats. It was clearly too painful for him to even hear about cats, much less handle his own pain. I soon saw how he used trains as means of shutting out the pain, and my heart hurt for him then. He was not a little robot—he was a very sad little boy.

Emotional regulation is the "processes of establishing, maintaining, or disrupting the relation" (Campos, Campos, & Barrett, 1989, p. 394) between the person and the environment. In other words, it's not the feelings themselves that create problems—it's the management of the emotions and how they relate to the environment. Emotional regulation develops along with the brain and the frontal lobe (Greenberg & Snell, 1997) and changes as the child develops and learns new ways of handling the overwhelming nature of her emotions. In typical children, this emotional regulation develops in predictable stages (Schetter, 2006):

- *Stage 1 (Birth to Age 2), Immediate*: The child is not aware of emotions as being something he can manage or even identify. He is aware of his physical and nurturing needs and asks for responses to fill those needs. When his needs are not met or he is overwhelmed, he may:

- cry,
- suck,
- disengage, or
- sleep.

- *Stage 2 (Ages 2–5), Physical*: Children become aware of their emotional states and seek physical actions to soothe themselves or to get rid of the emotions. These physical actions can look like:
  - snuggling with a "lovey,"
  - repetitive motions such as rocking in a rocking chair,
  - throwing a tantrum, or
  - hitting or biting.

- *Stage 3 (Ages 5–8), Verbal*: Children became better able to "use their words" to release their emotions. To release their pent-up emotions or to make themselves feel better, they may:
  - argue,
  - negotiate,
  - yell, or
  - tell someone about it.

- *Stage 4 (Ages 8+), Metacognitive*: Children and adults begin to take an active role in shaping their emotional experience and tell themselves what they are feeling and what actions they can take when they don't like the experience such as:
  - talking yourself "down,"
  - identifying changes to make, or
  - reframing the experience.

It is important to note that during times of perceived great emotional stress, typical children and adults will move backward in their coping mechanism. An adult who has a really challenging and difficult day may say, "Boy, I need a drink!" Drinking, eating, and smoking are examples of negative immediate physical coping strategies. Examples of more positive immediate physical coping strategies may include exercising or even sleeping. A person who goes to see a funny movie to get herself out of a funk is using the physical release of laughing to moderate her negative emotions. Or, she may decide to talk to someone; I am known for calling my girlfriends and talking something out for hours on the phone. These are backward coping strategies because the dialogue that occurs in our heads is not enough to release the flood of emotions. Our internal metacognitive discussion then selects which of the lower stage strategies are most likely to reduce and release the negative emotion.

This developmental sequence can only occur when children are taught to use their strategies—either through direct instruction or through experience (Greenberg & Snell, 1997). There is a reason that preschool teachers chant, like a mantra, "Use your words," to toddlers who are trying to release frustration and anger and desire. And counselors are always in demand to teach older children and adults how to reframe emotional issues and make conscious healthy coping choices.

The important thing to note about the use of this model is the importance of language, which is key to moving children along the developmental path toward healthy, adult emotional regulation. Without language, children cannot:

- name their emotions,
- ask for what they need,
- release or moderate negative emotions through conversation, or
- think themselves through decision-making processes.

Children with HFA have a very difficult time with emotional regulation, possibly because of their underlying difficulty with language. When they cannot access their language, they cannot handle emotional distress or anxiety in appropriate manners. Thus, children with HFA often will behave in immature manners—having tantrums, crying, disengaging, or seeking repetitive motions.

In addition to the regulation issues, children with HFA may exhibit rapid "escalation" cycles, in which they are triggered by an event, and begin the process of escalating to an emotional outburst. In practical terms, this can mean that a child can go from "zero to 60 in nothing flat," as one teacher told me. Please see Figure 8 for an example of what an escalation cycle can look like (Sugai, Horner, Lewis-Palmer & Todd, 2005). It is important to understand where a child is in the cycle, because intervention is only possible during the Agitation phase; once a child has started Accelerating, any intervention is only going to strengthen the intensity of the peak. Sometimes, you have to stand back and wait out a tantrum or a fit, and then attempt intervention during the Calming phase.

Children with HFA are more likely to "trigger" quickly, reach higher points of intensity during an outburst, and take longer to calm down (Aspy et al., 2007). There are also some classroom situations that are more likely than others to trigger an outburst or demonstration of anxiety or even rage. These include (Green et al., 2006):

- annoying behavior by a peer or adult that impacts the sensory system,
- losing a competition,
- running out of materials and not being able to complete a project,

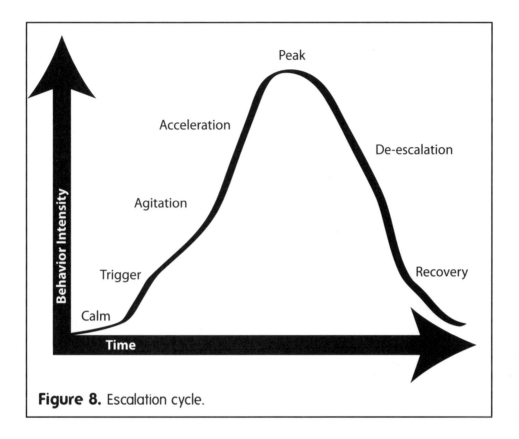

Figure 8. Escalation cycle.

- misplacing an item,
- interrupting an activity,
- cancelling an activity,
- delaying an activity,
- changing the sequence of an activity, and
- separating from a person or object of attachment.

One of the coping strategies that children with HFA use is repetitive behavior to moderate their own emotional intensities.

Repetitive Behaviors

All people feel stress. When typical children or adults experience stress, they have to release that stress, and they choose to do that through stimulating actions that soothe their jangled nerves. In biological terms, they are finding an activity that produces short bursts of neurotransmitters that moderate the overactive parts of the brain responsible for the feelings of stress and anxiety. The neurotransmitters allow the brain to then focus and sustain attention rather than being in a "fight or flight" mode (Attwood, 2008). In young children and infants, stress-releasing actions include lining up cars, stacking toys, banging things, and other actions that are "linked by repetitiveness, rigidity, invariance and inappropriateness" (Turner, 1999, p. 839). As children mature, they still seek out anxiety-reducing behavior, but it is often moderated by social norms. Thus, instead of lining up cars, adults straighten their desks; instead of banging their heads, they tap pencils or jiggle their legs. When my husband is anxious, he cleans (*I can't really complain about this coping strategy*). Video games provide some of this anxiety-reducing stimulation as well—the repetitive nature of the game produces pleasurable release from the moment.

It is important to note that *any* strong emotion can require a repetitive behavior to regulate it, even a good emotion. I distinctly remember watching my daughter make the winning soccer goal, and run back to the group with a big grin on her face, her arms flapping. The neurological system prefers balance and will seek to moderate any extreme.

When the repetitive behaviors interfere with daily functioning, or are considered highly socially inappropriate, they are considered a problem. Autism has at times been considered an anxiety disorder, significantly overlapping with both obsessive-compulsive disorder (Gillott, Furniss, & Walter, 2001) and Tourette's syndrome (Muris, Steernamen, Merckelbach, Holdrinet, & Meesters, 1998) because of the severity of the anxiety and the use of socially inappropriate, nonmeaningful repetitive actions to reduce that stress. The greater the impact of autism, the greater the level of stress, and the greater the need to seek stimulation to release that stress. This explains why some children with autism bang their heads or even bloody themselves—there is so much stress that they don't know how to release it all without a great deal of stimulation to counteract the negative flood of anxiety overwhelming them.

Sensory Integration Issues

Some theorists suggest that the level of stress arousal found in children with ASD is due to dysregulation of the seven systems of sensory information and processing (Iarocci & McDonald, 2006). The seven systems are:

1. Tactile (touch)
2. Vestibular (balance)
3. Proprioceptive (body awareness)
4. Visual (sight)
5. Auditory (hearing)
6. Gustatory (taste)
7. Olfactory (smell)

Sensory integration specialists tend to focus on the first three of the seven sensory systems because they believe that these three are the largest routes through which we gather information about the world around us (Ayers, 1979).

When children are taught about the five senses, they are not often taught about the vestibular and proprioceptive systems. To introduce teachers to these concepts, I ask teachers to stand on one foot and hold out one finger. This is not a difficult task for them. Then, I ask them to close their eyes—all of sudden, people are keeling over, unable to keep their balance. This inability to maintain your balance in the absence of visual cues is an issue of the vestibular system not communicating with the proprioceptive system. Often, children with vestibular issues are your climbers and balancers—the kids who are trying to balance their chairs on two legs or are climbing up on things. They want to get information to their system to determine where they are in space. By focusing their attention, such as balancing on a chair leg, they are stimulating their vestibular and proprioceptive sensory systems, just as someone else might eat Mexican food to stimulate their taste buds because they enjoy the spice. They may look like risks takers, but in reality, they're trying to arouse their nervous systems to determine where they are in space. I can always identify these children—they're the ones who have to hold on to the teacher to literally ground themselves.

Numerous studies have found that children with autism tend to notice details, not wholes, and that they perceive their interactions with the world through their senses in either heightened or reduced stimulation (Happé, Booth, Charlton, & Hughes, 2006; Iarocci & McDonald, 2006). As a result of their scrambled neurology, children with HFA may have difficulty with central coherence and joint attention, or as my grandmother would say, "finding the forest for the trees." Central coherence has to do with a focus on minutia, rather than focusing on the bigger picture; these are children who do not form an overall impression, but rather a sequence of parts (Happé, 1996). On the other hand, joint attention is being able to focus on and think about more than one thing at a time (Morgan et al., 2003). Children with HFA are easily distracted by small pieces of information and are then able to then shift their attention to other items to incorporate a whole concept. They also can get overwhelmed when the task they are focusing on changes or doesn't make sense to them.

As a teacher, this may mean that children with HFA can respond to minimal changes within the classroom or be completely oblivious to significant changes. Their sensory systems are more likely to be annoyed by new or different sounds, smells, tactile materials, and even the amount of light present in a room. It is a very good idea to ask the child's parents or previous teachers if there are certain sensory things that can upset a particular child. A questionnaire like the one in Figure 9 allows you to be better prepared for figuring out the particular puzzle that is your student. You can purchase formal sensory questionnaires, but I have found that it's

1. What rewards will motivate this child?
2. What rewards will backfire if attempted? What does not work?

	Specific items that may trigger anxiety or a response in the child	Size of response: Rate from 0–10 0 = nothing to 10 = uncontrollable outburst	Duration: Length of time of typical response until child calms down	What does the response look like?	How do you typically handle the reaction? How effective is intervention?	What will make the response continue? What does not work?
Auditory						
Visual						
Taste						
Tactile						
Smells						
Settings or places						
People						

Figure 9. Sensory questionnaire.

easier to make one that can reflect my own classroom needs. I encourage you to adapt the one I've created in Figure 9 to your own classroom.

I once worked with a preschool child who could not handle the feeling of the sand at the sand table. He would shriek and cry at even the sight of the table. Once, after being talked through it, he tried it, and had such a look of horror on his face, I soon quit and had him do something else. The same child had very little awareness of sound, would speak in a very loud voice, and was unfazed by the planes that would fly overhead because of our proximity to the airport. At the same time, I had another little boy who hated it when I sang. He liked songs, but the change in the sound of my voice when I sang was unbearable to him, and I am not that bad of a singer!

As teachers, we have to understand that the inappropriate behaviors that children with HFA are demonstrating aren't to get attention; in fact, they serve no social purpose whatsoever. The tantrums, the crying, the banging—all of this is an effort to get rid of overwhelming feelings. It is important that the adult moderate her own emotional responses, which will only fuel the fire of emotional distress of the child.

It is critical to understand that children with HFA act out because:
- They don't know what to do.
- They don't know how to make themselves feel better.
- They can't use language to help themselves or to ask for help.

Teaching Strategies

Teaching strategies are those strategies that have to be taught directly to a child. You can't ask a child to do something without providing direct instruction first. The first step in the modeling of emotional regulation is assisting children with HFA to identify what emotions they are feeling. Because language is a challenge, simply finding the name for emotions beyond "happy" and "sad" may be difficult for them. If words are not going to be the communication approach, visual images might be. In my classroom, I hung a chart that uses visual expressions with the name of the emotion under it. I encouraged children who were experiencing difficulty to point to the face that looked like how they felt. An example of this face chart can be found in Figure 10. This chart provides a visual link to the words for emotions and allows children to provide names to those feelings that they have. I have learned (the hard way) that I cannot offer verbal suggestions such as "Are you feeling scared? Sad? Lonely?" These are all words, and a child with HFA struggling with regulating an emotion may not have leftover cognitive energy to process the

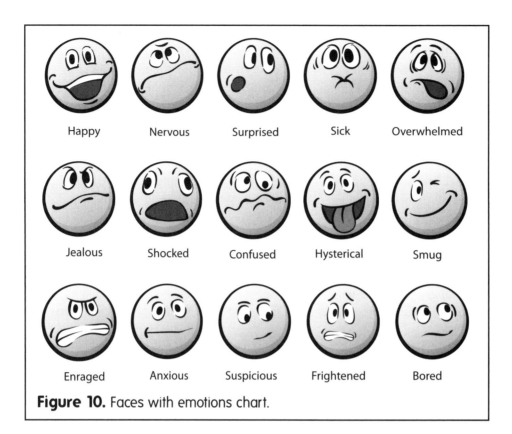

Figure 10. Faces with emotions chart.

language as well. I have learned to provide the pictures so that I can get some communication from the student and then determine what action I can take.

Some of the most frequently used strategies are those that help reduce stress in a child. These have to be very concrete and very specific. One of my favorites is teaching deep breathing. Breathing techniques are used in everything from yoga and prayer to meditation to assist people in centering themselves and stepping outside of the tumult of the emotional state. I have found that if I encourage "deep breathing," however, I get panting, and panting just makes things worse. I have learned to use the dual visual images of:

Smell the flower.
Blow out the candle.

This allows the child to fully inflate her chest and then to completely empty it. The increased oxygen allows her brain to move blood more easily into those regions that are affected by stress. In my classroom, I kept a plastic flower and a big, unlit candle handy together in a plastic bag, which provided the necessary visual reminder of what to do.

Replacement Behaviors

As a teacher, I had to recognize that I could not extinguish a child's need to release stress, I could only change how that child demonstrated his stress. I had to directly teach the child behaviors that would *replace* the undesirable behavior. So often, children act out simply because they don't know any other alternatives. The key is to find something that is close to the undesirable behavior but is appropriate:

- For a child who was hitting his head, I taught him to rub his head briskly.
- For a child who was gnawing off her fingernails, I taught her to press the tips of her fingers really, really hard on the table.
- I used gum frequently in my classroom to reduce the hair and clothes chewing.
- Another teacher I know who has "pickers," or kids who pick their skin, places stickers on plastic Easter eggs and styrofoam balls for kids to pick off.
- And yet another teacher I know has Velcro on the undersides of most of her desks for kids to pick at. She learned the hard way not to have both parts of the Velcro attached to the desk because the "rrrrriiiipppp" of the Velcro coming apart was very appealing to the children, but very irritating to her.
- This same teacher had an arrangement with the P.E. teacher to allow her to send her "runners" to him to run around the gym rather than having them bolt off away from the school. These children could still run when they felt the need to, but they had somewhere that was safe for them to release their feelings.

Because I am not a trained counselor, I would strongly encourage you to seek out assistance from a counselor or therapist who is accustomed to children with HFA. These professionals can also provide you with numerous ideas for helping teach emotional regulation strategies to a child. In addition, occupational therapists can assist with the challenges given to a child who has sensory overload or emotional overload and not enough language to moderate either one.

Timing Strategies

It is important to understand the escalation cycle of a child and those things that are most likely to "set off" a child. The data from the sensory questionnaire in Figure 9 becomes very useful in determining an improvement plan. A baseline of information can be gathered to determine what triggers a child and how long the cycles tend to be. I worked with a child who was slow to escalate, but once he hit the acceleration phase, he could take up to 3 hours to calm down. A 3-hour tantrum is indeed a sight to behold.

Once the environmental triggers and opportune moments of intervention are identified, then changes in the child's response can be initiated through careful selection of behavioral goals. If a child who used to lose his composure in moments and melt down for 45 minutes can maintain his composure for 5 minutes before melting down for 30 minutes, then he is demonstrating improvement. Both the Agitation stage and the Peak stage can be monitored for length of time and intensity of time. As improvement is shown, the child should be reinforced for his successful use of strategies.

Data collected about the escalation cycle must be precise; therefore, it might be somewhat difficult to monitor and measure. To alleviate this, the teacher can simply make a behavior contract like the one shown in Figure 2 on p. 79, using the behavior of emotional regulation as the goal.

It is important that the teacher demonstrate appropriate modeling of emotional regulation. He or she could use "talk aloud" strategies at times when the teacher is expressing frustration, modeling for the child what to say and how to moderate one's emotional state. See Figure 11 for an example of a "talk aloud" internal conversation. This modeling provides the student with an example of how to process internal dialogue to regulate his feelings.

The teacher can also praise and reward typical children who are using regulation strategies. Be specific in the praise: "Good job" has little meaning to typical children, much less to a child who is struggling with processing nonspecific language. "I like the way you took a deep breath before you started on this hard math work" is much more effective praise and feedback.

Training Strategies

There are a number of strategies that are designed to attract the attention of children with HFA and help them remember emotional regulation strategies, including the use of:
- "fidgets" or "stimming" activities,
- "calms" or sensory-reduction activities,
- music and movement, and
- visual cuing.

Stims

Some of the most helpful strategies in moderating a child's emotional state involve having materials and strategies available that will stimulate a child or arouse

Wow, this really frustrates me. I feel really angry when the school tells us about an assembly the same day that we're having one. I don't really have time to prepare anything else to do, and it's going to take away our math lesson. I'm very anxious and worried that we aren't going to get to the next chapter in time for our test.

Let me see. Do I have any control over this situation? No. Although math is important today, so is this assembly. We have to go to the assembly.

What are my choices here? I could scream and cry, but that won't help anything. I would just spend the assembly talking to the principal instead of watching the assembly.

I could refuse to go, but that won't be a good idea because then my class would miss the interesting things they're going to cover in the assembly.

I could skip that chapter, but that's not a good idea because we need to cover that material for the state test.

I could move the test, which I don't like to do because that pushes us off another day.

I don't really like any of these choices, but what is the best choice of the ones that I have? The best choice has got to be to move the test, because I don't want my students to miss the assembly or the material. Those are worse than getting off schedule.

That's what I'll do. It's my choice to do it that way from the choices that I have.

I don't feel frustrated anymore because I have made the best choice of the ones that I have. I don't need to feel angry because my students are still getting something good out of this. I can feel happy that I made a good choice and that my students are going to have an interesting experience.

Figure 11. Talk aloud model.

his underactive neurological system that is craving stimulation in order to regulate itself (Schetter, 2006).

Some children will need to alert themselves with rhythmic noise or gross motor movements. There are a variety of noisemakers and bouncy balls that can be purchased, but I would recommend that these only be available for recess or for breaks. There is a particularly nice octopus yo-yo toy that has lights and clackers on the ends of the "legs" that many of my children would stim on as they clacked away. Another favorite was the hands clapper that clapped as you shook it. You can find a list of companies that make toys and sensory stimulating activities for children with autism by doing a simple search online. To be honest with you, though, I usually find what I need at the dollar store.

Other stims or alerting activities include the use of cold water play and exercise (Schetter, 2006). When a class is on edge, and the weather permits, a game outside in chilly air wakes them up enough to be able to focus better for the rest of the day. On warmer days, I would ask some of my children to go to the bathroom to wash their hands in cold water. The stimulation of the cold water can also help them regulate a little bit better. Other teachers have shared that they have used peppermint candy or mint scents in the classroom as form of stimulation.

Occupational therapists will have a variety of official stims as well. My favorite is the seat cushion that looks like a half moon with raised knobs on it. As the child sits on the cushion, she can do a small, seated rumba motion and the cushion provides stimulation. I sometimes have large exercise balls available in a classroom as well, so that the act of sitting becomes a stimulating experience.

Calms

Some children, however, are so overstimulated that you don't need to arouse them; you need to calm them down. Particularly helpful when a child is becoming agitated is the use of "calms." Occupational therapists sometimes use weighted vests to ground a child. I have seen a teacher who just used large bags of rice in a fishing vest. When a child appeared to be triggered, she would recommend that he go and work in the "heavy corner" where the vest hung.

One of the most successful strategies I have seen is the use of "fidgets." Fidgets are small toys, generally purchased from the dollar store, that allow a child to squeeze, fiddle, pull, or otherwise take out their anxiety. They have been highlighted as effective strategies for use in keeping the attention of students with ADHD and learning disabilities (Lehrer, 2008), and I have found that they also help reduce the anxiety of students with HFA. I personally cannot do a presentation without a pencil or a key in my hand to gently prod myself with or to turn over and over again in my hand. It helps reduce my anxiety of public speaking. The keys to a successful fidget are that they are:

- small enough to not be a large visual distraction to the child or anyone else around him;
- inexpensive, because chances are very good that the child won't even be consciously aware that the fidget is in his hand and will wander off with it. I soon learned which of my students to keep an eagle eye on and to take back the fidget before they took it home with them or lost it on the playground;
- quiet, so that the fiddling does not distract anyone else with any resultant noise; and
- sturdy enough that it won't fall apart easily.

Examples include tennis balls, stress balls, little toys with varied edges, and LEGOs. LEGOs are particularly nice because students can them pick apart and put them back together, then pick them apart and put them back together again.

Another teacher I knew would work out an "antiseptic cleaning" strategy in collaboration with another teacher (Murawski, 2009)—preferably one whose classroom was all the way across the school—as a calming technique. When the emotional behavior of one child was about to spill out into the classroom, she would devise a very important errand that involved the child taking a note to the fellow teacher, hopefully resulting in a long, calming walk. She would seal it up in an envelope and send it with the child. Inside the note read "Antiseptic cleaning needed." The fellow teacher would ask the child to wait for 5 minutes while she wrote a note back. It didn't matter what the note said; the important part was the walk, the wait, and the walk back. One teacher I knew heard of this and added a component of heavy work to her "important errand." She had a pile of strategically placed books, and as a child was triggered and beginning to show signs of agitation, she would ask him to carry the books over to her fellow teacher. The fellow teacher would have a similarly stacked pile of books for the child to bring back. By the time the student returned, having carried two piles of books across the school twice, he often had worked off his agitation.

Movement and Music

Dancing and yoga appear to also be very effective means of moderating a child with HFA's emotional state (Levy & Hyman, 2009). I often meet some secondary teachers who turn up their noses at dancing in their classroom, perceiving that to be a preschool or primary activity. However, movement can be one of the most powerful means of learning, particularly for children for whom language is not their primary mode of understanding. Movement stimulates those neurotransmitters that provide emotional regulation (Zilius, 2010) and can open up neurological connections that allow learning to occur (Hannaford, 1997). It is very difficult to remain agitated and sensitive when one is boogieing on the dance floor—even if that dance floor is a classroom.

One strategy that is particularly effective to soothe emotional turmoil is the use of music. Children with HFA have been found to be particularly sensitive to music (Mottron, Peretz, & Ménard, 2003), and the selection of music can be a very powerful strategy. Music in the background can either highly agitate or significantly soothe a child. If you have two children—one whom it distracts and one whom it soothes—you can use earphones for either child. Noise-reducing earphones can be very helpful for the child who is overly attuned to sound, and earphones with music can soothe the child who needs background noise in order to reduce anxiety. It is important to note that the need for either sound or complete silence is highly individual; it's exacerbated by autism, but the need is very real. You can either spend your time fighting the need, or you can work with it.

In my classroom, I offer students three choices for independent work:
1. silence, achievable with noise-reducing headphones;
2. quiet background music, appropriate for quiet work; or

3. music of their choice—generally some radio station or an iPod selection that has to be approved by their parents—that they can listen to with earphones.

The rules are that they must work and behave appropriately. If they do not behave appropriately, they have to listen to music I select. I find that it takes only a couple of classes of Neil Diamond or country music to bring them back in line. (I happen to like both of these, but I find that students today tend to not appreciate the strains of "Sweet Caroline" as much I do!)

There are teachers who say that we're doing a child a disservice in providing these things because the real world won't be so accommodating. I beg to differ. As grownups, we regulate our environment all of the time. If I am asked to work in an environment where I cannot think, and it upsets me, I won't work there. If I am asked to perform tasks that I can't do, I won't go into that line of work. I have to learn to moderate my responses and advocate so that I can learn what to do when the environment is not optimal for me. We are providing children with the experiences that they need so that they can experience comfort when learning. We are not preparing them for the real world, but we are teaching them how to achieve their own reality.

It's important to understand that fidgets and weighted vests and exercise balls aren't going to end the emotional problems in the classroom, and there will be behavior management issues as you introduce them. I find that the first 2 weeks are very difficult as I teach the class how to use them. I have them available for use for everyone, with the following rules:

- Stims and calms are to be used only by you. If they get shared or become an object of conversation, they will be taken from you for today, and you may try again tomorrow.
- If a stim or a calm leaves your desk area for any reason, it becomes mine. You may try again tomorrow. *This is to stop the fidgets from being thrown, dropped, fought over, or reclaimed when another child wants to use them.*
- If the stim or calm becomes a weapon, it becomes mine for a week. Next week, you may select a different fidget.
- At the end of the class, or the end of the period, the stim or calm becomes mine.

I have found that I have to enforce these rules for about 2 weeks, while the objects are still a novelty. After this time, the children who are using them to get out of work or who can't control their impulsivity with them become tired of getting into trouble and stop picking them up. The children who need them to remain focused and find them useful continue to use them and the behavioral issues are reduced overall. I figure that it's better to have 2 weeks of enforcement and the rest of the year of good behavior.

Thinking Strategies

Aspy and colleagues (2007) noted the effectiveness of using sensory information to provide feedback to students with HFA. Because they are often unable to name emotions, they can transfer their ability to recognize sensory responses to emotional reactions. For example, a card that is located where a child could read it might state, "When I feel overwhelmed with the noise level in class or am very sensitive to people's touch—I am feeling anxious . . . Take two deep breaths. Press hands together and count to 10 slowly" (Aspy et al., 2007, Slides 28–29). Such a script allows the student to self-identify emotions though their manifestations and take preventative measures before an outburst.

Stress Thermometer

Another strategy that is used often is the concept of a "stress thermometer" (Aspy et al., 2007; Buron, 2004; McAfee, 2002). A stress thermometer doesn't ask children with HFA to name or identify their anxiety or stress, just to quantify it. A child is asked to rate his stress level from 1–5, with 1 being very mild and 5 being ready to blow. The visual cue of the thermometer allows the student to evaluate her own stress level and then take preventative measures. See Figure 12 for an example.

Reframing

Recent research studies in cognitive-behavioral interventions have found significant positive effects in a number of social and behavioral issues faced by children with anxiety-related disorders, including the reduction of motoric and vocal tics in children with Tourette's syndrome (Piacentini et al., 2010), decreases in obsessive-compulsive actions and thoughts in children with OCD (Piacentini, March, & Franklin, 2006), and decreases in manic and depressive states in children with bipolar disorder (Basco & Rush, 2007). A few studies are finding academic and emotional improvements in children with high-functioning autism as well (Sze & Wood, 2007; Wood et al., 2009).

Cognitive behavioral therapy involves the use of reframing, or acknowledging the impact that autism has on someone, but then asserting control over the emotion. It provides a script for children with HFA to follow to construct their thinking. Because language is not a strength of children with HFA, the scripted thoughts of reframing are useful tools to allow them to gain control of their emotional states. Figure 13 provides a simplistic version of this script that can be specifically taught to children with autism.

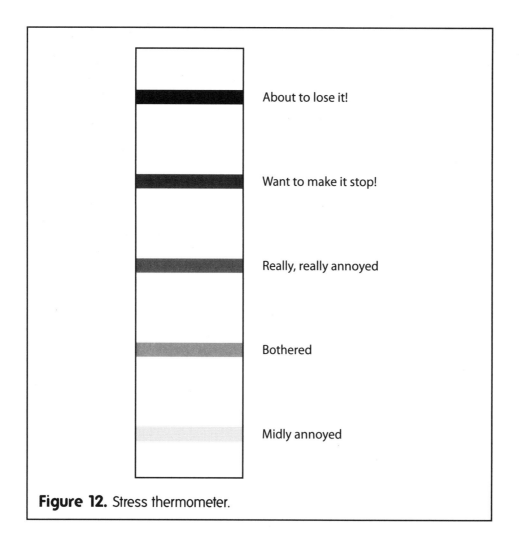

Figure 12. Stress thermometer.

Together Strategies

It is important that the climate and culture of the classroom is one in which the children all work together to help each other learn. This will mean acknowledging differences and understanding that differences are strengths within a classroom; once this occurs, then each child can feel recognized. Children with HFA are not the only different types of learners to be found within your classroom, but you—and the rest of the classroom—can work to accommodate them.

Peer partnerships can work very effectively to help a child with HFA feel connected to others. I have had the good fortune to work with numerous teachers at every level of schooling who truly made their classroom a place where students

> - I feel this way because my autism is making me feel this way with a bunch of chemicals in my brain. This isn't really how I feel.
>
> - I am in control of my behavior, not my autism. I can choose to feel something else. I will feel in control.
>
> - I will wait until the need to _____ passes, and I will win over my autism.
>
> **Figure 13.** Reframing script.

looked out for each other, and the teachers' caring attitudes extended to their students as well.

Within a classroom, there are numerous environmental strategies that can be used to create a classroom climate in which a child with HFA can learn. These include a strong supportive culture that does not accept bullying, physical environmental changes within a room to promote focus, a positive growth-oriented mindset, and the provision of a safe place.

Anti-Bullying Focus

A school environment that accepts and encourages students with HFA to develop emotionally is one in which bullying is unacceptable. Many children with HFA will either be the victim of a bully or become a bully themselves (van Roekel & Scholte, 2010). Often, children with HFA have flawed interpretations of bullying behavior. Most children with HFA who *are* bullies do not interpret their behavior as bullying; while conversely, children with HFA who are victimized perceive themselves to be bullied when they are not. The school community needs to become involved in a dialogue about what is considered bullying behavior, what is helpful behavior, and what can be done to reduce the bullying.

Environmental Issues

Perhaps one of the first things that a teacher can do in the classroom is to take out those things that will trigger a child's negative responses and to include those things that are soothing to him. You aren't preparing him for the real world by keeping things in your room that are annoying. If you lived near a train track and were driven crazy by trains, you would move. If a light hurt your eyes, you would turn it off. We should have such courtesy for our students as well, realizing that they aren't always in control of their sensory reactions. Knowing what can trigger an incident can alleviate much of your behavioral and emotional issues. You can't change the need to do a repetitive task or a sensory reaction, but you can replace the need or the reaction with a more appropriate one.

Classroom design is a significant factor in the comfort level of children with HFA. When children are over- or understimulated by sensory information, their ability to focus and concentrate becomes impaired. Consequently, the aesthetics of your classroom become very important. It is important to think of the things that stimulate and soothe your senses within your classroom.

1. Visual
    O   Some children need light—others find the light too bright. Fluorescent lights are notorious for setting off children with HFA. The child can "see" or at least sense the cycles and perceives the light as flickering, which is highly distractible and can cause headaches and disorientation (Grandin, 2004).
    O   Some students may be distracted by bright colors; others may need swirling colors to calm themselves down. I found that a lava lamp plugged in would soothe my children during meltdowns. I would then unplug it after they had calmed and I needed their attention for instruction.
    O   Some students may be so disturbed by books aligned in different heights or colors that they are unable to attend. As long as they weren't personal or confidential records, I tended to let my students organize things to their hearts' content—or in ways that made sense only to them. With one student, the need to have straight rows of desks was a problem during small-group activities. Therefore, I would provide this student with a time when he could go and straighten things out. Rather than saying "No," I learned the strategy of "Not now. Later (giving an exact time)." His frequent checking with me ("In 30 minutes, I can straighten the desks, right?") was not meant to be annoying—it was a means of helping him deal with his own anxiety. I found egg timers to be very helpful in this strategy.

2. Auditory
    O   Some children will be so distracted by the buzzing of electronics, that you might consider a white noise machine to drown out the ambient noise of a classroom in a busy school.
    O   Other children will respond with great passion and involvement with music; still others will shriek and cover their ears at the sound of music. You'll have to learn when music works to soothe and when it's too much.

3. Tactile
   - ○ Some children will need beanbag chairs in which to get cozy and to burrow. Others may need large pillows in a place where they can get underneath them.
   - ○ Some children respond well to small pieces of tape or Velcro taped to the bottom of their desks. If they're going to pick anyways, better to have them pick at a Velcro strip or tape than their own skin, or all of those little pieces of paper you might find in their desk.

4. Olfactory
   - ○ Some children will want fresh smells; others may be distracted by room deodorizers and cleaning products.
   - ○ Some children may be put off by your perfume or even your laundry soap.

5. Taste
   - ○ Some children will find the feel of certain foods in their mouth to be highly offensive and disgusting. They may start to act out the closer they get to lunchtime.
   - ○ Still other children may need to suckle or to have something in their mouths in order to regulate their emotions. Providing gum or mints can help them focus.

Mindsets

In her seminal work, Carol Dweck (2006) found that students were much more regulated and focused when the teacher used feedback that promoted a "growth" mindset, rather than a "fixed" mindset. A fixed mindset is one in which there is a limited amount of a characteristic—smarts, beauty, or capability—and the teacher expresses his or her belief that the student possesses enough of this characteristic to succeed. The student can then perceive that if she fails, then she must not have enough of that "ingredient" and is incapable of acquiring more. When a teacher states to a student that "You're so smart; you can do this!" he is in fact not raising the motivational level of the child, but reducing it. The child then perceives that if the work is hard, or heaven forbid, the child fails at it, then he or she must not be as smart as the teacher thought.

In contrast, Dweck (2006) advocated that teachers adopt a "growth mindset" in which children are encouraged to use effective strategies and to figure out which strategies are ineffective ones. Learning is presented not as a "got it or don't got it" activity, but a process of growing neurons, with the child in charge of growing those neurons. For a child with HFA, this mindset allows him to take control of his own emotional state, rather than feeling powerless and buffeted by outside forces. If he is encouraged to grow his neurons, and praised when he uses a successful strategy, then he is much more likely to attempt to control his learning and emotional status.

Safe Place

Because the world can be a very overwhelming place for a child who is dealing with language processing issues, sensory processing issues, and neurological storms, there is the need at times to find a safe place or a safe person to let jangled systems calm down (Moreno & O'Neal, 2002). In elementary classrooms, a safe place can be provided with cozy corners under a desk or in a darkened closet or quiet place. In middle and secondary schools, the safe place should be less public, but still provide a sensation-free, stimulus-free place where a child with HFA can collect him- or-herself. This can be another room, a reading corner away from the flow of the classroom, or a trusted teacher.

The characteristics of a safe place or person are that there be:
- few demands placed upon the child—sensory, communication, or emotional;
- an accepting attitude and one in which it is understood that this is necessary for the child to regain the ability to engage with the world; and
- a limited time frame. This is not an escape from schoolwork but there is emotional healing work to be done in this location.

Key Points From Chapter 8

- There are numerous emotional issues associated with high-functioning autism including emotional regulation, mindblindness, sensory integration, comorbidity with other mental and physical challenges, and rapidity of emotional escalation. In addition, students with HFA may not be as advanced as other students in the stages of self-soothing.
- *Teaching* strategies allow students to interpret specific emotions and responses using an emotion recognition chart and by the use of deep breathing. Also, identifying specific behaviors and replacement behaviors can be beneficial. It is important to recognize that you can't take away the need for the behavior, but you can teach an appropriate substitute for the behavior.
- *Timing* strategies allow teachers to determine appropriate modeling examples and then to promote appropriate soothing behaviors with specific praise. An example of a behavior contract is provided in Figure 2.

- *Training* strategies, such as a use of stimulating (stims) and calming (calms) activities, can provide a means for students with HFA to relieve their emotional tension in more socially acceptable manners. Music and movement have also been found to be useful in assisting students in their focus and emotional regulation.

- *Thinking* strategies provide ways for students to begin to self-regulate and to identify their own states of mind as well as communicate that state to others. Strategies such as the stress thermometer and reframing can facilitate a child being able to think through his own emotional state.

- *Together* strategies can mean that the classroom environment can be manipulated and amended to meet the unique learning needs of the child. Using the results from the sensory questionnaire, teachers can become more aware of the stressful components within their classroom. Physically arranging the classroom and promoting both a growth mindset and an anti-bullying climate among other students can establish the classroom as a safe place.

Chapter 9

Social Development: Autism Impacts How a Child Interacts

Social impairment is a defining feature of autism. Often, children with HFA will be able to understand how social behavior "should" be, but have a very difficult time actually behaving in socially appropriate manners (Hughes, 2011). The way in which this gap between understanding and demonstrating social skills is expressed can vary widely and is highly individual to the child. Unfortunately, few clear-cut, research-based social skills interventions have been found to be consistently effective within a school setting (Bellini, Peters, & Hopf, 2007). However, it is clear that teachers can't avoid the issue; I recommend that you research and just keep trying. Sometimes something works for one child that doesn't work for another. As Julia, a teacher friend of mine, says, "At least if you have a kid with HFA and you find the key—you've got it! They remember the path and they continue to use it. It's not like some other areas of disability where every day is a new day."

Causes

Often, children with HFA exhibit a condition called "mindblindness," where they lack "theory of mind" or the ability to understand someone else's thoughts and feelings when they are different than your own. Some researchers call this "mind reading," because of the assumptions that one must make about the other person (Baron-Cohen, 1997). Theory of mind is related to issues with mirror neurons (Iacoboni, 2008) or noisy brain networks (Dinstein, Thomas, Humphreys,

Behrmann, & Heeger, 2010) because interference with neurons that respond to someone else's pain or joy are impacted. Children with HFA are often very aware of their own emotions, but much less aware of others'. Or conversely, the emotion of others is so overwhelming to them, they don't know how to deal with the cascade of anxiety that they're feeling and therefore shut it out. Related to their issues with language, children with HFA may also have difficulty identifying and naming different emotions that they and other children are feeling. Some people perceive children with HFA to have no emotions, when in reality, they may be so overwhelmed by the whirlpools and eddies of emotions around them that they don't know how to respond.

Such lack of awareness of, or inability to name and handle, their own and others' emotions can lead to complications, particularly in the following aspects within a classroom:

- peer relationships;
- relationships with other, less familiar adults;
- group interactions, both in small and large groups;
- personal interactions such as greetings and extended conversations;
- conflict management such as avoiding or ending disagreements; and
- self-help skills such as asking for help or asking for directions.

Teachers can be one of the most powerful mediators in helping a child navigate through a development of social understanding (Hughes, 2011). The key to any successful behavior improvement program is to build from the student's strengths (Krasny, Williams, Provencal, & Ozonoff, 2003). Rather than trying to mold the child into another type of child, the goal is to help the child become the best that he can be. That means using his interests, obsessions, needs, and desires to help shape the way he interacts with you. In my presentations, I often tell teachers to "Stop fighting who the kid is—you can't change his autism. You *can* change how he deals with his autism."

One of the most important mantras I have learned to live by is the concept that "All behavior is communication." Behavior—good and bad—is an attempt to communicate something to the people around a child, whether it is her needs, wants, fears, or joys (Santrock, 2012). Rick Lavoie (2008) specified this even more, emphasizing the idea that all kids would rather be bad than dumb. What we as adults might see as "bad" behavior may often be a child avoiding the "dumb" label. I would go even further to say that "All kids would rather be bad than be lost in their own confusion." Acting out or being bad serves many purposes—we have to figure out what that purpose is for each child.

Teaching Strategies

Behavior-based strategies where the teacher teaches and then measures the results over time are the most heavily researched and most effective strategies in the literature. The Frank Porter Graham Center at the University of North Carolina has an extensive listing of strategies and training suggestions on its website: http://autismpdc.fpg.unc.edu. Although there is tremendous research for different strategies within clinical, therapeutic settings, this book will discuss the practical aspects of some of these in a classroom setting, with the teacher as a moderator. These include scripts; replacement behaviors; the Stay, Play and Talk strategy; and the use of Kohlberg's Moral Development model to facilitate interactions.

Scripts

Perhaps because children with HFA tend to have strong memories, scripts are one of the most successful and commonly used strategies for dealing with social situations. Michelle Garcia Winner's (2010) Social Scripts are well-used by speech language therapists for their training in use of certain scripts in certain places with an emphasis on generalization. A social script helps a child analyze and identify what type of social interaction she is being invited to engage in, from greetings to conversation to leave-taking. A script can provide openings and closings for a conversation of a particular type, as well as strategies that move the conversation along. Scripts provide cue words to the child to identify her role in the conversation and how to get what she wants.

Ms. Griffin: Now, to start a conversation, and because today is Monday, you might ask me, "How was your weekend, Ms. Griffin?"

Olivia (with HFA): How was your weekend, Ms. Griffin?

Ms. Griffin: And I might say, "It was very nice, Olivia! I went to the beach with my family. What did you do?" What am I doing here? I'm asking you a question about what?

Olivia: The beach?

Ms. Griffin: Not exactly. Listen for the cue words: "I went to the beach with my family. What did you *do*?" And what time frame are we talking about? Last month?

Olivia: No. Last weekend.

Ms. Griffin: Exactly! I'm asking you what *you* did last *weekend*.

Olivia: We went to the movies.

Ms. Griffin: I want you to extend that statement. You did go to the movies, but is there any other information I might want to know about that movie?

Olivia: Like the name of it?

Ms. Griffin: Exactly! Let's try that interchange again. "I went to the beach with my family. What did you do?"

Olivia: I went to the movies. I saw *Harry Potter.*

Ms. Griffin: Very nice! You figured out the right conversation initiation, you asked a leading question, and you answered the question appropriately with some information, but not more than might be wanted. If the person you're talking to wants more information, what will he or she do?

Olivia: Ask.

Often, scripts derive from the teacher observing the child's needs. One child I knew needed to socialize with his peers during free time. As a result, he was taught how to invite other children to play basketball with him—a skill highly sought after on the playground.

Too often, a child with HFA will move into a group of other students and either start discussing what she wanted to discuss or a topic of her interest, which can appear as domination, or not respond appropriately, which can then cause the other children to shun or avoid her. Either way, the child does not learn the appropriate social skills, resulting in a negative social standing with other children. However, with the use of memorable scripts, students with HFA can be taught social skills such as appropriately greeting someone else or asking to become part of the conversation by picking up on the conversational cues that were there earlier.

Replacement Behaviors

Replacement behaviors are the key to building social standing and social skills with the child with HFA. Most inappropriate behaviors come not from "meanness," but from the child not knowing what to say or do and not knowing how to handle his own emotions and the emotions of others. In fact, aggression in social situations has been found to be reduced when students with HFA are taught alternate ways to handle their emotions (Knapczyk, 1988). The teacher needs to ask not "What does this child need to stop doing?" but "What does this child need to do in place of the nondesired behavior?" The emphasis becomes placed on what the desired outcome is, not stopping a behavior.

It is important to pick those behaviors that are either the most serious or the easiest to change with the least amount of work. As Rick Lavoie (2008) said, "You don't have to accept every battle you're invited to" (p. 46). And as Stephen Covey and associates (Covey, Merrill, & Merrill, 1994) noted, "The main thing is to keep the main thing the main thing" (p. 75). There can be so many things that need to be worked on when it comes to social skills, but teachers should choose one or two of the most immediate behaviors to address first. For some children, that might be conflict management on the playground, for others that might be getting through the hallways during passing periods, and for others that might be eye contact.

Stay, Play and Talk

Stay, Play and Talk is a strategy devised by English, Goldstein, Shafer, and Kaczmarek (1997) that specifically teaches friendship skills. The process of developing buddies is broken into three stages:

1. Stay, which specifies that buddies stay in the same area, take turns playing, and not leave.
2. Play, which specifies that buddies share the same activities, bring activities to each other, or invite each other to play with other activities.
3. Talk, which specifies that buddies talk about the same subject until there is a pause in the conversation.

Moral Development

Lawrence Kohlberg (Kohlberg & Turiel, 1971) made famous the Stages of Moral Development by which he demonstrated that children (and adults) progress through certain stages in order to become fully mature and moral human beings. I have to admit that I never really paid attention to Kohlberg's developmental stages until I read Rafe Esquith's 2007 book *Teach Like Your Hair's On Fire*, where he uses Kohlberg as the basis for his classroom management, encouraging all of his students to get to at least Level 5, recognizing that not everyone will get to Level 6. Esquith changed the levels into kid-friendly terms, which are:

1. I don't want to get in trouble.
2. I want a reward.
3. I want to please someone.
4. I want to follow the rules.
5. I am considerate of other people.
6. I have a personal code of ethics that I follow ("It's the right thing to do").

These stages govern *all* behavior—the difference is who is being pleased and what rules are being presented. A child sharing his pencil, what we might call "good" behavior, might do this for a very low-level reason of "I just don't want to get into trouble." On the flip side, another child may get into trouble for taking a child's pencil because she wanted to help a fellow classmate who did not have any pencils.

This sequence is particularly important for the child with HFA for two reasons:
- the process of moral development is highly connected with language (it is difficult to have a moral code that one follows unless one is able to articulate a moral code), and
- there is an understanding of how one's own behavior is impacted by and impacts upon other people's behavior.

Both of these are skills that children with HFA may struggle with. However, when presented with a model that they can understand, children with HFA can attach meaning to the concepts, and we can start to get down to that mysterious "why" of their behavior. I have seen this model used as a visual for some students. When students have misbehaved in the classroom and are inarticulate (as so often happens), they are encouraged to point to the reason why they behaved a certain way and then elaborate on what they were trying to accomplish. By introducing the concept of moral development, we can begin to see growth in our children's behaviors.

A note here: Many children with HFA have a difficult time lying. Lying is actually a very complex task. You have to figure out (1) what the other person *thinks* is happening, (2) what really *is* happening, (3) alternatives to what the other person thinks is happening, (4) which of those alternatives the other person might believe, and (5) say it convincingly so that the person believes that you also believe it. Although we might condemn lying as bad, when the child with HFA begins to master lying, it is actually a step in the right direction—cognitively, that is. Lying requires a lot of perspective and language manipulation, and while you don't want to encourage it, you ironically need to recognize it for the great leap forward that it is, and then get the child to stop.

Timing Strategies

The key element of working with behavior strategies is the definition of the problem behavior, the use of replacement behaviors, and the documentation of the child's increased use of positive behaviors. There are numerous ways to document growth in a child with HFA. For example, using the process of social scripting, the teacher can focus on the number of interactions the child with HFA engages in with another person. These circles of communication can be measured and increased over time.

Motivation

When a child selects a behavior that is negative, or causes problems for himself or for others, the teacher has to play detective and determine the function of the negative behavior. Behavior managers note that all behavior is the process of either *getting* or *getting away from* something (Santrock, 2012). The key is to identify what it is that the child is either trying to get or trying to escape. In his book *Motivation Breakthrough*, Rick Lavoie (2008) identified six things that people are trying to get through their behavior:

1. *praise*, or to please someone;
2. *projects*, or the action of being engaged in something;
3. *people*, or involvement with others;
4. *prizes*, or the winning of achievement, titles, or other tangible objects;
5. *prestige*, or the recognition of others; and
6. *power*, or the right to make their own choices.

Lavoie (2008) noted that so often the one aspect of success that teachers have the most difficulty with is the issue of power. Teachers perceive power as an end sum—that by giving up some power, we are therefore losing it. In reality, we have the ability to provide a sense of power to a child through choice. Choices are very difficult for children with HFA because they require a manipulation of several possibilities. By providing limited choices to children with HFA, we can provide them experience with abstract concepts, thus empowering them to make decisions.

These six types of motivational rewards are the cornerstones of an Applied Behavior Analysis program that can identify what it is that a child is willing to work for. It is important to note that what works for one child is unlikely to work for another. Although some typical children may prefer prestige, children with HFA may be more motivated by visual and physical symbols of their limited interests.

Behavior Contracts

Teachers can make Lavoie's (2008) six motivational elements concrete in several ways, depending on their classroom. For example, a behavior contract that specifies a certain improvement in the use of a replacement behavior over time can offer the child a choice. Here's an example of a behavior contract that is written in first person to make the contract more personal and presents each of the six elements as options from which a child can choose:

I, Katie, will use my inside voice during lunchtime and at the library 4 days out of 5. If I can do that, I have the choice to:

- Have Ms. Brooke call my mom to tell her that I have accomplished my goal.
- Work on the computer for an extra 30 minutes.
- Invite two friends to eat lunch with me in the classroom.
- Get a prize from the prize closet.
- Be the first to leave the classroom for lunchtime.
- Choose what the class will do during free time.

The beauty of this choice menu is that it allows different children to work for their goals in different ways. Some of those choices will overwhelm some children; Nick is one child I know would choose to misbehave rather than lead the class in line. But he would do anything to get 30 more minutes on the computer! Computer games are one of his areas of obsession, and an opportunity to engage in his favorite activity is one that he would be very willing to work toward.

Power Cards

Identifying a child's area of interest can be one of the most powerful means of impacting his behavior. One of the ways in which teachers provide a use of these limited interests for students with HFA is through the use of power cards (Gagnon, 2001). Power cards are a means of modeling choices with students through the use of their areas of interest. Because children with HFA often have areas of interest, or even fixations, power cards provide a means of bridging that topic with behavior that the teacher is seeking.

The structure of a power card is simple in design and powerful in impact.

1. Select the area of interest.
2. Link the area of interest to a behavior that you *don't* want to see happen.
3. Link the area of interest to a replacement behavior, using the interest as a model.
4. End on a positive note of what will happen if the behavior is followed.
5. Provide a visual of the object of interest.

For example, for a secondary student obsessed with basketball, I created a card that linked an NBA player with attending class:

LeBron James never skips school.
LeBron James always comes to class.
LeBron James performs really well because he always comes to class.

For a younger child who loved Dr. Seuss, another teacher created cards with these sayings:

The Grinch never tears books.
The Grinch always keeps the books neat.
The Grinch has lovely, nice books to look at because he puts his books away after he looks at them.

Power cards allow a teacher to use the child's interest as a bridge to the world that he is trying to understand, but so often doesn't. Rather than fighting the interest, which can veer toward obsession, teachers can work with something that provides a sense of stability for the child. Lavoie (2008) noted that the key to creating success is by building on success. He added that "So often teachers say 'If he'd only try harder, he'd do better.' What [they mean is] 'If he'd only do better, he'd try harder'" (p. 21). Building upon interests has a stronger possibility of success, which then creates a stronger sense of motivation (Illinois State University, 2003).

Training Strategies

Most training strategies provide specific ways to structure students' thinking. Sometimes, the strategies use visual images, such as in comic book bubbles, and other strategies use sequenced events, such as Social Stories. Most of these use some form of prompting. Other strategies can use animals in lieu of people in order to begin the process of relationships, which can then be transferred over to people. Social autopsies can allow a student to use his logical abilities to analyze a nonsuccessful strategy and devise new strategies.

Social Stories

In contrast to Social Scripts, which follow a dialogued conversation or provide a set of tools to search for cues to continue social conversations, Social Stories (Gray, 2010) provide a sequence and context for a planned social encounter. The structure of the activity gives the child metacognitive prompts that she can then follow. Rather than a strict adherence to the interplay between two people engaged in conversation, Social Stories also help focus a child's attention on what to expect, how to plan ahead, and what she might be asked to do. Social Stories are formed by following a general pattern:

- The first sentence, typically initiated with a picture, sets the goal. The child herself must be part of this story.
- The second part describes the process of achieving this goal.
- The third part describes some obstacles to that goal and what the child with HFA can do.
- The fourth and final part describes how the goal was achieved and how all ended well.

An example might involve a situation that is anticipated to cause some anxiety such as the ringing of the fire alarm. It is *always* a good idea to tell your child with HFA who might exhibit anxiety about loud noises or fire about the planned fire alarm. A child with HFA who is surprised by the alarm and then triggered by one of her fears is oh-so-not a happy child. A teacher friend of mine experienced this once as she tried to dig her screaming, tantrumming 15-year-old student out from under a desk during a fire drill, and finally just decided to carry the child out with the desk. She realized later that it could have been prevented if she had read her e-mail that morning and cued the child in to the situation. The social story she had available for this very situation (but it was too late to use in the moment of crisis) went something like this:

1. Firemen and firewomen are here to help us. Firemen and firewomen will never hurt us. (We added the firewoman because if a woman were to show up, this story would end right here.)
2. When the alarm rings, it is there to tell the firemen and firewomen to hurry, hurry!
3. When students hear the bell, they are supposed to get out of the way to let the firemen and firewomen do their job.

4. When Kristy (the child with HFA) hears the bell, she is to calmly get up out of her seat.

5. She is to say in her head, "They're here to help. I have to go with everyone to get out of the way"

6. Kristy can look for Ms. Harper to help her get out of the building. If Ms. Harper is not there today, Kristy can look for the substitute or the aide. If they're hard to find, Kristy can find one of the other students in our class to follow.

7. We will follow the stairs down—even though they're normally the UP stairs. When we hear the alarm, they turn into the DOWN stairs.

8. We will go outside, where we will be safe. The firemen and firewomen will make the building safe.

9. When they tell us the building is safe, we can all go inside.

10. There will be some talking. Students and teachers are going to get a little louder than usual as everyone goes back to class.

11. Soon, the teachers will ask you to get started again on what you were already working on when the bell sounded. You remember what you were working on when the alarm sounded.

12. You can take a deep breath. You're safe. You're back in school. The firemen and firewomen made things safe. There is no fire and no more alarm.

Social stories are a very common suggestion for working with students with HFA, despite the relative limited research on their effectiveness (Kokina & Kern, 2010). For more examples, I would recommend that you check out Carol Gray's book, listed in the Resources section.

Prompts

When scripts, stories, or replacement behaviors are used to direct a child's attention to a particular course of action, it is important to review the process with the child. Although a child may need to have the script, story, or behavioral process explained several times, after a while, the teacher should fade the instruction until the child can recall the story and do the action independently. However, there is an in-between time where it cannot be expected that the child has mastered the behavior that is expected of him and so the use of prompts becomes very important.

Prompts need to be as visual as possible: a visual action or gesture, a picture, something that captures the elements of the instruction without repeating them. A common prompt that I have seen for helping a child with HFA make more appropriate eye contact is by first teaching him to look at the bridge of the receiver's nose. (Eye contact is very difficult for some children, and if you force them to look in someone's eye, they will get overwhelmed and miss the conversational flow. The trick is to make it *appear* like they are looking someone in the eye.) After instruction, the prompting cue was to tap the top of the nose when reminding the student to look between the eyes. Such a small action averted power struggles and frustration and reminded the child what he could do to improve communication with others.

Visual Cuing

Getting the attention of children with HFA in social situations can be difficult. There is so much stimuli and fear involved in social interactions that often there is little attention left over for instruction. However, there are a number of proactive things that a teacher can do.

One of the most common strategies I have seen is the use of duct tape to define personal space within the classroom. Because children with HFA can have limited understanding of personal or working space, numerous teachers have placed duct tape in a square around desks to separate children, reduce inappropriate social interactions, and provide a sense of security for the child.

I personally prefer the Montessori method of small rugs or carpet squares that define a "work space." The entire class respects one another's space in this manner. These can be moved as needed, and there is less of a sense of a barricade. However, many teachers have found the duct tape method to be more flexible in terms of size of space, so there are advantages to either method.

Whatever you do to provide cuing, prompts, and instruction, is it important to get the cooperation of the child—this cannot be during a period of escalation. The best time to work out an intervention that involves the child is right after an escalation moment, after the peak has passed, and the child moves into the calm phase. The memory of the experience is fresh, the need for intervention is apparent, and the child is the most open to changing his or her behavior. It's important to let the need and the choice of the child drive the intervention, rather than the teacher imposing the instruction upon a child. Results are likely to be much more positive if the child is involved.

Animals

Social interactions can involve more than people. Pet therapy has been found to be particularly effective with children with autism (Redefer & Goodman, 1989), particularly the use of equine therapy (Bass, Duchowny & Llabre, 2009). However, because most schools don't have their own stables, I tend to advocate for the use of animals that can be handled, but don't bite back. A classroom teacher I know has two rabbits, and those bunnies have been groomed, picked up, and petted to within an inch of their lives. The fear that rabbits have is one that children with HFA can relate to. Care should be taken, however, that the child does not try to dominate the animal through use of his own fear—one teacher I know had to protect her rabbit from a child with HFA who threatened to poke out the bunny's eyes. It soon became clear, however, that the child was using the rabbit as a way to "get to" the teacher. Horses tend to be highly effective simply because they are so large and thus gain respect from the child. But with caution, any animal that can be handled, cared for, and loved can impact a child.

Animals aren't judgmental about children's social skills and so children with HFA can find a safe place where they can be themselves. The rules with animals are simple, clear ones, and many children with HFA express an affinity for animals (Grandin, 1996). By teaching a child to train an animal through patience, rewards, and calmness, the child learns the same lessons. Animals have proven so effective at times that many therapy programs are using dogs as therapy tools to help a children with autism to navigate the world and reduce tantrums. Schools have been much less accommodating to the use of dogs as therapy tools (Associated Press, 2009), but I see them similar in need and use to a seeing-eye dog—they help the child negotiate through a world that he is unable to navigate himself. With assistance from the dog, the child can then learn to gradually navigate it on his own. Thinking of the dog as "unnecessary" or as "only a pet" for the child is like taking away a life preserver from someone who is drowning.

Social Autopsy

Many of these social strategies are proactive and help students plan for social engagement. However, oftentimes, a child will have a negative social interaction, and the use of "social autopsies" can allow a student and a facilitator to determine what happened and what can be changed for the next time (Myles & Adreon, 2001). A social autopsy asks the following questions:

1. What happened?
2. What was the social error?
3. Who was affected or hurt by the social mistake? How were they hurt?
4. What needs be done to fix the mistake?
5. What can be done next time?

Thinking Strategies

The history of social skills training programs for autism involve a heavily behavioristic model that promotes the specification of measureable goals and the provision of rewards as the child reaches those goals.

Sometimes, those goals are very specific and adult-focused as the source of intervention, as in the case of ABA, or sometimes, they're more naturalistic, as in the case of Pivotal Response Therapy (PRT; Koegel & Koegel, 2006).

PRT encourages the participation of the child in the naturalistic settings and responses provided by the adult or peer. The goals to be worked on are elicited from the child, as are the reinforcers that the child is working toward. This sense of self-direction that is employed increases motivation in the child to interact and engage in more appropriate manners. The role of the adult or peer is to provide naturalistic opportunities for the child to engage in positive manners, and then reward him appropriately when he does so.

Daniel, typical peer: Hey, Stephen!

Stephen, who has ASD: no response

Tyler, typical peer: Come on, Stephen! Wanna play some basketball?

Stephen: Okay.

Tyler: All right, I liked the way you said "Okay"! Can you look me in the eyes when you do, just so I know that it's me that you want to play ball with?

Stephen, briefly looking him in the eyes: Okay.

Tyler: Well, all right, then! Here, you get the first dribble! Do you think you might score?

Stephen: Yeah.

Daniel: Well, if you don't, remember how Ms. Weichel taught us to handle frustration? What do we say?

Stephen: We say, "I'll get that one sooner or later. I may have to practice some more."

Tyler: That's right! So, here! It's your ball!

This script has a number of elements, including 2-1 peer tutoring, scripting, and prompting, but the main focus is on the natural setting—kids going out to play basketball during recess, providing Stephen an opportunity to engage in that he had the choice to turn down, and responding positively to Stephen's attempts to engage, rather than treating him as different. Stephen is guiding the interactions through his choices, rather than following a rote script, although some rote scripts are invoked.

Comic Book Bubbles

Another strategy for teaching students how to think about social conversations is the use of comic book bubbles. Devised originally by Carol Gray (1994), this strategy allows a child to visually represent a conversation using comic book-like speech bubbles. The use of these bubbles can allow a child to visualize the differences between thoughts and words and to predict what might be said as a result of conversations. There is an app listed in Chapter 12 that allows students to interact with each other in comic strip fashion; such use of comic strips bubbles can facilitate the visual development of social behavior. Figure 14 shows some examples of how comic bubbles can be used to help students think about social engagement.

Use of Comic Bubbles for Social Instruction

When someone is interrupting, and one person is louder, it looks like this:

What are some problems with this? How can you get someone's attention without interrupting?

When someone is thinking one thing, and saying another, it might look like this:

Why might there be differences? How can someone think one thing and say something different?

When one person is talking, one person should be listening and thinking about what the other person is talking about. It looks like this:

Why is it important for the other person to be listening? Why is it important to think about the things we're listening to?

Figure 14. Comic book bubbles.

Self-Directed Modeling

PRT involves the directed focusing of the child on his or her own areas of challenge. Extending this naturalistic modeling, and still using the tools of behaviorism, self-directed behavioral training involves the child in determining goals, the length of time involved to achieve them, and the selection of appropriate cues. A teacher is thus a facilitator of social skills instruction, rather than the originator. This strategy is particularly useful for children with HFA because they can apply their strengths of memory and analysis to their own lives, using the tools that help them focus.

The teacher needs to sit down with the student and directly involve him with the tools helpful for improving behavior, including scripts, social stories, and behavior contracts. Rather than directing the student, the teacher needs to facilitate the problem-solving metacognitive strategies of the student, asking questions that include:

- What do you see as the problem?
- What behavior of yours might you change?
- What skills do you think you need to learn? (The teacher can help the student reach an appropriate goal here.)
- What do you need others to know and to be able to do?
- Rather than making huge changes at once, what small intermediate steps do you see that you could do?
- When do you want to have succeeded in this skill?
- What will be the end result?

Color-Coded Thinking

One of the strategies that I have seen used is the process of encouraging children with HFA to color code their thoughts before they speak them. Often, these kids are blunt, too honest perhaps, and thus break numerous social taboos by speaking their thoughts aloud. I remember one student, Jacob, a boy who was rather large and who was trying to run. Sean, a student with HFA, who was aware of small details to begin with, stated—out loud—how Jacob's fat was jiggling. Sean didn't mean it to be rude—it really was obvious and it really was just an observation, rather than a judgment, but his comment led to many hurt feelings. The other students laughed, because it was true, and it gave them an opportunity to pick on Jacob. However, at the same time, they were appalled that Sean had broken the social code.

We worked afterward with Sean on a task called Stoplight Your Thoughts.

- Green thoughts (we provided a lovely green thought bubble as a visual aid for the teaching of this) are those thoughts that are just fine to speak aloud.

They don't insult anyone, and they don't make any comments that might be personal about someone.

- Yellow thoughts (again, with a yellow speech bubble as a visual) are those "cautionary" thoughts that you might want to check with a teacher or a close friend before you say them to everyone.

- Red thoughts (with a bright red speech bubble) are those thoughts that you can think inside your head, but shouldn't come out of your mouth. Red thoughts will probably offend people if you say them aloud. You have every right to think your own thoughts, but red thoughts should stay inside.

Notice that the emphasis is not on controlling the child's thoughts; the child is free to have whatever thoughts he wants. This is not scripting thoughts or even conversations. This process is having the child examine his words before they are spoken through the use of color-coding—a metacognitive "brake" on their words. It's a useful skill . . . there are some typical adults I know who I wish would color-code their thoughts!

Together Strategies

The peer group is probably the most effective social skills strategy you have available. It is important that when a child with HFA is in a classroom, the rest of the class is aware that differences are to be not just tolerated, but accepted and not ridiculed. I cannot overemphasize the role of the teacher in the development of an open and caring climate. Teachers at every grade level influence students' attitudes toward each other and the differences they possess (Kirk et al., 2012).

It is important to note that any formal discussion of differences should involve the parents. Some parents are focused on trying to have their child "fit in" and are afraid that a label will work against their child by emphasizing differences. Social skills training can either directly instruct students about what labels mean and do not mean, or it can be done through a focus on behavior and not labels. Personally, I prefer the use of labels. It makes things less scary, gives reasons for behaviors that look intentional but are not, and provides an atmosphere of honesty. By acknowledging differences, you are providing a means of explanation and a way of approaching them. It also allows a child to begin the process of self-advocacy; she cannot advocate for what she does not understand. Yes, a child is more than her label—we all are. But children have to understand what the labels mean for themselves. However, ultimately, it is the legal and ethical decision of the parents whether or not to reveal their child's label.

The development of rules and procedures that provide stability, structure, and efficient means of communication and social interactions allows teachers to spend less time on disruptions and more time on academic work (Wong & Wong, 2009). So many teachers see social skills training as something beyond the scope of their job—*I was hired to teach geometry, not to show them how to get along with each other. Their parents should have taught them that!* In reality, the classroom environment is one more closely approximating a work environment and is completely unlike a home environment. Children with HFA have a difficult time generalizing; we might not like this characteristic, but we simply have to deal with it. No matter how the child responds to others at home or in previous classrooms, your classroom is a blank slate to him or her. It is up to you to create either an environment in which that child—and the other children in your classroom—can thrive and develop her abilities or to create one in which frustration and turmoil reign.

Your role as a teacher is critical to the way in which other children approach the child with HFA. Studies have found that even as young as kindergarten, typical children are unlikely to initiate conversation and social connections with children with autism without adult prompting (Laushey & Heflin, 2000), and this social isolation continues through adulthood (Howlin & Yates, 1999). Clearly, there is a need to involve the peers, and not just "pretend" that everything is all right: Children are aware of each other's differences, and we can either ignore the social issues, which will not get better on their own, or deal with them. And dealing with them means involving the child's peers.

There is some interesting research that shows that peer interventions are actually more effective than adult-led social skills interventions (Carter, Cushing, Clark, & Kennedy, 2005), and that social skills instruction that includes several children with HFA is even more effective (White, Koenig, & Scahill, 2007).

Circles of Support

Circles of Support are a way to analyze a child's level of support and which persons can be involved with a child's social development. When looking at a child with HFA's Circle of Support, it is helpful to specifically include several peers in addition to parents, aides, and teachers. According to Snow (1994), there are four circles that surround a person:

- Circles of Intimacy include those people who are very close to a person: his parents, his siblings, other family members, and very good friends. These relationships are deep and lasting and involve a significant level of trust.
- Circles of Friends are those people who are considered friends within a child's life, but not necessarily intimate friends; they are supportive and kind, but not necessarily part of deep and lasting relationships.
- Circles of Participants are those people within a person's life who are involved on a regular basis and are generally supportive, but are not necessarily aware of the level of details or the issues within someone's life. This group typically includes neighbors, store clerks, and classmates.

- Circles of Exchange are those people who are paid to be in one's life: doctors, nannies, teachers, and therapists. These people may know quite a bit about a person, but their interest and goals are of a professional nature.

One's mental health is often measured by the number of people in the first circle. Typical students have fairly large first and second circles and relatively restricted fourth circles. In contrast, students with HFA often have very small first and second circles and extensive fourth circles. Even if, for example, a teacher's aide becomes very close to a particular student, he will remain in the fourth circle while it is his job to care for the child. Often, the goal for social skills training is to increase the number of people within the second circle, and try to move one or two into the Circle of Intimacy.

It is more effective to have a larger group of general education peers, generally a 2-1 ratio, to work with a child with HFA (Carter et al., 2005). Carter and colleagues (2005) found that a single general education peer tends to get tired and overly aware of his own social standing. When the general education peer had a peer to support him as he worked with a child with autism, he tended to be much more empathetic and focused on teaching, rather than his own isolation.

Peer-Assisted Social Skills Training

When working with a peer group, the first step is to decide as a group—with the input of the child with HFA—what skills are to be worked on specifically. Common areas of focus include:
- eye contact,
- personal space,
- greetings, and
- dealing with frustration (e.g., that caused by losing a game).

Once the goal has been established, the children can work with and encourage each other through the use of a series of concrete, specific steps that can be memorized (Krasny et al., 2003). These steps should have visual cues attached to them as well and should be written down for reminding and instructional purposes. Children should practice in predictable situations, and encourage each other in the use of these strategies in more novel situations. It is important that social skills training be part of every day in a school-based setting and be practiced in community settings; weekly therapeutic sessions have been found to be mostly ineffective (Krasny et al., 2003).

Classroom Arrangement

Perhaps it goes without saying, but the worst thing that a teacher can do is place the child with HFA alone in the back of the room. I say this because I have been in so many classrooms where the child is placed in the back of the classroom, apart from the other children because the child "can't handle" being around other children. I am always so upset by this because although it appears to be for the consideration of the child, it is actually done for the teacher's sake—in order to reduce interactions. The child does not need to be isolated; the child needs to be in a small group where other students rotate in and out to help the child learn how to function in a group. Perhaps the child doesn't need to be in the middle of the room, but the student is still a valuable member of the class with interests and passions to share. Children with HFA have much to offer, and the classroom arrangement needs to facilitate this sharing and learning in both directions.

Key Points From Chapter 9

- Social difficulty is a defining feature of high-functioning autism, often linked to students' inability to recognize another's perspectives or emotions—a condition sometimes called "mindblindness." Although it is important to recognize differences within a classroom, parents have to be involved in the discussion of these differences. It is also very important when working with children with HFA that their significant strengths be built upon. There are few well-researched strategies available; however, social skills are a critical area for teachers to address. Social skills training programs have limited effectiveness data, but teachers have to do something to facilitate learning of the entire class.

- *Teaching* strategies can provide models of social and moral development so that the teacher and the students can understand the different levels of responses to social situations. Teachers and students can determine appropriate replacement behaviors to use. Kohlberg's Moral Development is one model that can be used to encourage children to examine their own behaviors. And although lying should not be encouraged, the use of lying as an interaction strategy is a relatively advanced skill and should be recognized as social growth.

- *Timing* strategies employ the use of behavioral techniques of identifying a specific target behavior, identifying a replacement behavior, identifying intervening steps, and creating rewards—the most effective strategies in the literature. Social contracts and power cards can be developed that use aspects that motivate a particular child.

- *Training* strategies, such as Social Stories, can use the strong memory of a child with HFA to remind himself of appropriate actions and words to use in particular situations. Animals can also be used to gain the attention and trust of children with HFA to develop skills that can then be transferred to others.

- *Thinking* strategies, such as Pivotal Response Therapy (PRT) and self-directed modeling, allow the child to analyze her own behavior and to set goals for herself, rather than the teacher controlling the child's behavior. Color-coded thinking is a way of making the thinking process visual for students.

- *Together* strategies focus the classroom on the learning of all students. Peer-assisted intervention is probably the most effective manner to involve the classroom in proactive social interactions. It is critically important that the child with HFA not be placed in the back of the classroom away from other children, but be placed in a moderately social environment so that the child can learn appropriate skills. Using the Circles of Support model, teachers can work on developing connections and relationships among students within the classroom.

Chapter 10

Cognitive Development: Autism Impacts How a Child Thinks and Learns

Teachers are ultimately responsible for teaching content. Teachers can use as many strategies as they like, but they are ultimately held responsible for how well a child does on a math test, a reading measure, or a writing activity. Thus, content has to be connected in meaningful ways to the strategies that are used. The ultimate goal of any strategy is to remove the disabling condition and allow the child to learn the content to the best of her ability. In the case of children with HFA, this ability may be quite high, indeed.

There are numerous issues that a child with HFA may face cognitively that will impact her learning of content. According to Dr. Dawson and her associates (2007), children with autism may have higher degrees of fluid intelligence rather than the more fixed intelligence related to memory and perception. As a result, not every child with HFA will have all of these issues, but they might have challenges with any of the following (Harris, Handleman, Gordon, Kristoff, & Fuentes, 1991; Myles, 2005):

- attention,
- memory—working and long-term,
- organization,
- processing speed,
- fixated interests,
- lack of creativity, and
- concrete operational thinking.

Responding to these can be a challenge; these are not gaps in content that can be fixed. However, there are numerous, numerous things you can do.

Teaching Strategies

Direct instruction is the process of explicitly teaching specific skills. Although that doesn't sound hard, many teachers don't "teach" as much as they provide experiences for children to discover information. Or, as is often the case, they assume that children have learned a skill when other skills were taught to them. However, many students with HFA are very, very, literal, and do not see beyond the single meaning of a word. Recently, I had a student with HFA who is extremely strong in math do poorly on a test. The directions on one activity were to "fill in the boxes." The teacher did not specify that the boxes were to have answers. So, the student very diligently colored in the boxes with his pencil. That student needed direct instruction that "fill in the boxes" meant to complete the boxes with the right answer.

Some aspects of learning will have to be explicitly taught that teachers often think students should get. I once worked with Aaron, a child who did not understand the concept of personal space. He would be excited, talking about something, and creep up on you until he was in your face. As other people edged backward, he would edge forward until he had his audience trapped. He needed to be taught the appropriate distance to stand away from others—it was not something he picked up. He would then be prompted that he was in a casual conversation, and he would carefully measure one arm's distance between himself and his conversational partner. If he was working in a group with someone, he would hug his elbow to his side and carefully measure out the distance of his forearm between him and his partners. This direct instruction of how far away one should be, based on type of conversation, reduced the shrieks of "Dr. Hughes! Aaron's bugging me!" considerably.

There are so many things that children with HFA might need direct instruction in doing:

- greeting someone or saying "Goodbye,"
- identifying key words in a math word problem,
- washing their hands after going to the bathroom,
- reading a table of contents,
- finding their way to their art classroom,
- checking out books from the library rather than just walking off with them,
- adjusting personal space for different relationships,
- looking for the meaning in a passage, or
- organizing their desk or their homework.

In all of these examples, it is recommended that the directions be short, sweet, and as visual as possible. Using one's arm to measure is better than "about 3 feet." Using a highlighter to underline the first sentence in a paragraph is better than asking "What is this sentence about?"

When designing a direct instruction model, I recommend that you break the steps of what it is that you're trying to teach into very specific parts. You will have to teach each part, and then determine if the child understands and is able to do the part. It provides a very quick question-response type of teaching. Please see Table 6 for an example of this quick give-and-take dialogue. Direct instruction can feel very painful in its level of detail, because teachers and other students may want to skip over steps the child ought to know.

"Oughtism" is one of the features of "autism," and it's important that teachers and parents work on getting past this. Yes, if the child were typical, she would know . . . but she has autism, and that means using direct instruction for content, information, and skills that the child ought to know—but doesn't—and needs to be taught.

It's important to recognize that direct instruction is not limited to concepts and skills that are remedial: Children with HFA are often very logical and responsive to patterns. Once they are presented with an idea in a manner that they can understand, they can often learn very quickly. Certainly, the areas of math and science seem to lend themselves to a more logical sequence of activities, and many children with HFA are very strong in these areas. It is important to offer *accelerated* opportunities to children as they learn the skills required in a content area. I've seen a child with HFA who was in the gifted range "figure out" the patterns of language that differentiated genres of books as well as writing essays that followed a predictable pattern. That child went on to win several writing awards, including a national poetry award. Although impromptu speaking was difficult for him, he could formulate his thoughts very coherently on paper by using logical patterns. He could apply his large vocabulary to the particular pattern of essays, poetry, and even short stories. But it took explicit instruction for him to learn these patterns.

Many children with HFA are very able to increase the level of their thinking and question asking once they are provided a template. I encourage teachers to share Bloom's taxonomy with children with HFA. Bloom's taxonomy provides a scaffold upon which students can link their thoughts. With such a scaffold, they learn how to ask critical question and to structure their own thinking. A question-based model of Bloom's taxonomy can be found in Figure 15.

I've found that I could even increase the creativity of students with HFA by directly teaching them strategies. Paul Torrance (1977) found that creativity could be measured and improved with specific instruction, and this certainly applies to children with HFA, who often suffer from lack of imagination. Torrance found that creativity can improve if you teach children to focus on:

Table 6

Give-and-Take Direct Instruction

Teacher	Student
The first thing you're going to do is look them in the eye. You can look at the bridge of their nose, if this helps.	
Which do you prefer—eyes or bridge of the nose?	Bridge of their nose
What's the first thing you do?	Look at the bridge of their nose.
Good! Then, you smile. What's the second thing you do?	Smile.
Good! Now, practice looking at the bridge of someone's nose and smiling.	*Practice*
Now, wait one second. How long are you going to wait?	One second.
If they say "Hi" or "Hello" first, you wait until they're done and respond with "Hello." If they don't, then you say "Hello."	
What do you say if they say "Hi," or "hello"?	Hello.
Good! What if they don't say "Hello"?	I wait and say "Hello."
Good! If they look at you and say something to you, you stop as well, and remain looking at the bridge of their nose.	
They are probably going to ask you "How are you?" or "How are you doing?"	
What are the two questions they are probably going to ask you?	"How are you?" or "How are you doing?"
Good! Your answer is going to be "Fine," if it's one of those questions.	
What is your answer going to be?	Fine. But what if I'm having a terrible day and I'm not fine?
Your answer is still "fine," unless it's your mom or dad or me, or your best friend. Everyone else gets your answer of "Fine."	
What do you tell someone, even if you're having a terrible day?	Fine.
Good! Then, you ask them, "How are you?" What do you ask them right after you've said "Fine"?	How are you? But they just asked me. Why do I ask them?
Because it's polite to ask them after you've answered their question. It's how we express interest in each other, even in small ways.	
Now, you're going to ask them "How are you?"	
What do you ask them, even if you're not really interested?	How are you?
Good! Then, if they don't say anything else, or they move away, you move away as well. What do you do if they move away or they stop talking?	Move away.
If they want to keep talking to you, they may ask another question, or make a comment. If they do that, you stay and talk with them. So, if they move away, what do you do?	Move away.
And if they start talking to you, what do you do?	What if I don't want to talk to them?
Then, you answer their question, smile at them, take your eyes away from their face, and move away. So, if they start talking to you, and you want to talk to them, what do you do?	Stay and talk.
Good! And if you don't want to talk to them, what do you do?	Smile, take my eyes away, and move away.
Good! Now practice.	*Practice*
Good! Now let's practice the whole exchange. I'll be the person who is coming at you in the hall.	

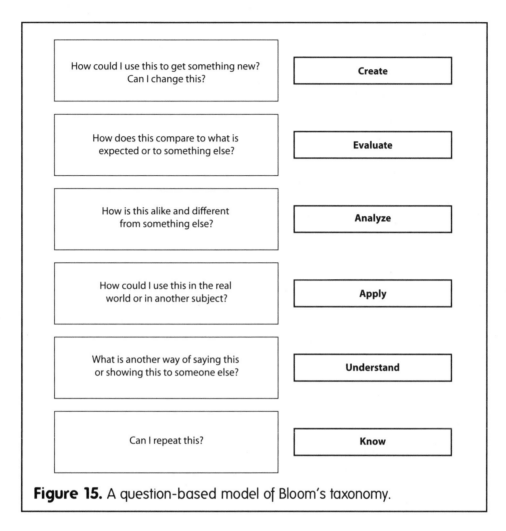

Figure 15. A question-based model of Bloom's taxonomy.

- fluency or increasing the number of ideas,
- flexibility or increasing the types of ideas,
- originality or trying to come up with something that no else has, and
- elaboration or trying to add detail to an idea.

Once children with HFA understand what creativity is, then they can use their analytical skills to become more creative, often making connections in ways that are completely unexpected. I remember teaching Jack, a highly musical child with HFA at the age of 8, the structure of a joke after he had been struggling with knock-knock jokes: "A joke is where you ask a question that you expect one answer to, but you provide another one. One that makes sense, but wasn't expected. It's the unexpectedness of the answer that makes it funny." After working with the concept for a while, Jack then proceeded to tell me:

Knock-knock!

Who's there?
Bonner!
Bonner who?
Bonnaroo is in Tennessee this year! (Bonnaroo is a music festival.)

All he needed was the framework and an understanding of how the structure worked. He didn't "get" it, but with direct instruction he was well able to create new jokes. Needless to say, there were days when he would be cracking jokes instead of paying attention to social studies when I wished I had never taught this structure to him!

Timing Strategies

The behavioral approach only works when a child is cognitively able to learn the material, but is lacking in motivation. Motivation only provides a reason for people to do something that they already know how to do; it can't teach them something they don't know how to do (Lavoie, 2008). Motivation is often the key to creating persistence in a task long enough for it to become automatic. However, care should be taken not to engage the child with HFA so much that the task itself becomes an object of fixation. I once struggled with teaching a boy who was having problems memorizing the multiplication tables. His difficulty with memory made any further mathematics skill difficult, and he would melt down in frustration. So I set about trying to improve his automaticity with multiplication, showing him the graph and promising him that he would be allowed to work on the computer—10 minutes for every five facts he could learn. Within 2 weeks, he had all 100 facts memorized. Not just memorized—mastered. Mastered to the point that he would retreat into chanting the multiplication tables when he was anxious and stressed. He would rock in his chair, ignoring his group work, chanting quietly "Six times six is 36. Six times seven is 42 . . ." I was never quite sure if I had done a helpful thing or a negative thing.

Areas of Interest

One of the most powerful motivators is allowing the student with HFA to connect what you are learning about with his area of interest. If you are studying percentages and the student is interested in quasars, the student might be encouraged to write percentage questions about quasars for other students to solve. There are often linkages between content areas that these students can find. However, if you cannot find a linkage, or it takes you too far off topic, students can be rewarded for completing assigned classroom work by being allowed to study more about their topic of interest (Heflin & Alaimo, 2007). Often, students with HFA will have extensive knowledge about some esoteric topic, and they can be rewarded for a certain behavior by being allowed to make a presentation to the class about their interest.

Charts and Graphs

From a behavioral perspective, you can select a specific skill such as organizing a desk and reward the child for keeping his or her desk clean. You can have a "check time" every afternoon, and if the desk is neat, you can provide a reward system. You can also chart progress. For example, if a child is trying to memorize the multiplication tables—a task that is difficult when there are memory challenges—you can provide a chart like the one in Figure 16 to document his or her progress. Charts are effective for children with HFA because they're visual, they explain progress more effectively than words, and everyone can see what skill is being worked on. Keeping data over time is a highly effective method of changing behaviors and increasing motivation for drill or uninteresting tasks. Plus, keeping such data is very handy for IEPs and other assessment monitoring programs.

Training Strategies

There are numerous interventions possible when using an information processing approach to cognitive challenges. The assumption of information processing is that children need to activate their brains without interference from other tasks or things. They must pay attention, be able to encode information, and then retrieve it when necessary. They have to be able to determine what the question is, what is important to know in the question, where information is in their minds, and what information will answer the question (Santrock, 2012).

In order to learn, children must pay attention, place new material learned into memory storages, and access old memory storage. When a child has HFA, these processes can be interrupted by brain and neurological interference (Attwood, 2008). This means that in order to teach a concept to a child with HFA, you can (a) remind her to pay attention or to remember, (b) reduce distractions to help her in this process, and (c) connect new learning and ideas to old ones.

Reminding

Reminding is the process of opening up the channels of attention and memory. It's a strategy to help students focus, determine their purpose, and find their way to a response. The most effective means of reminding is "selective reminding," in which teachers focus their reminding on those things that children do not know or are not doing, instead of general, overall reminding (Buschke, 1974).

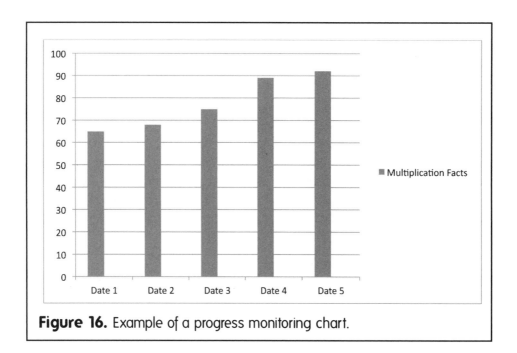

Figure 16. Example of a progress monitoring chart.

There are many, many ways to cue or to prompt children with HFA when trying to focus their attention on a skill. The key is to make it as visual as possible. I use a lot of timers and checklists in my work. I have a wide variety of timers that I bring out—groovy ones with swirling, settling sand, clocks that tick down the time left, clocks that tick out how long it's been, small clocks to go on an individual child's desk, and large digital clocks that go on the wall. I even have a Velcro "watch" where you can place pictures of tasks in the order that they are to be completed. These timers are all visual, so children can see how much time they are supposed to take, how much time they have left, how long a task is supposed to take, and in what order tasks are to be done. Some of these materials are listed in the Resources section. In addition to timers, I had checklists for tasks all over my classroom. See Figure 17 for an example of one of these checklists.

There are also numerous ways to cue students to find the information that has been previously stored in their minds. It's the "tip of the tongue" phenomenon: You know you know it, you just can't remember it right now. This means that you can't find the path to it in your head and sometimes a cue can help activate that neurological path of memory. Reminding provides a way for a child to access the information that she already knows, but has forgotten where in her memory it's located.

One interesting strategy is locational placing. Memory experts win awards for their tricks of placing a visual image of a number or a card in a familiar location, and then reviewing the walk in their minds to see what they placed there. I use it for grocery lists: I place a visual memory of a loaf of bread on my passenger side seat, a gallon of milk near the rear window, and butter on the dash, and then I cre-

```
Do I have the following:

_____ Clean desk on top?

_____ Organized desk inside?

_____ Chair on top of the desk?

_____ Homework written down in calendar?

_____ Books that I need for homework?

_____ A pencil to do homework?

_____ My coat?

_____ Any notes from the teacher to go home?

_____ My backpack?
```

Figure 17. Checklist for going home.

ate a story to go with it—the bread is going to be smashed if a passenger sits there, the butter's going to melt, and the milk is liquid like the gas that goes into the car. For other items like vanilla, I create an aroma in my head of the car smelling yummy, and for paprika, I visually imagine the top of the hood near the engine, which in some cars goes "pap . . . pap . . . pap . . ." As you can see, it's a whole sensory experience of a grocery list, but all centered on my car. I just have to look around my car in my mind's eye when I'm at the grocery store to remember my list.

Such locational prompting can be used in other ways such as placing important information on the walls of the classroom and prompting children during a test to remember where on the walls that information was, even if the information has been removed. You can have the children walk around the school, spelling their spelling words or reading over their spelling list. Then, they can remember their walk and what they were saying or reading at each place.

Mnemonics are a time-honored strategy for remembering things. I couldn't have gotten through music class without remembering Every Good Boy Does Fine (EGBDF) for the notes on the lines and FACE for the notes between the lines. But most mnemonics are oral. You might work on making some mnemonics visual as well. Figure 18 shows the Long Division Face. Mnemonics are ways to turn long steps and multiple facts into one piece of information so that the memory load is reduced.

Reducing Distractions

When reducing distractions, one question I have teachers ask themselves is "What can I add or subtract?" There are so many things that a teacher can add or take away from the task:

- increasing the size of fonts on worksheets or books;

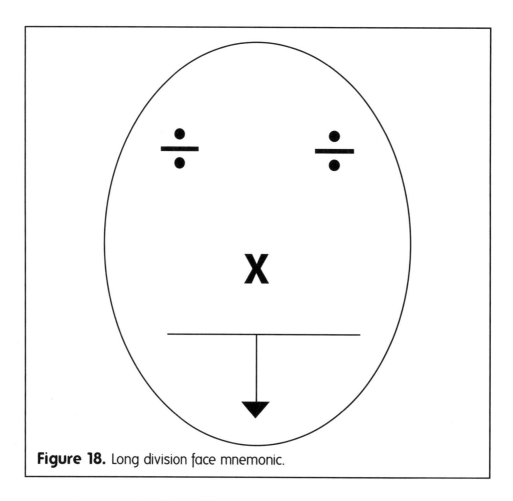

Figure 18. Long division face mnemonic.

- increasing time for problems;
- decreasing the number of problems;
- decreasing the words;
- increasing the pictures;
- decreasing the steps of an assignment;
- increasing the space available for writing;
- increasing the use of graph paper or lined paper (An easy way to get graph paper? Turn the lined paper on its side [see Figure 19]. You now have columns you can use for math problems, without having to buy special paper.); or
- allowing a peer to take notes or providing an outline for the student to fill out when taking notes. Note taking can be particularly difficult for some students who have difficulty processing oral information and require additional time to make it visual.

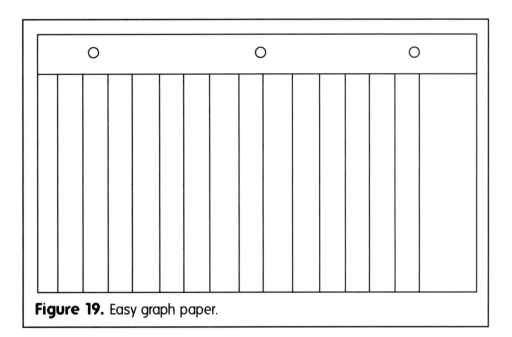

Figure 19. Easy graph paper.

Another strategy I've seen for keeping children's attention is the use of colored cups to ask for directions or for help during instruction (Murawski, 2009). When children have a question, the teacher typically requests that they raise their hand. With their hand raised, they then cease working; after all, they usually have raised the dominant hand that was doing the writing. They then sit and wait, sometimes distracting others around them because of the wait time. Instead of raising their hands, all children in the classroom can be encouraged to use three plastic colored cups on their desks. Green is the typical color and used when the child is focused on his work. However, if he has a question, he can restack the cups to have the red cup on top. Then, he is to continue working on the next problem, rather than stopping. The teacher can scan the room, and move to the child with the red cup on his desk, rather than moving to the noisiest child who is interrupting the thinking and quiet of other students. Finally, when a child is done with the task, and is either looking for something else to do, or can go and help other students, he can use the blue cup to signal his intentions to the teacher, rather than making a verbal request. This use of color-coded cups in the classroom reduces the talking level of a classroom—always a good idea for children with language processing difficulties—and allows the teacher to know what is going in his classroom with a single glance.

Connecting

When helping children learn new concepts, I have found that words often get in the way—I have to make the activity visual and kinesthetic for children to make the connections. There are a number of ways to make things active, reduce the language of teaching, and increase the visual and experiential aspects. One strategy is to make children move or act out part of the "story" that you're trying to teach them. I well remember the day I had kids rolling across the floor to demonstrate weathering of soil as it washes down to the ocean. I had them place stuff in their pockets and as they rolled, they shed small counters, markers—all sorts of things— all over my floor. They understood weathering after that activity. Even something as simple as cutting up a math worksheet and placing the problems into a brown paper bag (Murawski, 2009) for students to draw from is a means of getting children more actively engaged in a lesson.

One teacher I know uses a clothesline and clothespins to have kids come up to the front of the classroom and place their sequence in a timeline (Murawski, 2009). She uses this for order of operations, plot points in a story, and steps of the scientific process. That same teacher uses a "magic tablecloth," which is a cheap tablecloth with liquid adhesive sprayed on it (practical note—3M's Artist Adhesive works best to get papers off of the tablecloth). She does her KWL chart on it and as students learn new facts, they literally move the pieces of paper from the "What do I want to know?" column to the "What do I know?" column. I would strongly suggest that you encourage your students to draw out events, even if it involves stick figures. Math problems, story summaries, and social studies events—all of these can be represented with visual imagery rather than words.

Color-coding is another means of making connections using visual cuing. I knew a teacher who used Wikki Stix (see Resources section) to teach parts of speech, parts of a story, or key words in math problem solving. Wikki Stix are colorful, bendable, sticky sticks that lightly adhere to paper. You can use them as 3-D underlining, use different colors for different parts of speech, or to circle important information. When you don't have them available, colored pencils or markers can provide color-coding as well. Montessori educators knows this well: They use a triangle for the parts of speech system—a large blue triangle for a noun, a large purple triangle for a pronoun, a smaller blue triangle for an adjective, and a light blue, smallest triangle for articles. Their grammar worksheets are a dazzling array of shapes and colors. And let me tell you: Montessori-educated kids know their parts of speech and how they work as a system.

I cannot emphasize enough the importance of graphic organizers for helping students remember and connect new information to old learning. Children who have HFA are often very concrete thinkers and do not understand relationships unless they are shown to them, and a graphic organizer is a highly effective way of doing so. In addition, certain graphic organizers require different ways of thinking, and you can increase the flexibility of a child's thinking process by using different graphic organizers. Graphic organizers (see Figure 20) include:

- web maps for explaining relationships or parts to whole,

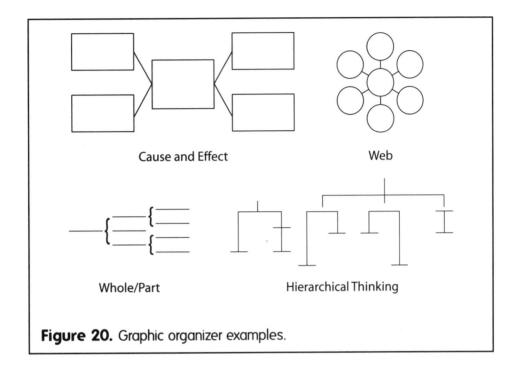

Figure 20. Graphic organizer examples.

- Venn diagrams and "double-bubble" organizers for comparing and contrasting,
- flow maps for showing sequencing, and
- family tree organizers for showing hierarchies.

Although they may be used in their pure, unadorned sense, there are a number of graphic organizers that use the basic shapes and translate them to more tangible items. Therefore, you might use the "hamburger model" of persuasive writing (VanTassel-Baska & Little, 2003), which is an amended version of the flow chart, or the "hand model," which is really a web, to help your students organize their ideas. I use a hand model to teach the five models of co-teaching (i.e., one-teach, one-support is on the thumb because it should be used the least because it's the shortest). Such use of graphic organizers has been found to be highly effective with visual learners (Hyerle, 2009). By reducing the importance of language and using the visual and logical strength of the child with HFA, you can transform his learning.

Thinking Strategies

It is important that direct instruction be provided not only by the teacher at a particular moment in time, but that the student continues with the use of these skills on her own. Teaching metacognitive strategies allows the student to remind herself about what to think in particular situations. Metacognitive strategies provide scripts for the student to follow in how to solve a problem or to perform a certain skill.

The Self-Regulated Strategy Development (SRSD) program directly teaches students how to write, solve math problems, and do a variety of specific cognitive tasks (Harris & Graham, 1999). The use of a set of scripted instructions frees up working memory for students and allows them to focus on what they're doing, instead of trying to remember how to do the task.

Providing step-by-step directions for umbrella terms is also critical. "Clean your desk" is not a single action, nor is "edit your writing." Both of these are a series of smaller skills that have to be explicitly described. See Figure 21 for an example of a visual checklist with a PSDSD-PPP mnemonic for "clean your desk." "Edit your writing" is a very good example of a learning strategy promoted by the University of Kansas. The University of Kansas Strategic Instruction Model (KU-SIM) is an amazing method of teaching students how to explicitly perform certain tasks such as editing a paper or reading for comprehension. My favorite strategy they use is COPS, used for editing writing (Reid & Lienemann, 1996). In my classroom, I amended it to COPSS. Rather than handing a paper back to a student and saying, "Edit this before you turn it in," I would ask the student, "Have you COPSSed it?"

- *C–Capitals*: Check to make sure beginnings of sentences are capitalized as well as names of things.
- *O–Overall appearance*: Is my name on it? Did I indent for paragraphs? Are things clean and completely erased?
- *P–Punctuation*: Did I end every sentence? Did I use commas correctly?
- *S–Spelling*: Are all of my words spelled correctly?
- *S–Sentences* (I added this one): Are all of my sentences complete sentences? Did I use a variety of types of sentences?

I have used this mnemonic strategy in classes I've taught from second grade through college. It's very helpful!

A hallmark of metacognitive, or self-directed, learning is the process of goal setting. The more a child is able to become directly involved in setting goals for himself, the more likely he is to achieve at a higher level (Dweck, 2006). However, it is critical that students with HFA set themselves *learning* goals rather than *performance* goals. A learning goal consists of determining what will be learned, rather than a "grade" or an outcome. Dweck's (2006) work found that students who were high achieving performed lower on tasks when their grades or results were praised. However, when their use of effective strategies or their effort was praised, their performance levels improved. Because students with HFA tend to have strong analytical skills, it is important to encourage them in their continued use of finding

Step	Action	
Prepare	Get your materials together, know where the trashcan is and where your backpack is.	
	Make sure you have enough room around you on both sides of your body to put stuff.	
Sort	Take things out of your desk, one by one.	
	As you look at what comes out, ask yourself, "Do I need to keep this, or is this trash?"	
	Place trash in a pile on your right side.	
	Place the rest of the stuff in a pile on your left side.	
	Continue until everything is out of your desk.	
Discard	Scoop up the trash pile and take it over to the trashcan.	
	Throw it away in the trashcan.	
	Go back to your desk.	
Sort, again	From the pile on your left side, find pencils, pens, and anything else that's small.	
	Place that on your right side.	
	Find the textbooks, folders, and notebooks for each subject area, then match math book with math folder, reading books with reading folder, and so on.	
	Make a small pile of each content area. No more than five piles should be made: math, reading, English/language arts, social studies, and science.	
	Take out the loose papers and place them in the appropriate pile: math papers in the math pile, and so on. Put papers that you aren't sure about in an "Other" pile.	
	Put the important papers in your folders. Important means unfinished work that has not been collected yet, or notes that you will need for future tests. If it's work you've already done, or random drawings, then you should place it in the "Other" pile.	
	The rest of the stuff is probably trash, or should go home.	
Discard, again	Decide what else needs to be thrown away, or what should go in your backpack. If it's something that your family needs to see, a note from your teacher, or finished work, it probably needs to go home in your backpack.	
	Place the stuff to go home in your backpack.	
	Throw the rest of it away. If you're not sure, ask your teacher. "What should I do with this?" He or she will tell you.	
Plan	Look at your five piles and your pencil pile and decide where each part should go in your desk—do not pick anything up yet.	

Figure 21. Explicit instructions for cleaning out a desk.

Place	Put your pencils and markers and pens in your pencil box. Place the pencil box near the very front of your desk	
	Place each pile of books and folder with papers inside of it carefully in its own pile in your desk.	
	Do not stack piles. You should have five piles in your desk along with your pencil box.	
	Look carefully at your desk. Note where your reading pile is, your math pile, and each of the other piles.	
Practice	Say to yourself, "Get out your social studies book."	
	Imagine that you are getting it out. Can you find it? Do you have to move anything to get to it?	
	If you can, and there aren't papers or books falling out, sit back and enjoy!	

Figure 21, continued.

patterns and use of strategies, rather than the outcomes of their efforts. Figure 22 shows an individual goal-setting contract for memorizing multiplication tables.

Another strategy for providing metacognitive coaching and learning opportunities for students with HFA who have trouble getting organized and staying motivated is through a café or choice menu (Tomlinson & Strickland, 2005). A choice menu allows students a choice in how they are going to accomplish the goal of the lesson. For example, in teaching math, students could write and solve their own problem, create a concrete example, or teach someone else. One method of providing choices within a classroom that has been very popular with the teachers I've trained has been the use of a tic-tac-toe board (Tomlinson & Strickland, 2005). You can use a variety of means of determining what activity goes into what square. The most common I've seen is using Bloom's taxonomy for each one of the squares or using multiple intelligences to distinguish activities. See Figure 23 for an example of a grammar tic-tac-toe board that was created using multiple intelligences. You can ask your students to complete the board, either by connecting three in a row, selecting two besides the required center square, or even doing blackout, with all of the squares completed. You can even require different groups of students differentiated by ability to complete different numbers of squares. It's entirely up to you and the nature of your class.

Another way of providing choice within a classroom environment is to provide students with a list or menu of activities that they have to complete within a certain amount of time. They can then select which ones they want to work on first, second, and so on. You can provide students with a packet of different activities to be done, and allow them the option of the order in which they want to accomplish

Monday:

Today, I scored ______________________________ .

Did I beat my record? Yes ❑ No ❑

I used ____ strategy.

Tomorrow, I want to try ____ .

Tuesday:

Today, I scored ______________________________ .

Did I beat my record? Yes ❑ No ❑

I used ____ strategy.

Tomorrow, I want to try ____ .

Wednesday

Today, I scored ______________________________ .

Did I beat my record? Yes ❑ No ❑

I used ____ strategy.

Tomorrow, I want to try ____ .

Thursday

Today, I scored ______________________________ .

Did I beat my record? Yes ❑ No ❑

I used ____ strategy.

Tomorrow, I want to try ____ .

Friday

Today, I scored ______________________________ .

Did I beat my record? Yes ❑ No ❑

I used ____ strategy.

Tomorrow, I want to try ____ .

Figure 22. Goal-setting example.

it. For example, a math unit might consist of having a student learn the concept of graphing in a whole group, and then choose the order in which they complete a worksheet, label the parts of a graph, conduct a survey, and explain how to determine increments. See Figure 24 for a menu approach that provides choice, but also allows students to determine their own learning preferences.

However you organize and manage metacognitive strategies, it's important to remember that the focus of instruction is on the child being able to complete the work independently. Rather than being frustrated when a child can't do the work, we have to provide strategies to allow him or her opportunities to learn how. In other words, we have to teach him.

Interpersonal	Intrapersonal	Logical-Mathematical
Tell a partner how adjectives and adverbs are alike and different.	Imagine you in your favorite place. What adjectives and adverbs would you use to describe you?	Find a favorite chapter book of yours. Count and graph how many adjectives are used on one page and how many adverbs. Why do you suppose that is? What conclusions can you draw about the use of adjectives and adverbs?
Spatial	**Required**	**Musical**
Draw a Venn diagram comparing and contrasting adjectives and adverbs.	Complete a worksheet from the State Standards workbook.	Pick a jazz standard and examine the use of adjectives in the lyrics. For example, "The Way You Look Tonight" and "Sophisticated Lady" both use really powerful adjectives. Can you think of five song titles that you might write that use adjectives and five that use adverbs?
Linguistic	**Bodily-Kinesthetic**	**Naturalist**
Write four sentences. 1. One should be "plain" with only verbs and nouns. 2. One should use at least three adjectives. 3. One should use at least two adverbs. 4. One should combine the above two sentences, with three adjectives and two adverbs. Now, write at least two sentences describing how the sentences are different. Which, if any, of the sentences is the "best" and why?	Pick two adjectives and two adverbs. With a partner, act out the adjectives and then the adverbs and have them try to guess what adjectives or adverbs you're demonstrating. Discuss how easy or hard it was to demonstrate the adjectives and adverbs.	It is important that scientists pick the absolutely correct word to describe what they see. Go out on the school playground and watch a bug or an ant that you see there. Describe what the ant does, using at least five adjectives and five adverbs.

Figure 23. Tic-tac-toe board example.

Together Strategies

There are numerous strategies within the classroom that can be implemented to develop the cognitive abilities of children with HFA that don't require direct intervention. These include designing the environment so that issues are not as significant and the involvement of peers.

One of the most significant ways to include a child with HFA is to develop an inclusive climate within the classroom where differences are tolerated, and it is

Dr. Hughes's Diner
Now Serving: Third-Grade Math

Appetizer
Small-group instruction on graphing

Entreé: Select one
- Complete a graphing worksheet for the state test.
- Label the parts of the graph worksheet.
- Determine the best increments to use in the example worksheets.

Side Dishes: Select one
- Conduct a survey of the third-grade classes' favorite ice creams.
- Survey the teachers to find out what subject they like to teach best.
- Survey your family members to determine which holiday they like best.

Dessert: Select one
- Present your survey results in a PowerPoint, using a graph.
- Present your survey results in a poster to the class, using a graph.
- Present your survey results on the class webpage, using a graph.

Figure 24. Choice menu example.

recognized that sometimes, people have to be treated differently to get what they need. One strategy I use to set a tone in my classroom that children would get what they need and to get past the complaints of "But it's not FAIR!" that we deal with so often, is described in Figure 25. The culture of inclusiveness is one that is larger than this book, but it is a critical building block to a classroom where a child with HFA can be accepted.

Cooperative grouping, in which every child is invited a role to play in a group process, is invaluable to children with HFA. They can be very task-oriented, so giving them the role of timekeeper is a natural place to start. However, it is important to teach them the roles outside of this one so that they can learn how to function in a group. Having a framework of cooperative grouping, in which there is a specified task, certain roles for the students, and individual accountability, is critical to the success of incorporating students with HFA into a group and raising the success level of the group (Slavin, 1991). Although such a grouping method is not effective for the academic development of gifted students (Rogers, 2002), it does play a role in the cognitive development of children with HFA through social engagement. Great care should be taken, however, that children with HFA are also provided opportunities to work alone and with like-ability peers (Rogers, 2002). Flexible grouping patterns appear to be the keys to stabilizing and working with children with HFA.

Included with flexible grouping and cooperative grouping is the concept of peer tutoring. It is critical that the child with HFA be both the one being tutored and a tutor himself. If the child is able to have value to the class by explaining a concept to someone else, it can raise the child's self-esteem, as well as his own level of understanding (Santrock, 2012). For a child with HFA who may have the concept, but not the language, it also allows him an opportunity to learn the language that connects to content that he already knows. If he doesn't understand the concept, then being tutored allows him a different way of seeing the material and provides some one-on-one instruction and time to reflect. Peer tutoring can allow the child to use the didactic language that may come naturally to him, but have it be of use to the classroom, rather than a hindrance. Great care should be taken that the child is also learning social skills in the context of instruction.

Another way of encouraging a child with HFA to use his formal, didactic language as a means of strength is to encourage brainstorming and open-ended thinking within the classroom. Asking students "How many ways can we . . . ?" or "In what way might we . . . ?" encourages creativity and flexibility of thought. Open-ended, brainstorming questions include:

- In what way might we . . . ?
- How many ways could we . . . ?
- Can anyone think of a different way to . . . ?
- What is another possible answer?
- Are there any other reasons that _____ might have happened?

Other ways of managing the environment within the classroom and encouraging the cognitive growth of children with HFA involve classroom arrangement. Within the classroom, schedules and rules should be clearly posted, as well as procedures. In addition to the words that describe these aspects, a visual cue of a pic-

Scene: My classroom.

Teacher: *Tone of great excitement*. Guess what? I just got the greatest tool that is going to help all of you learn to read! I thought that I read pretty well, and it helped even me! Do you want to hear about it?

Students: Okay!

Teacher: *Confiding tone*. Well, I went to this doctor and he gave me this tool that he said was going to help me read. I didn't believe him, because I read pretty well—I mean, I teach reading!—and guess what? It helped me read better. It did! And guess what? I've ordered one for every single one of you! Or should I order just one and have you share? Would it be fair for only some of you to get one?

Students: No! One for each of us!

Teacher: Do you all want to learn how to read better?

Students: Yeah!

Teacher: Well, I got the first tool in the mail today—it's just a demo. But it will let you all know what's in store for you. And I ordered one for all of you—it's coming. Because it wouldn't be fair for me to hog this all to myself.

Teacher takes out reading glasses. Now in my case, I have normal vision in my left eye, while my right eye is close to 20/200—coke bottle glasses have nothing on me. However, for teachers who have better vision than I do, they can find a pair of strong reading glasses at a pharmacy.

Teacher: *Puts on glasses and nods wisely*. Wow! What a difference! I can totally see better! Here, I'll pass it around so that you can see this amazing new tool that helps me read better!

Pass to child. Children pass around. Children being children, there will likely be some who dramatically take off the glasses. Others will get teary-eyed. There will almost always be the "tough" guy who says "What? These don't do anything!" Just smile.

Teacher: *As glasses are going around*. I'm hearing that some of you don't want to use this. Why not?

Student: Because these were made for your eyes, and boy, you've got bad eyes!

Teacher: You're absolutely right—these *were* made for me! Where did I go to get these?

Student: The eye doctor!

Teacher: You're right. I went to someone who is a specialist in helping eyes read better. All right, I'll cancel the order. But guess what? Do you realize that *I* am a specialist in education? It's my job, just like the eye doctor's job is to figure out how to help you read better, only I work with your brains, not your eyes. And you can have complete confidence in me because it says right here, proven with my education diploma, that I know what I'm doing. What it means is that I might give some of you something different to help you learn—some of you might get different assignments, some of you might get different grading rubrics, and some of you might use different materials. And you know why?

Students: Either "Why?" *or silence as they're getting the message*.

Teacher: Because it's my job to help you read and learn and I don't ever want to hear "But it's not *fair* that so-and-so is doing such-and-such"! Because each of you will get what you need—not what everyone else is getting. Just like the glasses—not everyone needs the same thing to help learn.

Teacher: *Brings out a large poster of a pair of glasses over the phrase "Fair is when everyone gets what they need to learn."*

End of scene.

Figure 25. Script for inclusive classrooms.

Note. The greatest challenge will come not from the children who can be cued by pointing at the poster during the school year every time they start to say, "It's not *fair*!", but from the parents and the other teachers. I would recommend you do this same activity with parents at the beginning of the school year.

ture or a symbol helps as well. With clearly observable rules and procedures, the child with HFA can monitor himself better so that he has a visual representation of what to do—whether that is where he's supposed to be, what he's supposed to be doing, or how he's supposed to interact with others. An example of a picture schedule is found in Figure 26. These can be individualized for the child to be on his desk, or they can be posted for other students to use as well.

Cognitive development is likely to be a strength area of a child with high-functioning autism. She may not get concepts unless they are explicitly taught or unless visual images are used, but typically, underlying intelligence allows a child to understand the content. Getting children to understand facts, concepts, and skills is critical to a teacher's success. If you have a child with HFA, there are a variety of ways to go about linking the child to the content.

Key Points From Chapter 10

- Cognitive skills such as memory and spatial relationships are likely to be strength areas of children with HFA. Often, science and math are strong areas, but language arts can be as well, if the skills of analysis and language rules are specifically taught.
- However, children with HFA often have difficulty processing and organizing verbal information. In addition, a child with HFA may be so constrained by his fixated interests that it is difficult to confer meaning in other subject areas.
- *Teaching* strategies can reduce the frustration that teachers feel when they experience "oughtism" or feel that a child should be able to do a skill. The use of Bloom's taxonomy and Torrance's creativity model can provide access to students to think of content in structured manners. Acceleration should be provided to students with HFA in their areas of talent and strength.
- *Timing* strategies can be used in almost every subject area. Care should be taken that students are first provided direct instruction before they are rewarded for skills that they have. If reward systems are offered for skills that students do not have, the result can be frustration.
- *Training* strategies, such as the use of timers and mnemonics, can help students organize their thinking. Color-coding materials, activities, and instruction can help direct attention and provide a means of remembering things. Graphic organizers are powerful ways of connecting content to visual means of organizing a child's thinking.
- *Thinking* strategies are used in the University of Kansas Strategic Instruction Model and the Self-Regulated Strategy Development model to provide metacognitive scaffolding for students. In addition, providing

Time	Activity	Picture Cue
8:00–8:15	Daily board work	
8:15–8:35	Calendar work	
8:35–9:05	Special Monday/Wednesday: PE Tuesday: Art Thursday: Music Friday: Computer	
9:05–10:10	Reading	
10:10–10:25	Brain break: Recess	
10:25–11:15	Language arts	
11:15–11:45	Science	
11:45–12:15	Lunch	
12:15–12:30	Read-aloud	
12:30–12:45	Recess	
12:45–1:30	Math	
1:30–2:00	Social studies	
2:00–2:15	Announcements/clean up	
2:15–2:30	Dismiss	

Figure 26. Picture schedule example.

students choice through tic-tac-toe boards or choice menus allows them ways of organizing their own time and thought processes to connect to content.

- *Together* strategies need to be balanced between the use of cooperative learning strategies and alone time for learning. The classroom can be constructed using visual schedules in the classroom that allow a child to connect her sense of space and time to let her know what is coming up and where she should be.

Chapter 11

Autism in the Schools: The Level of School and Content Area Affects How We Deal With Autism

Most of the described strategies in Chapters 5–10 are appropriate for students of all ages in all content areas, with some specific modifications. A child with autism is taught within a context of a particular school level and within a particular content area. Ultimately, teachers are responsible for teaching a child academic content at the appropriate grade level. The level of schooling can change the way in which strategies are applied, as can the particular content area that is being addressed. This chapter describes some of those modifications.

Adaptations From Primary to Secondary

Clearly, teachers, classrooms, and schools are different at different levels. For the sake of this book, I will discuss four groups that will overlap, depending on the age of the child and the requirements of the state:

- preschool and early elementary, grades K–3;
- upper elementary, grades 3–6;
- middle school, grades 6–9; and
- secondary or high school, grades 9–12.

Preschool and Early Elementary Grades

Most of the emphasis at the preschool and primary levels is on the development of relationships, early literacy and math concepts, and learning how to learn (National Association for the Education of Young Children, 2002). Children are learning the alphabetic concept of connecting various shapes to specific meanings, ordinal order, one-to-one correspondence, and appropriate classroom behaviors. There is a significant focus on learning to read at these stages, beginning with phonemic awareness and moving to the alphabetic principles and phonics.

This is probably the opportune time for children with HFA to be identified. Speech therapy is the most effective at young ages, and early intervention is designed to work with children in naturalistic settings. Typical children are developmentally not as aware of the negativity of differences (Santrock, 2012) and are fairly open to working with a friend who is struggling, often because their own development is so widely varied. If a teacher starts noticing differences, it is important that he or she start making notes and working toward identification so that services can be provided. There are a number of children (my daughter was one) who, if they receive services early and intensely enough, can learn to cope with their autism very effectively in later grades. Not all can, but the provision of early services can only help. According to a 2009 study by Dr. Fein of the University of Connecticut and colleagues, between 10%–20% of children diagnosed with high-functioning autism between the ages of 1 and 3 no longer qualified as having autism by the age of 9.

Upper Elementary

Although this is often not a formal section of school, it is probably one of the most critical phases for children with HFA. Most children with Asperger's syndrome and other forms of HFA are not identified until ages 8–9 because it is at this point that their differences become much more noticeable and cannot be explained by developmental lags or quirks. It is in the upper part of elementary school when so many children with HFA start receiving services.

During the upper end of elementary school, most children have made the developmental leap from Piaget's Pre-Operational stage to the Concrete Operations stage, in which children learn to manipulate time and space (Santrock, 2012). Children with autism appear to be mixed in their ability to move through Piagetian stages (Morgan, 1986), typically being behind in their use of understanding of multiple perspectives, but progressing in terms of figurative or theoretical understandings. Such differences become more apparent in upper elementary as other children finish making the complete leap into manipulating perspectives, symbols, and figurative elements, while children with HFA are often lagging in their social understandings, which affects their ability to develop higher order understandings (Hughes, 2011).

Although speech and occupational therapy are probably most effective with younger children, they are still critically needed for children in the upper grades of elementary school. The services have the added ability to build off of children's experiences and their increased ability to conceptualize and think beyond their immediate experience. Because children with HFA have significant abilities, it is likely that by the upper end of elementary school, both the areas of challenge and the areas of strength are more easily identified and both can be developed.

Middle and High School

Children who are not identified until secondary school are probably the most high functioning of all—able to hide their areas of difficulty behind their significant strengths. In many of these cases, teachers and parents were able to overlook many of the child's social and emotional issues simply because the gifts and academic abilities masked the problematic areas. The emotional and social differences can become most apparent at ages in which social issues dominate the school culture. As a friend of mine with HFA stated, "I find and identify my emotions through logic, rather than analyzing what I am feeling. Logic precedes emotion for me."

There are other issues involved with the structure of secondary school that impact services and how a teacher can work with a child (Dieker & Murawski, 2003). Because teachers focus so heavily on content in secondary settings, there is sometimes an effort to push services back onto the speech therapist or to blame the elementary teachers for their lack of "fixing" the child. At the same time, many secondary settings are operating within block periods of time to provide an intense amount of information related to the content standards to students—content that is required for the heavy testing pressures often found in secondary settings.

Simultaneously, while preparing students to succeed in secondary school, teachers are preparing students to succeed in life after high school through transition plans. Students with HFA often have a strong possibility of attending college because of their strengths, and higher education should be addressed within their transition plans (Sherman, 2007), in addition to self-help skills and work-related skills. Sherman (2007) noted that schools are responsible for meeting the goals that are determined by the IEP transition team, and must provide services to the student until he is 21 if the goals are not met by the time he turns 18. However, once a child has moved into the college environment, the IEP no longer applies, and the student is covered under Section 504 of the Americans with Disabilities Act, which prohibits discrimination, but does not provide the same level of requirements or legal rights. There are numerous colleges that are making efforts to meet the needs of students with HFA, and guidance counselors and parents should research what programs are available. Landmark College in Vermont, in particular, specializes in students with learning differences. And it isn't only teachers who are impacted: Parents of children with autism are often much more trepidacious and anxious about the success of their child beyond high school than typical parents (Whitney-Thomas & Hanley-Maxwell, 1996).

At the same time, secondary teachers are faced with increasing and widening diversity in student preparation and backgrounds. What were small differences in primary and early elementary are enormous gaps between students in secondary settings. Although all students can learn, the rate of learning is not the same, and as a result, the distance between students becomes significantly wider at secondary levels.

Differences at Different Ages

Some of the strategies will be less effective at different ages. Many of the thinking strategies will be less immediately effective at younger grades, simply because children have not yet reached the Piagetian stage of Formal Operational thinking in which they can begin to take in or analyze other points of view. It may be difficult for them to think about their own thinking. However, because children with HFA often have prodigious memories, if they are taught the scripts and the self-reflection methods early, there is a strong chance that they will be able to incorporate the strategies at younger ages. Students with HFA often have to be taught the words to think, and this thinking is more easily taught the younger they are.

Although the strategies themselves may not have to be altered significantly, the language that is used to describe the strategies and the use of peers will have to be altered for the different age groups. A younger child may not object to having a stress thermometer in public view for his peers to see and assist him with, but an older child may need more private instruction about its use. Similarly, while peers need to be involved at every level, how they are involved and their level of understanding will change at every level. Teachers should adapt the ideas to their particular level of school and the conceptual and developmental levels of the children with HFA and their peers.

Content-Related Adaptations

Just as the level of schooling will affect how teachers can adapt the strategies, the teaching of various content areas will also affect how students with HFA are presented with the strategies discussed in this book. Education is a process of bridging the gap between content and students, and teachers are ultimately responsible through assessment to bring all students to higher levels of learning. Table 7 connects the strategies to the specific content areas.

Table 7

Strategies Applied to Content Areas

Content Area		Instructional Approaches				
		Teacher Focus		Student Focus		Social Focus
Broad Area	Content Skills:	Instruction *Teach*	Behavioral *Time*	Attention/Memory *Train*	Metacognition *Think*	Environment *Together*
Reading	Phonological awareness Phonics Vocabulary Comprehension Fluency	Tiered reading activities Reading centers Vocabulary development	Motivational rewards Modeling Charting Progress monitoring Fluency graphs	Assistive technology Learning styles Cuing Prompting Mnemonics Reading level +− Time + Spacing	SRSD KU-SIM Choice menus	Choral reading
Language Arts	Composition Listening Speaking Prosody	Speech therapy Specific skill instruction	Modeling prosody	Assistive technology Visual cues Prompts	SRSD KU-SIM Cue words Scripts Visualization techniques	Group stories Writers' workshop model
Math	Numbers and operations Geometry Measurement Algebra Probability and statistics Data analysis	Task analysis Tiered math activities Math centers Math literacy development Acceleration	Motivational rewards Modeling Progress monitoring Fluency graphs	Mnemonics for procedures Songs for procedures	Singapore Math Cue words Goal-setting Problem Finding/ Solving Graphic organizers	Group solving processes Problem-based learning
Science and Social Studies	Question finding and solving Data analysis Critical thinking Creative thinking	Question-response Tiered instruction Acceleration Enrichment Creativity skills	Motivational rewards Modeling	Learning styles Cuing Prompting Mnemonics	Color-coded thinking Goal-setting Problem finding/solving Visual organizers Graphic organizers	Problem-based learning Classroom arrangement

Reading and Language Arts

Children with HFA are more likely to experience difficulties with reading comprehension and imaginative writing than with more technical skills such as spelling and oral reading—tasks at which they are likely to excel (Schwartz, 2011). It isn't the process of decoding or writing that tends to produce difficulties, but the use of language to achieve a certain goal.

Reading, which includes the skills of phonological awareness, phonics, vocabulary development, reading comprehension, and oral reading fluency, can be further developed with the five strategies through the use of:

- Teaching strategies:
  - Tiered reading activities and centers allow the incorporation of areas of interest and multiple reading levels to further develop reading skills as well as meet the child where she is academically.
  - Vocabulary development activities that include visual elements and visual connections to prior learning should be utilized.
  - Adjusting the writing instruments can be helpful, because many students with HFA have difficulty feeling the correct pressure of their pencils. Felt-tip pens are often used because of their ease of flow and the dramatic difference of the ink on the paper (Heflin & Alaimo, 2007).

- Timing strategies:
  - Modeling of appropriate reading rate and expression, using both teachers and peers for modeling purposes, should be provided.
  - There are numerous opportunities for charting and graphing with fluency activities, comprehension questions, and phonics-based skills.
  - In addition, an overall rewards-based system to develop the increased use of skills can be developed using the interests and passions of the child. There are numerous children who will do what they have to do in order to learn more about their area of interest.

- Training strategies:
  - Attracting and keeping the attention of students with HFA on the written words and on their writing can be done with numerous activities such as increasing font size and increasing or decreasing the reading level. Often, students with HFA can pay attention to more complex material simply because it captures their attention, while simpler material may bore them into behaving inappropriately.
  - In addition, teaching students to read for comprehension by having them identify and visually underline, represent, or otherwise note transition and direction words can be very helpful.

- Writing strategies can be used through the teaching and use of order words and words that signal shifts and direction in writing such as the use of "first," "second," and "next."
- Finally, the use of assistive technology to maintain attention and interest cannot be overestimated. In the Resources section, there is a list of apps that have been reviewed favorably to assist with writing.

- Thinking strategies:
  - There are a number of writing and reading strategies developed by the University of Kansas, Vanderbilt University, and Georgetown University that are quick mnemonics for prompting student thinking in reading strategies, reading comprehension, and writing composition—all areas in which children with HFA tend to struggle.
  - At the same time as specific skill-based instruction, teachers can create a menu or tic-tac-toe board of available activities that allow students to engage with materials in ways that are meaningful to them.
  - Finally, encouraging students to follow a process of "read, visualize, respond" will allow them to connect their abilities for visualization to language—a process that is difficult for them and requires additional time.

- Together strategies:
  - Turning reading and writing into group activities can facilitate not only the content skills, but also the group dynamics of the class.
  - Choral reading can allow the child with HFA to hear models of appropriate prosody, rhythm, and intonations, particularly if the teacher provides appropriate feedback and specific praise for the use of selected strategies and skills.
  - Group writing processes, such as a writers' workshop, allow students to become engaged in each other's writing and to provide that often-missing element of writing—an audience. Children with HFA often need to see a connection between what they are writing and a bigger purpose.

Math

Math tends to be a strength among children with HFA. Many children with HFA are able to visually represent the various geometric and measurement concepts while manipulating numbers in their head. Numbers often appear to make sense to children with HFA, perhaps because of their foundation in concrete objects, rules, and logic, rather than conceptual language and the vagaries of human expression.

The most significant area of challenge often occurs in the literacy and language of mathematics and the higher level, conceptual, more probabilitistic math found in calculus and higher level courses. Because children can struggle in so many other areas, it is critically important that areas of strength are developed as well. Children form self-concepts from what they *can* do (Santrock, 2012), and it is necessary that they perceive themselves as strong in the areas in which they excel.

It is also important to note that not all children with HFA will excel in math or science—and some will need support in these areas as well. However, because American math curricula cover so many concepts (up to 30 per year) and then tend to review those concepts over and over (Schmidt, Houang, & Cogan, 2002), math remediation is often a process of identifying the area of difficulty and then filling that "hole," which can then vault a student with HFA ahead quickly because of the linear and logical process of math itself.

- Teaching strategies:
  o Certainly the specific skills of algebra, computation, and all of the various mathematical number operations can be directly taught.
  o It is strongly encouraged to have a variety of tiered math activities and centers to develop the mathematical talents of children. Often, they learn computation skills so quickly that they need continued acceleration opportunities.
  o Programs such as Touch Math (see Resources in Chapter 12) can provide students a multisensory means of connecting meaning to symbols and functions of math.
  o It should also be noted that the child should not be held back in his computation skills if he does not demonstrate mathematical literacy—often, it isn't the math process that's at issue but the words used to describe or specify the task. Mathematical terms should be taught clearly and using similar visual supports as language literacy vocabulary.

- Timing strategies:
  o Certainly, math is an area that is easily measured and tracked over time. The number of problems done correctly, the number of pages completed, and the rate of memorizing facts are all common measurements that can be tracked using a program such as Excel or a simple graph on a child's desk.
  o Because of its common linear process, it is more difficult to enrich math and easier to accelerate.
  o Even if a child is several grade levels behind her age peers, the amount of information that she is missing is actually less that it might appear. The American math program is recursive and tends to repeat a great

deal of information from year to year (Schmidt et al., 2002). If a child gets stuck on a particular concept or linguistic term, the holes in her thinking can set her back significantly until they are filled, when she can then make tremendous leaps and gains.

- Training strategies:
  - Memory is often a strength of students with HFA. Thus, while they may get tangled up in the language of mathematics, they often can clearly remember the process of mathematics. Mnemonics and songs can help them remember the procedures as well as the use of the specific language of math.

- Thinking strategies:
  - Although students with HFA may be able to develop their mathematical abilities in typical classrooms, the Singapore method of math instruction is particularly suited for them because of its highly visual nature (Hoven & Garelick, 2007). The Singapore method of math takes math concepts that are often algebraically and linguistically explained in the United States and makes them more simplistic using visual and symbolic means—strategies that use the strengths of the student with HFA.
  - Using cue words and the goal statement of "What is this problem asking?" for problem solving, students can learn explicit patterns of math language to help them solve word problems—often the most difficult area for students with HFA to master. I remember teaching a student that "(number) *of* (group word) and (number) on *each*" was a common formula for multiplication word problems. After that, he color-coded the cue words and figured out how to solve word problems. There are a number of problem-solving strategies that can be used to help students with HFA and certainly other struggling students. The difference between a child with HFA and a child struggling with math is often that it is the language, not the mathematical concept, that is a stumbling block for the student with HFA.
  - Using graphic organizers and visualization techniques, students with HFA can learn problem-finding and problem-solving strategies that allow students to manipulate concepts and numbers. Time has to be provided to allow the student to translate the mathematical words into symbols and visual representations.

- Together strategies:
    - When students are encouraged to solve complex problems together, there are several advantages for students with HFA. First, they often get to be the "expert"—a role that they may not often get to fill. And secondly, they can use language, an area of difficulty, to communicate mathematical concepts, an area of strength, to their peers. Using strengths to develop areas of challenge is a particularly effective form of remediation.
    - A highly recommended strategy to involve students in real-world uses of math and other skills is the use of Problem-Based Learning (PBL; Ronis, 2007). PBL engages students in the use of math in realistic situations and allows a student with HFA to connect his or her knowledge with real-world demands and group dynamics. Such skills will be invaluable in later life, when a student will have to learn how to function in the adult world.

Science and Social Studies

Math and language arts are sets of skills that can be applied. In contrast, science and social studies are the use of those skills to solve specific types of questions (Vacca & Vacca, 2005). Both science and social studies involve the use of problem identification, problem solving, and data analysis to understand different phenomena. Science is often an area of strength for children with HFA because of the connection to observable phenomena and to math, whereas social studies tends to be more difficult because it focuses on the impact of human actions—issues that students with HFA have a difficult time with in their own lives. However, social studies is an excellent way to study human interaction from an analytical manner—skills that can only help the child understand his own experiences.

- Teaching strategies:
    - Perhaps the most significant content application of strategies for students with HFA is through the use of differentiated questions; questions that require higher order thinking and analytical processes are particularly suited to their strengths of memory and analysis.
    - Such questions can be used in tiered activities and centers in which directions are written down; questions that are verbally asked will be more difficult for the child with HFA to process, whereas a written question may provide a visual cue for the thinking process.
    - Creativity skills can be further developed in the context of specific content such as science and social studies. Students with HFA tend to need a purpose for creativity because of their practical natures. The development of fluency skills is more easily produced in realistic settings than in fun brainstorming experiences.

- Timing strategies:
  - Science or social studies topics will often be an area of interest for a child. I worked with children who were passionately interested in—to name a few obsessions—every battle of World War II, the war in Afghanistan, astronomy, and the history of the train. These areas of interest can be used as rewards for other work or encouragement to develop research skills and offered as enrichment and acceleration opportunities. Rather than fighting the passion, teachers can harness the areas of interest and, by using the internal motivation, encourage the student to develop communication and research skills.
  - Other aspects of timing strategies include the use of modeling appropriate question-asking and problem-solving strategies. Exposing students with HFA to adults who may have HFA and work in the science and social studies fields may be an excellent way to encourage them to pursue academic directions in these areas. Many adults with HFA have found success in fields that perceive their abilities as assets rather than deficits, and these people can be used as role models. Certainly Temple Grandin, who holds a Ph.D. in animal science, is an example of a person with HFA who has learned to use her autism to her advantage in her chosen field.

- Training strategies:
  - Science tends to lend itself to greater understanding by students because of its concrete and hands-on approach. However, science, particularly at lower grades, often is taught primarily as a vocabulary exercise and neglects the importance of inquiry and thoughtful processes (Anderson, 2002). When taught appropriately for greater scientific understanding, students with HFA have a greater ability to connect the vocabulary with the concepts being taught. In contrast, social studies, in order to impact students with HFA, needs to take a more interactive, concrete, and visual approach in order to effect change. I have had intense conversations with students with HFA in fourth grade about economic supply and demand after doing a quick trip to a store and a review of real estate listings.
  - It is essential, because of their concrete abilities and visual memories, that instruction be accompanied by a visual prompts. These visual prompts can guide instruction through the use of memory triggers, focusing strategies, and access to content. When studying the development of democracy in Ancient Greece, a third-grade standard, we brought in scale models of the Parthenon and reenacted debates. When discussing the Periodic Table of Elements, I had the class build

it by presenting some of the models of the atoms and asking students to develop an organization of them. After manipulating models, the students could then present the beauty of the Periodic Table and the words became part of the visual elements.

- Thinking strategies:
  - Using color-coded elements, teachers can engage students in the various processes of content-oriented thinking. For example, each of the various steps of the scientific process can be assigned a different color.
  - I have had success teaching students to engage with science and social studies topics using Edward deBono's Thinking Hats (1985). The different hats are different colors and are visual, color-organized cues for different types of thinking, such as a green hat for new ideas, a red hat for emotions, and a white hat for finding facts and information. By switching the hats, you can request that students be flexible in their responses and thinking patterns.
  - Because of their content focus, it is also helpful for students with HFA to set themselves learning goals and determine progress toward their goals. When a new unit is introduced, the teacher can share the required standards goal with students, and then, perhaps using a visual KWHL chart (What do we Know?, What do we Want to Learn?, How can we find out?, What have we Learned?), work with students to set individual learning goals.
  - Similarly, working with students to connect content using various problem-finding and problem-solving strategies, such as Creative Problem Solving (Isaksen, Dorval, & Treffinger, 2000), can help students organize their thinking processes using a visual guide and sequential steps.

- Together strategies:
  - Teachers can use group processes to facilitate both social skills and content acquisition for students with HFA. Many of the peer support activities can be implemented using the content as the vehicle of communication. Many teachers may feel that they don't have time to teach social skills in addition to content; teaching social skills within content allows both goals to be met simultaneously.
  - A strategy that allows the development of group interaction and deepening of content knowledge is the teaching strategy of Problem-Based Learning (Ronis, 2007). In PBL, students work together to solve realistic problems that engage students in the application of specific content. The role of the teacher is not the "sage on the stage," nor

the "guide on the side," but the "meddler in the middle" (McWilliam, 2005, p. 1), in which the teacher takes an active role to provide content; facilitate student engagement, discussion, and thinking; and encourage positive student interactions.

Assessment Issues

There are numerous forms of assessment. Special education or Response to Intervention (RtI) processes often use progress monitoring of IEP or RtI goals to determine how well students are progressing on specific goals. The progress monitoring and/or IEP goals and objectives are clearly stated and specific to the individual child. A teacher must be aware of what measures are being taken when and what decisions will be made based on the results.

However, beyond IEP and RtI assessments, there are state tests. Clearly, tests rule. Having students do well on state-level tests is becoming more and more critical to student success and teacher evaluations (Koebler, 2011), despite significant resistance (Darling-Hammond, 2011). There are several issues related to the assessment of students with HFA, including behavioral, academic, relational, and other issues, including medical issues.

Behavioral

If a child is in meltdown mode, there will be little opportunity to engage with him for testing purposes. It is critical that the stress level of the teacher be under control so that the student with HFA does not reflect the teacher's stress level and act out accordingly. When a child is highly anxious, learning and memories that were previously accessible become unavailable due to the fight or flight response. Teaching the child stress-relieving strategies and following behavioral management practices that allow the student to calm or stimulate her nervous system will be invaluable. *And I would recommend that if the teacher is feeling stressed, he or she try some of these strategies as well!* Prior to testing situations, it is very important that the student become familiar with the room setup and the process and that any changes of schedule because of testing be reviewed and placed into social stories for students.

Similarly, testing behaviors should be reviewed and scripted. If the child finishes early or doesn't think that she will finish, strategies to alleviate anxiety or boredom need to be planned ahead of time. I would recommend that the student have practice sessions so that the process is recognized for its importance, but does not become a source of high anxiety—*even though it may be for everyone involved.*

It is very important that testing be perceived as part of the "normal" educational process by students who have difficulties managing anxiety.

Similarly, teachers and schools will have to work with parents who will also be significantly anxious about their child's performance on tests. I would recommend that the whole school learn anxiety-reducing techniques!

Academic

Because of the varied academic abilities of students with HFA, it becomes important to determine growth in each area, rather than lumping together assessment scores. Children with HFA often will have "mountain" type scores rather than flat profiles (Schwartz, 2011), and overall grade-level growth can be difficult to determine. When discussing academic growth, therefore, it is very important to look at each factor individually. Often, students with HFA, like other children with disabilities, have difficulties qualifying for gifted education services because of the erratic nature of their academic skills (Trail, 2011).

Relational

Because students with HFA often have difficulty managing their emotional relationships with others, I would suggest that in order to raise academic test scores—which will determine teacher evaluations—teachers focus on the development of group dynamics. The Together strategies therefore become not "touchy-feely" strategies, but strategies that will allow the smooth operation of a classroom. I often tell my preservice teachers, "Spend a little time early, or spend a lot of time later." If the classroom environment can become one in which all members of the community support one another, help one another, engage with each other, and focus on each other's progress, academic growth can happen (Stronge, 2007).

Medical

There may be medical issues to consider during assessment periods, including timing of medication, food allergies, and fatigue. Teachers need to consider these carefully when arranging testing situations. It is very, very important for teachers to understand that often, there is a biological underpinning to a child's anxiety, hyperactivity, and irritability. Such behaviors are created through biological issues, triggered by anxiety or timing and are *not* a child being "bad" or "mean." Forcing a child to do something or responding with frustration will simply aggravate the situation—a situation that can be sometimes be alleviated with food, medication, or a removal of the stimulus.

Key Points From Chapter 11

- The level of schooling will affect how strategies are implemented; however, all strategies can be adapted for different levels.
- There are different issues and concerns at different levels of schooling; strategies have to be adapted for these relative issues.
- The strategies of teaching, timing, training, thinking, and together can be integrated into all academic content areas. Different content areas will have different emphases.
- Students with HFA often have very high and very low academic strengths and weaknesses. These differences have to be understood when developing both acceleration and remediation activities. Tiered activities are key to developing these differing abilities.
- Students with HFA have to be prepared for taking assessments, particularly state tests. Behavioral, academic, relational, and medical issues have to be considered.

Chapter 12

Resources and Materials: Autism Impacts What Materials You Select

Technology

Technology plays a significant role in the educational process of children with autism. There are devices that can monitor the level of a child's physical stress, such as the recent MIT-developed Q sensor (Grifantini, 2010). Such a device can alert a teacher or a caregiver that a child is about to have a tantrum or is experiencing significant anxiety—emotions that the child may be unable to communicate. Certainly, many schools and institutions have jumped on board with the use of the iPad for its programs, such as Proloquo2go, which allow students with limited speech to select icons for use.

The iPad and other tablet computers have received tremendous attention recently because of their relative ease of use, their "coolness" factor in the classroom, and their applications that can meet so many needs. Not only can iPads be used for typical classroom activities, such as recording notes, using colors to take notes, and other academic tasks, they have some very specific applications that may be appropriate for students with HFA. It should be noted that many of the apps found on the market reflect things that can be made by clever teachers and parents. Although there may be a perception that the iPad can "fix" a child, the tablet computer can only reinforce what is already being taught—it cannot replace a good teacher. What it can do is to centralize the instruction, not be invasive, raise the child's social factor, and provide a means of tracking learning over time.

Table 8

Apps Recommended for Students With HFA

Academic	Language	Social	Behavioral
Look 2 Learn	ProLoquo2go	Social Stories	Angry Octopus Book
Stories 2 Learn	Larry the Talking Parrot	All About Me	First, Then Visual Schedule
Picture Planner	Tom the Talking Cat	Smile at Me	iReward Chart
	Augie AAC	Look in My Eyes and Look in My Eyes Toys	Autism Xpress: Facial Expressions
	Communicating Basic Needs	SOSH: Social Skills for Children and Adolescents	Model Me and Model Me: Going Places
	Speech Tutor: Pocket SLP	Recite, Relax, Regulate, Reason and Recognize	ABA Receptive
	Speech With Milo	iAdvocate	ABA Therapy Images
	Tap Speak Button	Quick Cues	Behavior Tracker Pro
	Builder Series: Question Builder, Sentence Builder, Conversation Builder		Choice Board Maker and My Choice Board
			My Healthy Smile
			iEarned That
			iDress for Weather

At the time of this book, the apps market was exploding, with literally thousands of apps that have been developed in the past year. Table 8 includes a list of apps that have been reviewed either by Squidalicious (2011), a mother of a child with HFA; those available through Oceanhouse Media (http://www.oceanhouse-media.com/products), an app development company that specializes in educational apps; or those that have been mentioned in other blogs of parents and teachers of children with HFA. However, it should be noted that this list is already outdated, and readers should research what else may be available. I am not listing apps that are of general interest, such as books and academic sites, simply because those apps have such broad interest to so many teachers and students. I have chosen to list apps in Table 8 that are focused on the areas of challenge that students with HFA may face, including visual learning styles, communication issues, social issues, and behavioral issues. Many of the apps out there are more appropriate for children of specific ages; however, most of the ones that I have listed are appropriate for students of all ages with some instruction provided. Before schools or parents invest significant money, they should make sure that the app is:

- *Age appropriate*: Tom the Talking Cat is probably focused more on younger students than older ones, while SOSH is focused more on adolescents.
- *Cost appropriate*: There are a number of free apps, and if you can find an app that is less fancy but focuses on the same skill, save your money.

- *Reinforcing of the instructional objectives*: There is no point in buying an app that focuses on question building, if the SLP is focusing on conversation skills instead of questions.
- *Interest appropriate*: The purpose of any app is to use it. If the child does not engage with the material, then there is little reason to use it.

Resources

The following is a list of resources that I found helpful in my instruction of children with high-functioning autism. There are many, many others out there. Please do research and determine what speaks to you!

Materials for Teaching Children With Autism and Asperger Syndrome

ABA Materials—http://www.aba-materials.com

Autism Teaching Tools—http://www.autismteachingtools.com

Different Roads to Learning—http://www.difflearn.com

Do2Learn—http://www.do2learn.com

Edmark Reading Program—http://www.proedinc.com/customer/productview.aspx?id=1068

HearthSong—http://www.hearthsong.com

Highlights Merchandise—http://www.highlights.com/merchandise

Melissa & Doug Toys—http://www.melissaanddoug.com

Model Me Kids—http://www.modelmekids-store.com

Natural Learning Concepts—http://www.nlconcepts.com

Palmetto Pearl—http://www.palmettopearl.com

Picture Exchange Communication System (PECS)—http://www.pecs.com

Signing Time!—http://www.signingtime.com

SmileMakers—http://www.smilemakers.com

Stand Up for Learning (Stand-up desks with swinging footrests)—http://www.standupforlearning.com

Teacher Created Resources—http://www.teachercreated.com

Thinking Maps—http://www.thinkingmaps.com

Toys for Autism—http://www.toysforautism.com

Treatment and Education of Autistic and Related Communication-Handicapped Children (TEACCH)—http://www.teacch.com

University of Kansas Strategic Intervention Model—http://www.kucrl.org/sim

WikkiStix—http://www.wikkistix.com

Workbook Window—http://www.workbookwindow.com

Buron, K. D., & Curtis, M. (2004). *The incredible 5-point scale: Assisting students with autism spectrum disorders in understanding social interactions and controlling their emotional responses.* Overton Park, KS: Autism Asperger.

Gagnon, E. (2001). *Power cards: Using special interests to motivate children and youth with Asperger syndrome and autism.* Overton Park, KS: Autism Asperger.

Gray, C. (2010). *The new social story book.* Arlington, TX: Future Horizons.

Winner, M. G., & Crooke, P. (2010). *You are a social detective: Explaining social thinking to kids.* Great Barrington, MA: North River Press.

Organizations Specific to Autism and Asperger Syndrome

Asperger Association of New England—http://www.aane.org

Autism Europe—http://www.autismeurope.org

Autism National Committee—http://www.autcom.org

Autism Research Institute (ARI)—http://www.autism.com

Autism Society of America (ASA)—http://www.autism-society.org

Autism Speaks—http://www.autismspeaks.org

Autism Treatment Center—http://www.autismtreatmentcenter.org

Autism-Watch—http://www.autism-watch.org

Biofeedback—http://www.eegspectrum.com

Childnett.tv—http://www.childnett.tv

CHIME Institute at Woodland Hills—http://www.chimeinstitute.org

Dan Marino Foundation—http://www.danmarinofoundation.org

Families for Early Autism Treatments—http://www.feat.org

Father's Network—http://www.fathersnetwork.org

First Signs—http://www.firstsigns.org

Global and Regional Asperger Syndrome Partnership—http://www.grasp.org

Global Autism Collaboration—http://www.autism.org

Indiana Resource Center for Autism—http://www.iidc.indiana.edu/index.php?page Id=32

International Society for Autism Research (INSAR)—http://www.autism-insar.org

More Advanced Individuals With Autism, Asperger Syndrome and Pervasive Developmental Disorder (MAAP)—http://aspergersyndrome.org

National Autism Association (NAA)—http://www.nationalautismassociation.org

National Autistic Society—http://www.nas.org.uk

National Dissemination Center for Children with Disabilities—http://www.nichcy.org

National Institute of Mental Health (NIMH)—http://www.nimh.nih.gov

A Little Wiggle Room at Pleasant Grove Elementary School, Greenwood, IN—http://www.alittlewiggleroom.com

Talk About Curing Autism (TACA)—http://www.talkaboutcuringautism.org

University of California-Davis Medical Investigation of Neurodevelopmental Disorders Institute (UC-Davis MIND)—http://www.ucdmc.ucdavis.edu/MIND Institute

United States Autism and Asperger Association (USAAA)—http://www.usautism.org

Wright's Law—http://www.wrightslaw.com

National Organizations for Exceptionalities

ARC (Formerly known as the Association for Retarded Citizens)—http://www.thearc.org

Beach Center on Disability—http://www.beachcenter.org

Center for Disease Control and Prevention—http://www.cdc.gov/ncbddd/autism/index.htm

National Association for Gifted Children—http://www.nagc.org

Blogs by Parents of and People With Autism and Asperger

Autism's Edges—http://autismsedges.blogspot.com

Autism Hub—http://www.autism-hub.co.uk

Ballastexistenz—http://ballastexistenz.autistics.org

Day Sixty Seven—http://daysixtyseven.blogspot.com

Hopeful Parents—http://hopefulparents.org

Left Brain, Right Brain: Autism News, Science and Opinion—http://leftbrainrightbrain.co.uk

MOM – Not Otherwise Specified—http://www.momnos.blogspot.com

One Dad's Opinion—http://onedadsopinion.blogspot.com

Online Asperger Syndrome Information and Support—http://www.aspergersyndrome.org

University Students With Autism and Asperger's Syndrome—http://www.users.dircon.co.uk/~cns

IRC Chat Channels

Asperger—http://www.inlv.demon.nl/irc.asperger

Autism—http://www.theautismchannel.com

Books by Parents of Children With Autism

Collins, P. (2005). *Not even wrong: A father's journey into the lost history of autism.* New York, NY: Bloomsbury.

Gardner, N. (2008). *A friend like Henry: The remarkable true story of an autistic boy and the dog that unlocked his world.* Naperville, IL: Sourcebooks.

Gaston, L., & Gaston, R. (2009). *Three times the love: Finding answers and hope for our triplets with autism.* New York, NY: Avery.

Grinker, R. R. (2008). *Unstrange minds: Remapping the world of autism.* New York, NY: Basic Books.

Iverson, P. (2006). *Strange son: Two mothers, two sons and the quest to unlock the hidden world of autism.* New York, NY: Penguin Books.

Kephardt, B. (1999). *A slant of sun: One child's courage.* New York, NY: Harper Perennial.

Maurice, C. (1994). *Let me hear your voice: A family's triumph over autism.* New York, NY: Ballantine.

McCarthy, J. (2006). *Louder than words: A mother's journey in healing autism.* New York, NY: Plume.

McCarthy, J. (2008). *Mother warriors: A nation of parents healing autism against all odds.* New York, NY: Dutton.

Merchent, T. (2007). *He's not autistic, but . . . How we pulled our son from the mouth of the abyss.* Noblesville, IN: Joyous Messenger Books

Notbohm, E. (2005). *Ten things every child with autism wishes you knew.* Arlington, TX: Future Horizons.

Paradiz, V. (1996). *Elijah's cup: A family's journey into the community and culture of high-functioning autism and Asperger's syndrome.* Glencoe, IL: Free Press.

Senator, S. (2005). *Making peace with autism: One family's struggle, discovery and unexpected gifts.* Boston, MA: Trumpeter.

Seroussi, K. (2002). *Unraveling the mystery of autism and pervasive developmental disorder: A mother's story of research and recovery.* New York, NY: Broadway Books.

Stacey, P. (2003). *The boy who loved windows.* New York, NY: De Capo Press.

Whiffen, L. (2009). *A child's journey out of autism.* Naperville, IL: Sourcebooks.

Books by People With High-Functioning Autism and Asperger's

Barron, J., & Barron, S. (2002). *There's a boy in here: Emerging from the bonds of autism.* Arlington, TX: Future Horizons.

Carley, M. J. (2008). *Asperger's from the inside out: A supportive and practical guide for anyone with Asperger's syndrome.* New York, NY: Perigee.

Grandin, T. (1996). *Thinking in pictures and other reports on my life with autism.* New York, NY: Vintage.

Grandin, T. (2004). *Animals in translation: Using the mysteries of autism to decode animal behavior.* New York, NY: Scribner.

Jackson, L. (2002). *Freaks, geeks and Asperger Syndrome: A user guide to adolescence.* London, England: Jessica Kingsley.

Lawson, W. (2001). *Understanding and working with the spectrum of autism: An insider's view.* London, England: Jessica Kingsley.

Lawson, W. (2010). *The passionate mind: How people with autism learn.* London, England: Jessica Kingsley.

Mukhopadhyay, T. (2000). *The mind tree: A miraculous child breaks the silence of autism.* New York, NY: Riverhead Books.

Mukhopadhyay, T. (2008). *How can I talk if my lips don't move?: Inside my autistic mind.* New York, NY: Arcade.

Page, T. (2009). *Parallel play: Growing up with undiagnosed Asperger's.* New York, NY: Doubleday.

Robison, J. E. (2007). *Look me in the eye: My life with Asperger's.* New York, NY: Three Rivers Press.

Stillman, W. (2008). *The soul of autism: Looking beyond labels to unveil spiritual secrets of the heart savants.* New York, NY: Career Press.

Stillman, W. (2009). *Demystifying the autistic experience: A humanistic introduction for parents, caregivers and educators.* London, England: Jessica Kingsley.

Tammet, D. (2006). *Born on a blue day: Inside the extraordinary mind of an autistic savant.* New York, NY: Free Press.

Willey, L. H. (1999). *Pretending to be normal: Living with Asperger's syndrome.* London, England: Jessica Kingsley.

References

Adee, S. (2011, July). Specs that see right through you. *New Scientist*. Retrieved from http://www.newscientist.com/article/mg21128191.600-specs-that-see-right-through-you.html

Allen, J. (1999). *Words, words, words: Teaching vocabulary in grades 4–12*. York, ME: Stenhouse Publishers.

American Academy of Pediatrics. (2004). *Guidance for effective discipline*. Retrieved from http://aappolicy.aappublications.org/cgi/content/full/pediatrics;101/4/723

American Psychiatric Association. (2011). *Autism disorder: Proposed revision*. Retrieved from http://www.dsm5.org/proposedrevision/pages/proposed revision.aspx?rid=94

American Speech-Language-Hearing Association. (2011). *What is language? What is speech?* Retrieved from http://www.asha.org/public/speech/development/language_speech.htm

Anderson, R. D. (2002). Reforming science teaching: What research says about inquiry. *Journal of Science Teacher Education, 13*(1), 1–12.

Aspy, R., Grossman, B. G., & Myles, B. S. (2007). *Behavior interventions for individuals with high-functioning autism and Aspergers*. Paper presented at the Council for Exceptional Children Annual Convention, Louisville, KY.

Associated Press. (2009, August 21). *Schools fight families over autism service dogs*. Retrieved from http://www.MSNBC.msn.com/id/32511651/ns/health-childrens_health/t/schools-fight-families-over-autism-service-dogs/#. TlanttnPT79E

Associated Press. (2010, July 14). Autistic adults in Ohio have a hard time finding work. *Sandusky Register.* Retrieved from http://www.sanduskyregister.com/jobs/2010/jul/14/autistic-adults-ohio-have-hard-time-finding-work

Attwood, T. (2008). *The complete guide to Asperger's syndrome.* London, England: Jessica Kingsley.

Autismhealingthresholds.com. (2011). *Autism therapy: Drug.* Retrieved from http://autism.healingthresholds.com/therapy/drug

Ayers, A. J. (1979). *Sensory integration and the child.* Los Angeles, CA: Western Psychological Services.

Baron-Cohen, S. (1997). *Mindblindness: An essay on autism and theory of mind.* Boston, MA: MIT Press.

Basco, M. R., & Rush, A. J. (2007). *Cognitive behavioral therapy for bipolar disorder* (2nd ed.). New York, NY: Guilford Press.

Bass, M. M., Duchowny, C. A., & Llabre, M. M. (2009). The effect of therapeutic horseback riding on social functioning in children with autism. *Journal of Autism and Developmental Disorders, 39,* 1261–1267.

Bellini, S., Peters, J. K., & Hopf, A. (2007). Meta-analysis of school-based social skills interventions for children with autism spectrum disorders. *Remedial and Special Education, 28,* 152–162.

Bettleheim, B. (1962). *Dialogues with mothers.* Glencoe, IL: The Free Press.

Blischak, D. M., & Schlosser, R. W. (2003). Use of technology to support independent spelling by students with autism. *Topics in Language Disorders, 23,* 293–304.

Boushey, A. (2001). The grief cycle: One parent's trip around. *Journal of Autism and Other Developmental Disabilities, 16,* 27–30.

Brice, J. (2007, October). *Physicians rely on psychiatric drugs to treat autism spectrum disorders.* Presentation at the American Academy of Pediatrics annual conference, San Francisco, CA. Abstract 472. Retrieved from http://www.medscape.com/viewarticle/565002

Bureau of Labor Statistics. (2011). *Occupational outlook handbook* (2010–2011 ed.). Retrieved from http://www.bls.gov/oco/ocos078.htm

Buron, K. D. (2004). *The incredible 5-point scale: Assisting students with autism spectrum disorders in understanding social interactions and controlling their emotional responses.* Overton Park, KS: Autism Asperger.

Buschke, H. (1974). Components of verbal learning in children: Analysis by selective reminding. *Journal of Experimental Child Psychology, 18,* 488–496.

Butterworth, J., Hall, A. C., Smith, F. A., Migliore, A., Winsor, J., Timmons, J. C., & Domin, D. (2011). *StateData: The national report on employment services and outcomes.* Boston: Institute for Community Inclusion, University of Massachusetts Boston.

Campos, J. J., Campos, R. G., & Barrett, K. C. (1989). Emergent themes in the study of emotional development and emotion regulation. *Developmental Psychology, 25,* 394–402.

Cardoso-Martins, C., & da Silva, J. R. (2008). Cognitive and language correlates of hyperlexia: Evidence from children with autism spectrum disorders. *Reading and Writing, 23,* 129–145.

Carr, E. G., Horner, R. H., & Turnbull, A. E. (1999). *Positive behavior support for people with developmental disabilities.* Washington, DC: American Association on Mental Retardation.

Carter, E. W., Cushing, L. S., Clark, N. M., & Kennedy, C. H. (2005). Effects of peer support interventions on students' access to the general curriculum and social interactions. *Research and Practice for Persons With Severe Disabilities, 30*(1), 15–25.

Center for Gifted Education, The College of William and Mary. (1996a). *Literature web.* Retrieved from http://cfge.wm.edu/curriculum.htm

Center for Gifted Education, The College of William and Mary. (1996b). *Vocabulary web.* Retrieved from http://cfge.wm.edu/curriculum.htm

Centers for Disease Control and Prevention. (2009). Prevalence of autism spectrum disorder. *Morbidity and Mortality Weekly Report, 58*(SS-10). Retrieved from http://www.cdc.gov/mmwr/pdf/ss/ss5810.pdf

Cermak, S. (1985). Developmental dyspraxia. In E. A. Roy (Ed.), *Neuropsychological studies of apraxia and related disorders* (pp. 225–243). New York, NY: Elsevier.

Champagne, T., & Stromberg, N. (2004). Sensory approaches in inpatient psychiatric settings: Innovative alternatives to seclusion and restraint. *Journal of Psychosocial Nursing and Mental Health Services, 42*(9), 34–41.

Covey, S., Merrill, A. R., & Merrill, R. R. (1994). *First things first.* New York, NY: Free Press.

Cutright, C. (2010, December 28). Proud of their progress: Whatever happened to Molly and Audreanna? *Roanoke Times.* Retrieved from http://www.roanoke.com/news/wht/wb/272043

Darling-Hammond, L. (2011, May 25). Teacher evaluation through student testing. *Education Nation: Guest Blog.* Retrieved from http://www.educationnation.com/index.cfm?objectid=E730EFBA-86ED-11E0-B74E000C296BA163

Dawson, G., Rogers, S., Munson, J., Smith, M., Winter, J., Greenson, J., . . . Varley, J. (2009). Randomized, controlled trial of an intervention for toddlers with autism: The Early Start Denver Model. *Pediatrics, 125*(1), 17–23.

Dawson, G., Toth, K., Abbott, R., Osterling, J., Munson, J., Estes, A., & Liaw, J. (2004). Early social attention impairments in autism. *Developmental Psychology, 40,* 271–283.

Dawson, M., Soulières, I., Gernsbacher, M. A., & Mottron, L. (2007). The level and nature of autistic intelligence. *Psychological Science, 18,* 657–662.

de Bono, E. (1985). *Six thinking hats: An essential approach to business management.* New York, NY: Little, Brown.

Demboski, A. (2010, November 1). At the age of peekaboo, in therapy to fight autism. *New York Times.* Retrieved from http://www.nytimes.com/2010/11/02/health/02autism.html?pagewanted=1&_r=1

Deshler, D. D., & Lenz, B. K. (1989). The strategies instructional approach. *International Journal of Disability, Development, and Education, 36,* 203–224.

Dieker, L. A., & Murawski, W. W. (2003). Coteaching at the secondary level: Unique issues, current trends and suggestions for success. *High School Journal, 86*(4), 1–8.

Dinstein, I., Thomas, C., Humphreys, K., Behrmann, M., & Heeger, D. (2010). Normal movement-selectivity in autism. *Neuron, 66,* 461–469.

Dweck, C. S. (2006). *Mindset: The new psychology of success.* New York, NY: Random House.

Elbaum, B., Moody, S. W., Vaughn, S., Schumm, J. S., & Hughes, M. (2009). *The effect of instructional grouping format on the reading outcomes of students with disabilities: A meta-analytic review.* Retrieved from http://www.ncld.org/at-school/especially-for-teachers/effective-teaching-practices/the-effect-of-instructional-grouping-format-on-the-reading-outcomes-of-students-with-disabilities

Emory Autism Center. (2009). *Frequently asked questions about autism.* Retrieved from http://www.psychiatry.emory.edu/PROGRAMS/autism/autismFAQs.html

English, K., Goldstein, H., Shafer, K., & Kaczmarek, L. (1997). Promoting interactions among preschoolers with and without disabilities: Effects of a buddy skill-training program. *Exceptional Children, 63,* 229–243.

Esquith, R. (2007). *Teach like your hair's on fire.* New York, NY: Penguin Classics.

Faller, M. B. (2010, November 12). Autism therapy group says it cured 6 kids. *Arizona Republic.* Retrieved from http://www.azcentral.com/arizonarepublic/local/articles/2010/11/12/20101112autism-study-arizona.html

Fein, D., Barton, M., Eigsti, I. M., Naigles, L., Rosenthal, M., Tyson, K., & Helt, M. (2009, May). *Cognitive and behavioral profiles of children who recover from autism.* Presentation at the International Society for Autism Research Annual Conference, Chicago, IL.

Fitzgerald, W. F. (1995). Is mercury increasing in the atmosphere? The need for an atmospheric mercury network (AMNET). *Water, Air and Soil Pollution, 80*(1), 245–254.

Friend, M., & Cook, L. (2007). *Interactions: Collaboration skills for school professionals* (5th ed.). White Plains, NY: Longman.

Frith, U. (2001). Mind blindness and the brain in autism. *Neuron, 32,* 969–979.

Frombonne, E. (2002). Prevalence of childhood disintegrative disorder. *Autism: The International Journal of Research and Practice, 6,* 149–157.

Gabel, S. (2005). Introduction: Disability studies in education. In S. Gabel (Ed.), *Disability studies in education: Readings in theory and method* (pp. 1–18). New York, NY: Peter Lang.

Gagnon, E. (2001). *Power cards: Using special interests to motivate children and youth with Asperger syndrome and autism.* Overton Park, KS: Autism Asperger.

Ghaziuddin, M. (2005). *Mental health aspects of autism and Asperger syndrome.* Philadelphia, PA: Jessica Kingsley.

Ghaziuddin, M., Ghaziuddin, N., & Greden, J. (2002). Depression in persons with autism: Implications for research and clinical care. *Journal of Autism and Developmental Disorders, 32,* 299–306.

Gillott, A., Furniss, F., & Walter, A. (2001). Anxiety in high functioning children with autism. *Autism, 5,* 277–286.

Grandin, T. (1996). *Thinking in pictures and other reports on my life with autism.* New York, NY: Vintage.

Grandin, T. (2004). *Animals in translation: Using the mysteries of autism to decode animal behavior.* New York, NY: Scribner.

Granpeesheh, D., Tarbox, J., & Dixon, D. R. (2009). Applied behavior analytic interventions for children with autism: A description and review of treatment research. *Annals of Clinical Psychiatry, 21,* 162–173.

Gray, C. (1994). *Comic strip conversations.* Arlington, TX: Future Horizons.

Gray, C. (2010). *The new social story book.* Arlington, TX: Future Horizons.

Green, V. A., Sigafoos, K. A., Pituch, K. A., Itchon, J., O'Reilly, M., & Lancioni, G. E. (2006). Assessing behavioral flexibility in individuals with developmental disabilities. *Focus on Autism and Other Developmental Disabilities, 21,* 230–236.

Greenberg, M. T., & Snell, J. (1997). The neurological basis of emotional development. In P. Salovey (Ed.), *Emotional development and emotional literacy* (pp. 92–119). New York, NY: Basic Books.

Greenwood, S. C. (2002). Making words matter: Vocabulary study in the content areas. *The Clearing House, 75,* 258–263.

Grifantini, K. (2010, October 26). Sensor detects emotions though the skin. *MIT Technology Review.* Retrieved from http://www.technologyreview.com/biomedicine/26615/

Hallahan, D., Fuchs, D., Gerber, M., Scruggs, T., & Zigmond, N. (2010, April). *The LD construct: Can it be saved? Is it worth saving?* Presentation at the annual meeting of Council for Exceptional Children, Nashville, TN.

Hannaford, C. (1997). *Smart moves: Why learning is not all in your head.* Arlington, VA: Great Ocean Publishers.

Hansson, S. L., Röjvall, A. S., Rastam, M., Gillberg, C., Gillberg, C., & Anckarsäter, H. (2005). Psychiatric telephone interview with parents for screening of childhood autism—tics, attention-deficit hyperactivity disorder and other comorbidities (A–TAC). *British Journal of Psychiatry, 187*, 262–267.

Happé, F. G. E. (1996). Studying weak central coherence at low levels. *Journal of Child Psychology and Psychiatry, 37*, 873–877.

Happé, F., Booth, R., Charlton, R., & Hughes, C. (2006). Executive function deficits in autism spectrum disorders and attention-deficit/hyperactivity disorder: Examining profiles across domains and ages. *Brain and Cognition, 61*, 25–39.

Harris, K., & Graham, S. (1999). Programmatic intervention research: Illustrations from the evolution of self-regulated strategy development. *Learning Disabilities Quarterly, 22*, 251–262.

Harris, S. L., Handleman, J. S., Gordon, R., Kristoff, B., & Fuentes, F. (1991). Changes in cognitive and language functioning of preschool children with autism. *Journal of Autism and Developmental Disorders, 21*, 281–290.

Heflin, L. J., & Alaimo, D. F. (2007). *Students with autism spectrum disorders: Effective instructional practices.* Upper Saddle River, NJ: Merrill/Prentice Hall.

Hehir, T. (2002). Eliminating ableism in education. *Harvard Educational Review, 72*, 1–25.

Henderson, L., & Hughes, C. E. (2011, March). *Autism IEPs: Factors involved in the parental and professional satisfaction of the IEP process.* Poster presented at the annual Gatlinburg Conference, San Antonio, TX.

Hensley, S. (2010, February 2). Lancet renounces study linking autism and vaccines. *Shots: NPR Health Blog.* Retrieved from http://www.npr.org/blogs/health/2010/02/lancet_wakefield_autism_mmr_au.html

Heward, W. (2008). *Exceptional children: An introduction to special education.* Upper Saddle River, NJ: Prentice Hall.

Hoven, J., & Garelick, B. (2007). Singapore math: Simple or complex? *Educational Leadership, 65*(3), 28–31.

Howlin, P., & Yates, P. (1999). The potential effectiveness of social skills groups for adults with autism. *Autism, 3*, 299–307.

Hughes, C. (2011). *Social understanding and social lives: From toddlerhood through to the transition to school.* New York, NY: Psychology Press.

Hughes, C. E. (2010a, December). Gifts of autism. *Parenting for High Potential*, 15–19.

Hughes, C. E. (2010b). Twice-exceptional children: Twice the challenges, twice the joys. In J. Castellano & A. D. Frazier (Eds.), *Special populations of gifted children: understanding our most able students from diverse backgrounds* (pp. 153–173). Waco, TX: Prufrock Press.

Hughes, C. E., & Murawski, W. W. (2001). Lessons from another field: Applying co-teaching strategies to gifted education. *Gifted Child Quarterly, 45*, 195–204.

Hughes-Lynch, C. E. (2010). *Children with high-functioning autism: A parent's guide.* Waco, TX: Prufrock Press.

Hyerle, D. (2009). *Visual tools for transforming information into knowledge.* Thousand Oaks, CA: Corwin Press.

Iacoboni, M., (2008). *Mirroring people: The new science of how we connect with others.* New York, NY: Farrar, Straus & Giroux.

Iarocci, G., & McDonald, J. (2006). Sensory integration and the perceptual experience of persons with autism. *Journal of Autism and Developmental Disorders, 36,* 77–90.

Illinois State University. (2003). *Power cards fact sheet.* Retrieved from http://autismspectrum.illinoisstate.edu/resources/factsheets/powercard.shtml

Individuals with Disabilities Education Improvement Act, Pub. Law 108-446 (December 3, 2004).

Isaksen, S. G., Dorval, K. B., & Treffinger, D. J. (2000). *Creative problem-solving: An introduction.* Waco, TX: Prufrock Press.

Joffe, V. L., Cain, K., & Marić, N. (2007). Comprehension problems in children with specific language impairment: Does mental imagery training help? *International Journal of Language and Communication Disorders, 42,* 648–664.

Joyce, B. R., & Weil, M. (2009). *Models of teaching* (8th ed.). New York, NY: Allyn & Bacon.

Jurvetson, S. (2010, September 29). *Meaning innovation: Whether to design or evolve?* [Video file]. Retrieved from http://www.youtube.com/watch?v=WOwcDr-A3to

Kanner, L. (1943). Autistic disturbances of affective contact. *Nervous Child, 2,* 217–250.

Kaplan, M., Carmody, D. P., & Gaydos, A. (1995). Postural orientation modifications in autism in response to ambient lenses. *Child Psychiatry and Human Development, 27,* 71–91.

Karnes, F. A., Shaunessy, E., & Bisland, A. (2004). Gifted students with disabilities: Are we finding them? *Gifted Child Today, 27*(4), 16–21.

Karp, H. (2009). *Cracking the autism riddle: Toxic chemicals, a serious suspect in the autism outbreak.* Retrieved from http://www.huffingtonpost.com/harvey-karp/cracking-the-autism-riddl_b_221202.html

Kirk, S. A., Gallagher, J. J., Coleman, M. R., & Anastasiow, N. J. (2012). *Educating exceptional children* (13th ed.). Independence, KY: Cengage.

Klausmeier, H. J., & Frayer, D. A. (1970). *Cognitive operations in concept learning.* Madison: Wisconsin Research and Development Center for Cognitive Learning. (ERIC Document Reproduction Services No. ED045467)

Knapczyk, D. R. (1988). Reducing aggressive behaviors in special and regular class settings by training alternative social responses. *Behavioral Disorders, 14,* 27–39.

Koebler, J. (2011, July 6). NEA says testing may play role in teacher evaluations. *US News and World Report: High School Notes.* Retrieved from http://

www.usnews.com/education/blogs/high-school-notes/2011/07/06/nea-says-testing-may-play-role-in-teacher-evaluations

Koegel, R. L., & Koegel, L. K. (2006). *Pivotal response treatments for autism.* Baltimore, MD: Brookes.

Kohlberg, L., & Turiel, E. (1971). Moral development and moral education. In G. Lesser (Ed.), *Psychology and educational practice.* Glenview, IL: Scott Foresman.

Kokina, A., & Kern, L. (2010). Social Story ™ interventions for students with autism spectrum disorders: A meta-analysis. *Journal of Autism and Developmental Disorders, 40,* 812–826.

Koshino, H., Carpenter, P. A., Minshew, N. J., Cherkassky, V. L., Keller, T. A., & Just, M. A. (2004). Functioning connectivity in an fMRI working memory task in high-functioning autism. *NeuroImage, 24,* 810–821.

Krasny, L., Williams, B. J., Provencal, S., & Ozonoff, S. (2003). Social skills interventions for the autism spectrum: Essential ingredients and a model curriculum. *Child and Adolescent Psychiatric Clinics of North America, 12*(1), 107–122.

Kübler-Ross, E. (1973). *On death and dying.* London, England: Routledge.

Kübler-Ross, E. (2005). *On grief and grieving: Finding the meaning of grief through the five stages of loss.* New York, NY: Simon & Schuster.

Kulik, C.-L., & Kulik, J. A. (1984). *Effects of ability grouping on elementary school pupils: A meta-analysis.* Paper presented at the annual meeting of the American Psychological Association, Toronto. (ERIC Document Reproduction Service No. ED255329)

Laurent, A. C., & Rubin, E. (2004). Challenge in emotional regulation in Asperger syndrome and high functioning autism. *Topics in Language Disorders, 24,* 286–297.

Laushey, K. M., & Heflin, L. J. (2000). Enhancing social skills of kindergarten children with autism through the training of multiple peers as tutors. *Journal of Autism and Developmental Disorders, 30,* 183–193.

Lavoie, R. (2008). *The motivation breakthrough.* New York, NY: Touchstone.

Learning Disabilities Association of America. (2004). *Principles of IDEA.* Retrieved from http://www.ldanatl.org/aboutld/parents/special_ed/print_principles.asp

Ledgin, N. (2005). *Asperger's and self-esteem: Insight and hope through famous role models.* Arlington, TX: Future Horizons.

Lehrer, S. (2008). Inexpensive sensory ideas for the special education classroom. *Journal of Occupational Therapy, Schools, and Early Intervention, 1,* 238–245.

Levy, S. E., & Hyman, S. L. (2009). Complementary and alternative medicine therapies for children with autism spectrum disorders. *Child and Adolescent Psychiatric Clinics of North America, 17,* 803–820.

Leyfer, O. T., Folstein, S. E., Bacalman, S., Davis, N. O., Dinh, E., Morgan, J., . . . Lainhart, J. E. (2006). Comorbid psychiatric disorders in children with autism: Interview development and rates of disorder. *Journal of Autism and Developmental Disorders, 36,* 849–861.

Maqbool, S. (2009). *67m children affected by autism.* Retrieved from http://www.thenews.com.pk/daily_detail.asp?id=170476

Mayes, S. D., & Calhoun, S. L. (2007). Learning, attention, writing, and processing speed in typical children and children with ADHD, autism, anxiety, depression and oppositional-defiant disorder. *Child Neuropsychology, 13,* 469–493.

McAfee, J. (2002). *Navigating the social world: A curriculum for individuals with Asperger's syndrome, high functioning autism and related disorders.* Arlington, TX: Future Horizons.

McCauley, R., Strand, E., Lof, G. L., Schooling, T., & Frymark, T. (2009). Evidence-based systematic review: Effects of non-speech oral motor exercises on speech. *American Journal of Speech-Language Pathology, 18,* 343–360.

McWilliam, E. (2005). Unlearning pedagogy. *Journal of Learning Design, 1*(1), 1–11.

Mesibov, G. B., Shea, V., & Schopler, E. (2004). *The TEACCH approach to autism spectrum disorders.* New York, NY: Springer Science + Business Media.

Mirenda, P. (2001). Autism, augmentative communication and assistive technology: What do we really know? *Focus on Autism and Other Development Disabilities, 16,* 141–151.

Moreno, S., & O'Neal, C. (2002). *Tips for teaching high-functioning people with autism.* BBB Autism Support Network. Retrieved from http://www.bbbautism.com/pdf/article_41_tips_for_teaching_ppl_with_HFA.pdf

Morgan, B., Mayberry, M., & Durkin, K. (2003). Weak central coherence, poor joint attention, and low verbal ability: Independent deficits in early autism. *Developmental Psychology, 39,* 646–656.

Morgan, S. B. (1986). Autism and Piaget's theory: Are the two compatible? *Journal of Autism and Developmental Disorders, 16,* 441–457.

Mottron, L., Peretz, I., & Ménard, E. (2003). Local and global processing of music in high-functioning persons with autism: Beyond central coherence? *Journal of Child Psychology and Psychiatry, 41,* 1057–1065.

Murawski, W. W. (2009). *Collaborative teaching in elementary schools: Making the co-teaching marriage work.* Thousand Oaks, CA: Corwin Press.

Muris, P., Steernamen, P., Merckelbach, H., Holdrinet, I., & Meesters, C. (1998). Comorbid anxiety symptoms in children with pervasive developmental disorders. *Journal of Anxiety Disorders, 12,* 387–393.

Myles, B. S. (2005). *Children and youth with Asperger syndrome: Strategies for success in inclusive settings.* Thousand Oaks, CA: Corwin Press.

Myles, B. S., & Adreon, D. (2001). *Asperger syndrome and adolescence: Practical solutions for school success.* Shawnee Mission, KS: Autism Asperger.

Nation, K., Clark, P., Wright, B., & Williams, C. (2006). Patterns of reading ability in children with autism spectrum disorder. *Journal of Autism and Developmental Disorders, 36,* 911–919.

National Association for the Education of Young Children. (2002). *Early learning standards: Creating the conditions for success.* Retrieved from http://www.naeyc.org/files/naeyc/file/positions/position_statement.pdf

National Children's Study. (2011). *Study overview.* Retrieved from http://www.nationalchildrensstudy.gov/about/overview/Pages/default.aspx

National Institute of Mental Health. (2008). *The numbers count: Mental disorders in America.* Retrieved from http://www.nimh.nih.gov/health/publications/the-numbers-count-mental-disorders-in-america/index.shtml

National Institute of Mental Health. (2009). *Treatment options for autism.* Retrieved from http://www.nimh.nih.gov/health/publications/autism/treatment-options.shtml

National Public Radio. (2010, August 23). *Autism gives woman an "alien view" of social brain.* Retrieved from http://www.npr.org/templates/story/story.php?storyId=129379866

New America Foundation. (2011). *Individuals with Disabilities Education Act: Funding distribution.* Retrieved from http://febp.newamerica.net/background-analysis/individuals-disabilities-education-act-funding-distribution

Norbury, C. F., & Bishop, D. V. M. (2002). Inferential processing and story recall in children with communication problems: A comparison of specific language impairment, pragmatic language impairment and high-functioning autism. *International Journal of Language and Communication Disorders, 37,* 227–251.

Oberman, L. M., Hubbard, E. M., McCleery, J. P., Altschuler, E. L., Ramachandran, V. S., & Pineda, J. A. (2005). EEG evidence for mirror neuron dysfunction in autism spectral disorders. *Cognitive Brain Research, 24,* 190–198.

O'Keefe, M. J., & McDowell, M. (2004). Bridging the gap between health and education: Words are not enough. *Journal of Pediatrics and Child Health, 40*(5), 250–262.

Ormrod, J. E. (2010). *Educational psychology: Developing learners.* Upper Saddle River, NJ: Prentice Hall.

Peppé, S., McCann, J., Gibbon, F., O'Hare, A., & Rutherford, M. (2006). Assessing prosodic and pragmatic ability in children with high-functioning autism. *Journal of Pragmatics, 38*(10), 1776–1791.

Piacentini, J. C., March, J. S., & Franklin, M. E. (2006). Cognitive behavioral intervention for youths with obsessive-compulsive disorders. In P. C. Kendall (Ed.), *Child and adolescent disorders* (pp. 297–321). New York, NY: Guilford Press.

Piacentini, J., Woods, D. W., Scahill, L., Wilhelm, S., Peterson, A. L., Chang, S., . . . Walkup, J. T. (2010). Behavior therapy for children with Tourette's syndrome. *Journal of the American Medical Association, 303,* 1929–1937.

Reaven, J. A., Blakeley-Smith, A., Nichols, S., Dasari, M., Flanigan, E., & Hepburn, S. (2009). Cognitive-behavioral group treatment for anxiety symptoms in children with high-functioning autism spectrum disorders. *Focus on Autism and Other Developmental Disabilities, 24*(1), 27–37.

Redefer, L. A., & Goodman, J. A. (1989). Pet-facilitated therapy with autistic children. *Journal of Autism and Developmental Disorders, 19,* 461–467.

Reid, R., & Lienemann, T. (1996). *Strategy instruction for students with learning disabilities.* New York, NY: Guilford Press.

Rimland, B. (1964). *Infantile autism: The syndrome and its implication for a neural theory of behavior.* New York, NY: Appleton-Century-Crofts.

Rimland, B., Crook, W., & Crook, C. (2001). *Tired—so tired!: And the "yeast connection."* Newtown, PA: Future Health.

Rinehart, N. J., Tonge, B. J., Bradshaw, J. L., Iansek, R., Enticott, P. G., & McGinley, J. (2006). Gait function in high-functioning autism and Asperger's disorder: Evidence for basal-ganglia and cerebellar involvement? *European Child and Adolescent Psychiatry, 15,* 256–264.

Roberts, J. M. A. (1989). Echolalia and comprehension in autistic children. *Journal of Autism and Developmental Disorders, 19,* 271–281.

Robison, J. E. (2007). *Look me in the eye: My life with Asperger's.* New York, NY: Three Rivers Press.

Rogers, K. (2002). *Reforming gifted education: Matching the program to the child.* Scottsdale, AZ: Great Potential Press.

Ronis, D. (2007). *Problem-based learning for math and science: Integrating inquiry and the internet.* Thousand Oaks, CA: Corwin Press.

Rudacille, D. (2011). X-linked variants may up autism, schizophrenia risk. *Simons Foundation Autism Research Initiative: News and Commentary.* Retrieved from https://sfari.org/news-and-commentary/open-article/-/asset_publisher/6Tog/content/x-linked-variants-may-up-autism-schizophrenia-risk?redirect=%2Fnews-and-commentary%2Fall

Santrock, J. (2012). *Educational psychology* (6th ed.). Saddle River, NJ: McGraw Hill.

Schetter, P. (2006). *Improving the behavior and academic success of students with high-functioning autism and Asperger syndrome: Strategies that work (Grades K–12).* Bellevue, WA: Bureau of Education and Research.

Schmidt, W., Houang, R., & Cogan, L. (2002, Summer). A coherent curriculum: The case of mathematics. *American Educator,* 10–26.

Schopler, E., Mesibov, G., & Hearsey, K. (1995). Structured teaching in the TEACCH system. In N. E. Schopler & G. Mesibov (Eds.), *Learning and cognition in autism* (pp. 243–267). New York, NY: Plenum.

Schwarber, L. A. (2006). *A comparison of general education and special education teachers' knowledge, self-efficacy, and concerns in teaching children with autism*

(Unpublished master's thesis). Miami University, Oxford, OH. Retrieved from http://etd.ohiolink.edu/send-pdf.cgi/Schwarber%20Laura%20A.pdf?miami 1154641936

Schwartz, J. (2011). Academic performance and cognitive abilities in children with ASD. *Center on Human Development and Disabilities Outlook, 4,* 1–2.

Senator, S. (2005). *Making peace with autism: One family's struggle, discovery and unexpected gifts.* Boston, MA: Trumpeter.

Seroussi, K. (2002). *Unraveling the mystery of autism and pervasive developmental disorder: A mother's story of research and recovery.* New York, NY: Broadway Books.

Shaw, W., Rimland, B., Scott, P., Seroussi, K., Lewis, L., & Semon, B. (1998). *Biological treatments for autism and PDD.* Manhattan, KS: Sunflower Press.

Sherman, D. A. (2007). *Autism: Asserting your child's right to a special education.* New York, NY: Oxford Churchill.

Siegel, B. (2003). *Helping children with autism learn.* New York, NY: Oxford University Press.

Simpson, R. (2005). *Autism spectrum disorders: Interventions and treatments for children and youth.* Thousand Oaks, CA: Corwin Press.

Sinclair, J. (1999). *Why I dislike person-first language.* Retrieved from http://web.syr.edu/~jisincla/person_first.htm

Slavin, R. (1991). Synthesis of research on cooperative learning. *Educational Leadership, 48*(5), 71–82.

Snow, J. (1994). *What's really worth doing and how to do it.* Toronto, Canada: Inclusion Press.

Speech Therapy on Video. (2006). *Speech terms explained.* Retrieved from http://www.speech-therapy-on-video.com/speechterms.html

SpeechPathology.com. (2005). *Apraxia v. dyspraxia.* Retrieved from http://www.speechpathology.com/askexpert/display_question.asp?question_id=119

Squidalicious. (2011). *iPad apps for autism.* Retrieved from http://www.squidalicious.com/2011/01/ipad-apps-for-autism-spreadsheet-of.html

Sternberg, R. J., & Williams, W. M. (2010). *Educational psychology* (2nd ed.). Upper Saddle River, NJ: Merrill.

Straker, D. (2007). *The Kübler-Ross grief cycle.* Retrieved from http://changingminds.org/disciplines/change_management/kubler_ross/kubler_ross.htm

Stronge, J. H. (2007). *Qualities of effective teachers.* Alexandria, VA: Association of Supervision and Curriculum Development.

Sugai, G., Horner, R., Lewis-Palmer, T., & Todd, A. (2005). *Schoolwide positive behavior support team training manual.* Retrieved from http://pbismanual.uoecs.org

Szatmari, P., Archer, L., Fisman, S., & Streiner, D. L. (1995). Asperger syndrome and autism: Differences in behavior, cognition and adaptive functioning. *Journal of the American Academic of Child and Adolescent Psychiatry, 34,* 1662–1671.

Sze, K. M., & Wood, J. J. (2007). Cognitive behavioral treatment of comorbid anxiety disorders and social difficulties in children with high-functioning autism: A case report. *Journal of Contemporary Psychotherapy, 37,* 133–143.

Tammet, D. (2006). *Born on a blue day: Inside the extraordinary mind of an autistic savant.* New York, NY: Free Press.

Tannenbaum, A. I., & Baldwin, L. J. (1983). Giftedness and learning disability: A paradoxical combination. In L. H. Fox, L. Brody, & D. Tobin (Eds.), *Learning disabled/gifted children: Identification and programming* (pp. 11–36). Baltimore, MD: University Park Press.

Tomlinson, C. A., & Strickland, C. A. (2005). *Differentiation in practice: A resource guide for differentiating curriculum.* Alexandria, VA: Association for Supervision and Curriculum Development.

Torrance, E. P. (1977). *Creativity in the classroom: What research says to the teacher.* New Haven, CT: National Education Association.

Trail, B. A. (2011). *Twice-exceptional gifted children: Understanding, teaching, and counseling gifted students.* Waco, TX: Prufrock Press.

Turner, M. (1999). Annotation: Repetitive behavior in autism: A review of psychological research. *Journal of Child Psychology and Psychiatry, 40,* 839–849.

United States Department of Education. (2004). *Individuals with Disability Act, Section 300.8.* Retrieved from http://idea.ed.gov/explore/view/p/,root,regs,300,A,300%252E8

Vacca, R. T., & Vacca, J. A. L. (2005). *Content area reading: Literacy and learning across the curriculum* (8th ed.). New York, NY: Longman.

van Roekel, E., & Scholte, R. H. J. (2010). Bullying among adolescents with autism spectrum disorders: Prevalence and perception. *Journal of Autism and Developmental Disorders, 40,* 63–73.

VanTassel-Baska, J., & Little, C. A. (Eds.). (2003). *Content-based curriculum for high-ability learners.* Waco, TX: Prufrock Press.

Webb, J., Amend, E., Webb, N., Goerss, J., Beljian, P., & Olenchak, R. (2005). *Misdiagnosis and dual diagnoses of gifted children and adults: ADHD, bipolar, OCD, Aspergers, depression, and other disorders.* Scottsdale, AZ: Great Potential Press.

White, S. W., Koenig, K., & Scahill, L. (2007). Social skills development in children with autism spectrum disorders: A review of the intervention research. *Journal of Autism and Developmental Disorders, 37,* 1858–1868.

Whitney-Thomas, J., & Hanley-Maxwell, C. (1996). Packing the parachute: Parents' experiences as their children prepare to leave high school. *Exceptional Children, 63,* 75–87.

Williams, D. (1995). *Somebody somewhere: Breaking free from the world of autism.* New York, NY: Crown.

Winebrenner, S. (2001). *Teaching gifted kids in the regular classroom* (2nd ed.). Minneapolis, MN: Free Spirit.

Winner, M. G. (2010). *You are a social detective: Explaining social thinking to kids.* Great Barrington, MA: North River Press.

Wong, H. K., & Wong, R. T. (2009). *The first days of school: How to be an effective teacher.* Mountain View, CA: Harry K. Wong.

Wood, J., Drahota, A., Sze, K., Har, K., Chiu, A., & Langer, D. (2009). Cognitive behavioral therapy for anxiety in children with autism spectrum disorders: A randomized, controlled trial. *Journal of Child Psychology and Psychiatry, 50,* 224–234.

Zilius, M. N. (2010). Dance/movement therapy in pediatrics: An overview. *Alternative and Complementary Therapies, 16*(2), 87–92.

About the Author

Claire E. Hughes-Lynch, Ph.D., has her doctoral degree from the College of William and Mary in the areas of gifted education and special education and is an associate professor of teacher education in the early childhood/special education program at the College of Coastal Georgia.

As a former Visiting Fellow at Oxford University in the area of autism, she researches and publishes in the areas of educational interventions for children with autism, gifted children with disabilities, and inclusive practices. She is the author of *Children With High-Functioning Autism: A Parent's Guide* and *Teaching Children With High-Functioning Autism*.

She lives with her husband, two children, two cats, a dog, and a variety of fish on the beach in Georgia, loves to travel, and is absolutely passionate about teaching.